PAGODA TOEFL Actual Test Listening

3rd Edition

파고다교육그룹 언어교육연구소 | 저

PAGODA Books

PAGODA TOEFL
3rd Edition

Actual Test Listening

초 판	1쇄 발행	2014년 12월 15일
개정 2판	1쇄 발행	2021년 2월 26일
개정 3판	1쇄 인쇄	2025년 4월 21일
개정 3판	1쇄 발행	2025년 4월 30일

지 은 이 | 파고다교육그룹 언어교육연구소
펴 낸 이 | 박경실
펴 낸 곳 | PAGODA Books 파고다북스
출판등록 | 2005년 5월 27일 제 300-2005-90호
주   소 | 06614 서울특별시 서초구 강남대로 419, 19층(서초동, 파고다타워)
전   화 | (02) 6940-4070
팩   스 | (02) 536-0660
홈페이지 | www.pagodabook.com

저작권자 | ⓒ 2014, 2021, 2025 파고다아카데미, 파고다에스씨에스

이 책의 저작권은 저자와 출판사에 있습니다. 서면에 의한 저작권자와 출판사의 허락 없이
내용의 일부 혹은 전부를 인용 및 복제하거나 발췌하는 것을 금합니다.

Copyright ⓒ 2014, 2021, 2025 by PAGODA Academy, PAGODA SCS

All rights reserved. No part of this publication may be reproduced, stored
in a retrieval system, or transmitted, in any form, or by any means, electronic,
mechanical, photocopying, recording or otherwise, without the prior written
permission of the copyright holder and the publisher.

ISBN 978-89-6281-938-0 (13740)

파고다북스	www.pagodabook.com
파고다 어학원	www.pagoda21.com
파고다 인강	www.pagodastar.com
테스트 클리닉	www.testclinic.com

| 낙장 및 파본은 구매처에서 교환해 드립니다.

2023년 7월
New iBT TOEFL®의 시작!

TOEFL 주관사인 미국 ETS(Educational Testing Service)는 iBT TOEFL® 시험에서 채점되지 않는 더미 문제가 삭제되면서 시간이 개정 전 3시간에서 개정 후 2시간 이하로 단축됐으며, 새로운 라이팅 유형이 추가되었다고 발표했다. 새로 바뀐 iBT TOEFL® 시험은 2023년 7월 26일 정기 시험부터 시행된다.

- 총 시험 시간 기존 약 3시간 …▸ 약 2시간으로 단축
- 시험 점수는 각 영역당 30점씩 총 120점 만점으로 기존과 변함없음

영역	2023년 7월 26일 이전	2023년 7월 26일 이후
Reading	지문 3~4개 각 지문 당 10문제 시험 시간 54~72분	지문 2개 각 지문 당 10개 시험 시간 36분
Listening	대화 2~3개, 각 5문제 강의 3~5개, 각 6문제 시험 시간 41~57분	28문제 대화 2개, 각 5문제 강의 3개, 각 6문제 시험 시간 36분
Speaking	*변함없음 4문제 독립형 과제 1개 통합형 과제 3개 시험 시간 17분	
Writing	2문제 통합형 과제 1개 독립형 과제 1개 시험 시간 50분	2문제 통합형 과제 1개 수업 토론형 과제 1개 시험 시간 30분

목차

이 책의 구성과 특징	5
4주 완성 학습 플랜	7
iBT TOEFL® 개요	8
iBT TOEFL® Listening 개요	15

PART 01 Question Types — 18

01 Main Idea	20
02 Details	26
03 Function & Attitude	32
04 Connecting Contents	38
05 Inference	44

PART 02 Actual Tests — 50

Actual Test 01	52
Actual Test 02	64
Actual Test 03	76
Actual Test 04	88
Actual Test 05	100
Actual Test 06	112
Actual Test 07	124

해설서

이 책의 구성과 특징

▶▶ New TOEFL 변경사항 및 최신 출제 유형 완벽 반영!
2023년 7월부터 변경된 새로운 토플 시험을 반영, iBT TOEFL®의 출제 경향을 완벽하게 반영한 문제와 주제를 골고루 다루고 있습니다.

▶▶ 예제를 통한 문제 유형별 공략법 정리!
본격적으로 실전에 들어가기에 앞서, iBT TOEFL® Listening의 5가지 문제 유형을 정리해 자주 나오는 질문을 파악하고 예제를 풀어보면서 iBT TOEFL® 전문 연구원이 제시하는 문제풀이 필수 전략을 학습할 수 있도록 하였습니다.

▶▶ 7회분의 Actual Test로 실전 완벽 대비!
실제 시험과 동일하게 구성된 7회분의 Actual Test를 수록해 실전에 철저하게 대비할 수 있도록 구성하였습니다.

▶▶ 추가 3회분의 Actual TEST 온라인으로 제공!
교재 외에 추가 3회분의 Actual TEST를 파고다북스 홈페이지에서 PDF로 다운로드 받으실 수 있습니다. (총 10회분의 Actual TEST 제공)

▶▶ 그룹 스터디와 독학에 유용한 단어 시험지 생성기 제공!
자동 단어 시험지 생성기를 통해 교재를 학습하면서 외운 단어 실력을 테스트해 볼 수 있습니다.

▶ 사용 방법: 파고다북스 홈페이지(www.pagodabook.com)에 로그인한 후 상단 메뉴의 [모의테스트] 클릭 > 모의테스트 메뉴에서 [단어 시험] 클릭 > TOEFL - PAGODA TOEFL Actual Test Listening 를 고른 후 원하는 문제 수를 입력하고 문제 유형 선택 > '단어 시험지 생성'을 누르고 별도의 브라우저 창으로 뜬 단어 시험지를 PDF로 내려 받거나 인쇄

▶▶ 무료 MP3 다운로드 및 바로듣기 제공
파고다북스 홈페이지(www.pagodabook.com)에서 교재 MP3 다운로드 가능합니다.

▶ 이용 방법: 파고다북스 홈페이지(www. pagodabook.com)에서 해당 도서 검색 > 도서 상세 페이지의 '도서 자료실' 코너에 등록된 MP3 자료 다운로드(로그인 필요) 또는 바로듣기

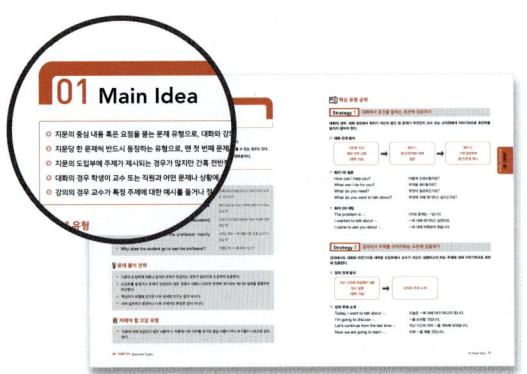

PART 01 Question Types

iBT TOEFL® 전문 연구원이 제안하는 5가지 문제 유형별 고득점 전략을 학습할 수 있습니다.

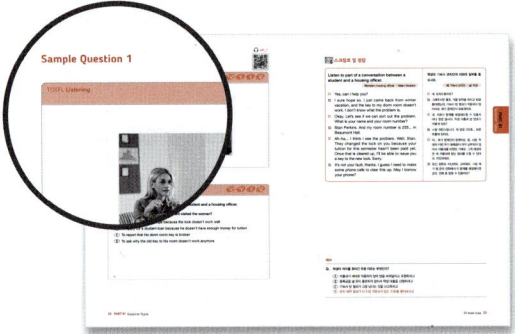

Sample Question

앞에서 배운 Lesson별 문제풀이 전략을 적용하여, 점진적으로 난이도가 높아지는 연습문제를 풀어보며 해당 문제 유형을 집중 공략합니다.

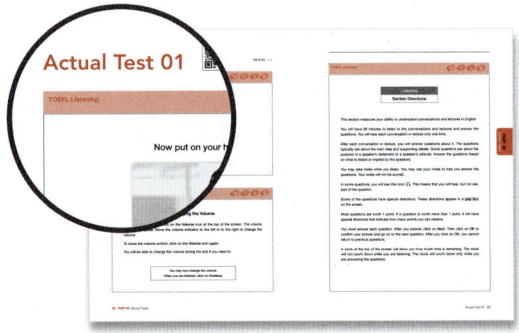

PART 02 Actual Test

실제 시험과 동일하게 구성된 7회분의 Actual Test를 통해 실전에 대비합니다.

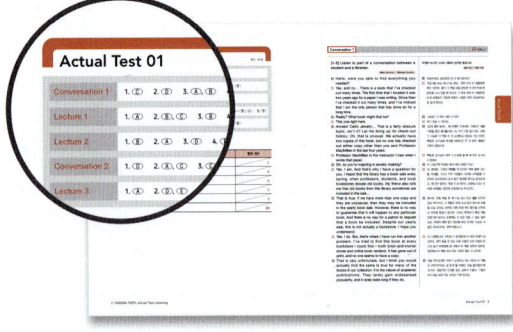

정답 및 해석

지문 및 문제에 대한 정답과 해석, 지문에서 등장한 주요 어휘 정리를 수록했습니다.

4주 완성 학습 플랜

DAY 1	DAY 2	DAY 3	DAY 4	DAY 5
PART 01				
01 Main Idea • 문제 유형 및 전략 • Sample Questions	02 Details • 문제 유형 및 전략 • Sample Questions	03 Function & Attitude • 문제 유형 및 전략 • Sample Questions	04 Connecting Contents • 문제 유형 및 전략 • Sample Questions	05 Inference • 문제 유형 및 전략 • Sample Questions
DAY 6	**DAY 7**	**DAY 8**	**DAY 9**	**DAY 10**
PART 01	PART 02			
PART 01 Review • PART 1 전체 복습하기	Actual Test 01 • 문제 풀이	Actual Test 01 Review • 틀린 문제 확인하기 • 어휘 재정리하기	Actual Test 02 • 문제 풀이	Actual Test 02 Review • 틀린 문제 확인하기 • 어휘 재정리하기
DAY 11	**DAY 12**	**DAY 13**	**DAY 14**	**DAY 15**
PART 02				
Actual Test 03 • 문제 풀이	Actual Test 03 Review • 틀린 문제 확인하기 • 어휘 재정리하기	Actual Test 04 • 문제 풀이	Actual Test 04 Review • 틀린 문제 확인하기 • 어휘 재정리하기	Actual Test 05 • 문제 풀이
DAY 16	**DAY 17**	**DAY 18**	**DAY 19**	**DAY 20**
PART 02				
Actual Test 05 Review • 틀린 문제 확인하기 • 어휘 재정리하기	Actual Test 06 • 문제 풀이	Actual Test 06 Review • 틀린 문제 확인하기 • 어휘 재정리하기	Actual Test 07 • 문제 풀이	Actual Test 07 Review • 틀린 문제 확인하기 • 어휘 재정리하기

iBT TOEFL® 개요

1. iBT TOEFL® 이란?

TOEFL은 영어 사용 국가로 유학을 가고자 하는 외국인들의 영어 능력을 평가하기 위해 개발된 시험이다. TOEFL 시험 출제 기관인 ETS는 이러한 TOEFL 본연의 목적에 맞게 문제의 변별력을 더욱 높이고자 PBT(Paper-Based Test), CBT(Computer-Based Test)에 이어 차세대 시험인 인터넷 기반의 iBT(Internet-Based Test)를 2005년 9월부터 시행하고 있다. ETS에서 연간 30~40회 정도로 지정한 날짜에 등록함으로써 치르게 되는 이 시험은 Reading, Listening, Speaking, Writing 총 4개 영역으로 구성되며 총 시험 시간은 약 2시간이다. 각 영역별 점수는 30점으로 총점 120점을 만점으로 하며 성적은 시험 시행 약 4~8일 후에 온라인에서 확인할 수 있다.

2. iBT TOEFL®의 특징

1) 영어 사용 국가로 유학 시 필요한 언어 능력을 평가한다.

각 시험 영역은 실제 학업이나 캠퍼스 생활에 반드시 필요한 언어 능력을 측정한다. 평가되는 언어 능력에는 자신의 의견 및 선호도 전달하기, 강의 요약하기, 에세이 작성하기, 학술적인 주제의 글을 읽고 내용 이해하기 등이 포함되며, 각 영역에 걸쳐 고르게 평가된다.

2) Reading, Listening, Speaking, Writing 전 영역의 통합적인 영어 능력(Integrated Skill)을 평가한다.

시험이 4개 영역으로 분류되어 있기는 하지만 Speaking과 Writing 영역에서는 [Listening + Speaking], [Reading + Listening + Speaking], [Reading + Listening + Writing]과 같은 형태로 학습자가 둘 또는 세 개의 언어 영역을 통합해서 사용할 수 있는지를 평가한다.

3) Reading 지문 및 Listening 스크립트가 길다.

Reading 지문은 700단어 내외로 A4용지 약 1.5장 분량이며, Listening은 3~4분 가량의 대화와 6~8분 가량의 강의로 구성된다.

4) 전 영역에서 노트 필기(Note-taking)를 할 수 있다.

긴 지문을 읽거나 강의를 들으면서 핵심 사항을 간략하게 적어두었다가 문제를 풀 때 참고할 수 있다. 노트 필기한 종이는 시험 후 수거 및 폐기된다.

5) 선형적(Linear) 방식으로 평가된다.

응시자가 시험을 보는 과정에서 실력에 따라 문제의 난이도가 조정되어 출제되는 CAT(Computer Adaptive Test) 방식이 아니라, 정해진 문제가 모든 응시자에게 동일하게 제시되는 선형적인 방식으로 평가된다.

6) 시험 응시일이 제한된다.

시험은 주로 토요일과 일요일에만 시행되며, 시험에 재응시할 경우, 시험 응시일 3일 후부터 재응시 가능하다.

7) Performance Feedback이 주어진다.

온라인 및 우편으로 발송된 성적표에는 수치화된 점수뿐 아니라 각 영역별로 수험자의 과제 수행 정도를 나타내는 표도 제공된다.

3. iBT TOEFL®의 구성

시험 영역	Reading, Listening, Speaking, Writing
시험 시간	약 2시간
시험 횟수	연 30~40회(날짜는 ETS에서 지정)
총점	0~120점
영역별 점수	각 영역별 30점
성적 확인	응시일로부터 4~8일 후 온라인에서 성적 확인 가능

시험 영역	문제 구성	시간
Reading	• 독해 지문 2개, 총 20문제가 출제된다. • 각 지문 길이 700단어 내외, 지문당 10개 문제	36분
Listening	• 대화(Conversation) 2개(각 5문제씩)와 강의(Lecture) 3개(각 6문제씩)가 출제된다.	36분
Break		10분
Speaking	• 독립형 과제(Independent Task) 1개, 통합형 과제(Integrated Task) 3개 총 4개 문제가 출제된다.	17분
Writing	• 통합형 과제(Integrated Task) 1개(20분) • 수업 토론형 과제 (Writing for Academic Discussion) 1개(9분)	30분

4. iBT TOEFL®의 점수

1) 영역별 점수

Reading	0~30	Listening	0~30
Speaking	0~30	Writing	0~30

2) iBT, CBT, PBT 간 점수 비교

기존에 있던 CBT, PBT 시험은 폐지되었으며, 마지막으로 시행된 CBT, PBT 시험 이후 2년 이상이 경과되어 과거 응시자의 시험 성적 또한 유효하지 않다.

5. 시험 등록 및 응시 절차

1) 시험 등록

온라인과 전화로 시험 응시일과 각 지역의 시험장을 확인하여 신청할 수 있으며, 일반 접수는 시험 희망 응시일 7일 전까지 가능하다.

❶ 온라인 등록

ETS 토플 등록 사이트(https://www.ets.org/mytoefl)에 들어가 화면 지시에 따라 등록한다. 비용은 신용카드로 지불하게 되므로 American Express, Master Card, VISA 등 국제적으로 통용되는 신용카드를 미리 준비해 둔다. 시험을 등록하기 위해서는 회원 가입이 선행되어야 한다.

❷ 전화 등록

한국 프로메트릭 콜센터(00-7981-4203-0248)에 09:00~17:00 사이에 전화를 걸어 등록한다.

2) 추가 등록

시험 희망 응시일 3일(공휴일을 제외한 업무일 기준) 전까지 US $60의 추가 비용으로 등록 가능하다.

3) 등록 비용

2023년 현재 US $220(가격 변동이 있을 수 있음)

4) 시험 취소와 변경

ETS 토플 등록 사이트나 한국 프로메트릭(00-7981-4203-0248)으로 전화해서 시험을 취소하거나 응시 날짜를 변경할 수 있다. 등록 취소와 날짜 변경은 시험 날짜 4일 전까지 해야 한다. 날짜를 변경하려면 등록 번호와 등록 시 사용했던 성명이 필요하며 비용은 US $60이다.

5) 시험 당일 소지품

❶ 사진이 포함된 신분증(주민등록증, 운전면허증, 여권 중 하나)

❷ 시험 등록 번호(Registration Number)

6) 시험 절차

❶ 사무실에서 신분증과 등록 번호를 통해 등록을 확인한다.

❷ 기밀 서약서(Confidentiality Statement)를 작성한 후 서명한다.

❸ 소지품 검사, 사진 촬영, 음성 녹음 및 최종 신분 확인을 하고 연필과 연습장(Scratch Paper)을 제공받는다.

❹ 감독관의 지시에 따라 시험실에 입실하여 지정된 개인 부스로 이동하여 시험을 시작한다.

❺ Reading과 Listening 영역이 끝난 후 10분간의 휴식이 주어진다.

❻ 시험 진행에 문제가 있을 경우 손을 들어 감독관의 지시에 따르도록 한다.

❼ Writing 영역 답안 작성까지 모두 마치면 화면 종료 메시지를 확인한 후에 신분증을 챙겨 퇴실한다.

7) 성적 확인

응시일로부터 약 4~8일 후부터 온라인으로 점수 확인이 가능하며, 시험 전에 종이 사본 수령을 신청했을 경우 약 11-15일 후 우편으로 성적표를 받을 수 있다.

6. 실제 시험 화면 구성

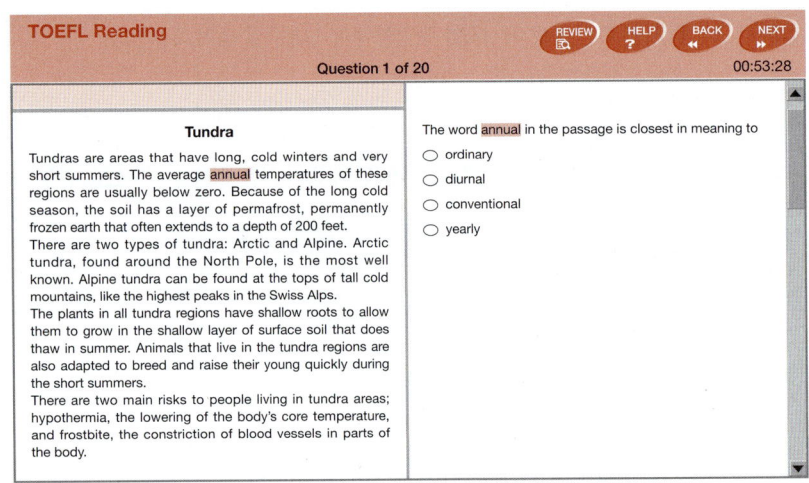

전체 Direction

시험 전체에 대한 구성 설명

Reading 영역 화면

지문은 왼쪽에, 문제는 오른쪽에 제시

Listening 영역 화면

수험자가 대화나 강의를 듣는 동안 사진이 제시됨

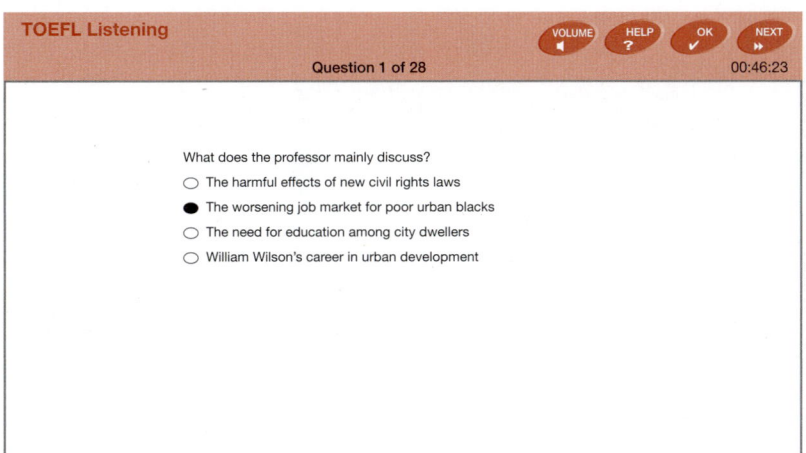

Listening 영역 화면

듣기가 끝난 후 문제 화면이 등장

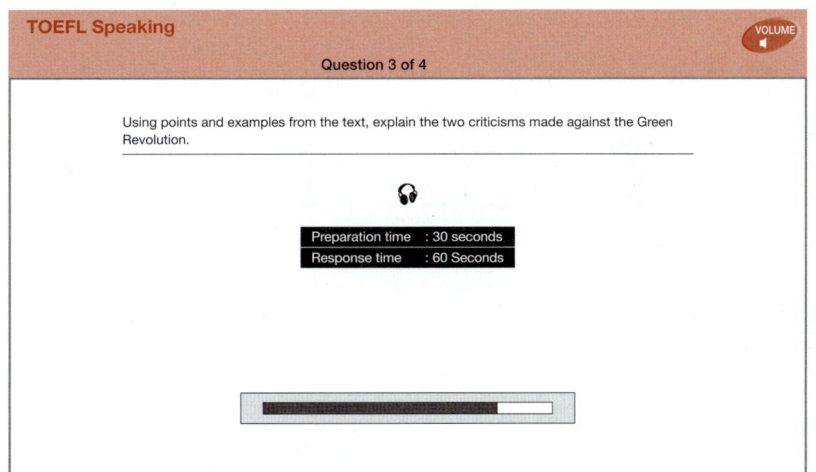

Speaking 영역 화면

문제가 주어진 후, 답변을 준비하는 시간과 말하는 시간을 알려줌

TOEFL Writing

Question 1 of 2

In the late 14th century, an unknown poet from the Midlands composed four poems titled *Pearl, Sir Gawain and the Green Knight, Patience,* and *Cleanness*. This collection of poems is referred to as Cotton Nero A.x and the author is often referred to as the Pearl Poet. Up to this day, there have been many theories regarding the identity of this poet, and these are three of the most popular ones.

The first theory is that the author's name was Hugh, and it is based on the *Chronicle of Andrew of Wyntoun*. In the chronicle, an author called Hucheon (little Hugh) is credited with writing three poems, one of which is about the adventures of Gawain. Not only that, but all three poems are written in alliterative verse, as are all four of the poems in *Cotton Nero A.x*. Since they are written in the same style and one poem from each set concerns Gawain, some people contend that all of the *Cotton Nero A.x* poems were written by Hugh.

The second theory is that John Massey was the poet, and it is supported by another poem called *St. Erkenwald* and penmanship. Although the actual authorship of *St. Erkenwald* is unknown, John Massey was a poet who lived in the correct area and time for scholars to attribute it to him. This manuscript was written in very similar handwriting to that of the Pearl Poet, which indicates that one person is likely the author of all five of the poems.

The third theory is that the poems were actually written by different authors from the same region of England. This comes from the fact that there is little linking the poems to each other. Two are concerned with the Arthur legends, but the only link connecting the other two is that they describe the same area of the countryside. They also seem to be written in the same dialect. Taken together, these facts indicate that they were written in the same region, but they probably were not written by the same person.

Writing 영역 화면

왼쪽에 문제가 주어지고 오른쪽에 답을 직접 타이핑할 수 있는 공간이 주어짐

복사(Copy), 자르기(Cut), 붙여넣기(Paste) 버튼이 위쪽에 위치함

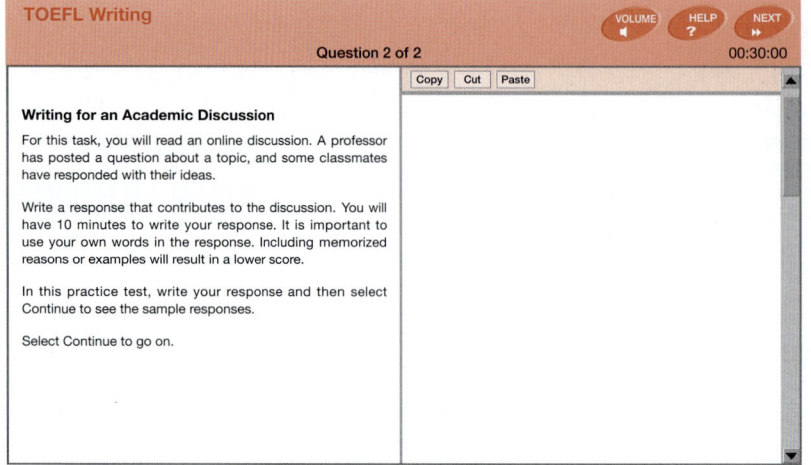

Writing 영역 화면

왼쪽에 문제가 주어지고 오른쪽에 답을 직접 타이핑할 수 있는 공간이 주어짐

복사(Copy), 자르기(Cut), 붙여넣기(Paste) 버튼이 위쪽에 위치함

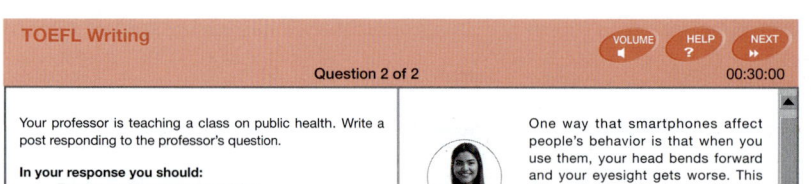

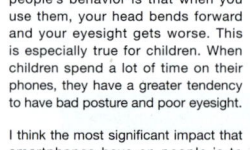

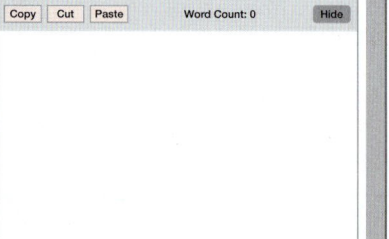

Writing 영역 화면

왼쪽에 문제가 주어지고 오른쪽에 답을 직접 타이핑할 수 있는 공간이 주어짐

복사(Copy), 자르기(Cut), 붙여넣기(Paste) 버튼이 타이핑하는 곳 위쪽에 위치함

iBT TOEFL® Listening 개요

1. Listening 영역의 구성

Listening 영역은 약 2개의 파트로 구분되며, 각 파트에는 대화(Conversation), 강의(Lecture) 및 토론(Discussion)의 청취 지문이 등장한다. 대화 지문은 2개가 출제되며, 강의 지문은 3개가 출제된다.

* Conversation 지문 2개, 지문당 각 5문제 출제

* Lecture 지문 3개, 지문당 각 6문제 출제

2. Listening 영역의 특징 및 학습 방법

1) 반드시 노트 필기를 한다.

iBT TOEFL®에서는 청취 지문을 듣는 동안 주어진 필기 용지(Scratch Paper)에 들은 내용을 필기할 수 있다. 따라서 강의나 토론과 같은 긴 지문을 들을 때, 기억력에 의존하기보다는 강의의 중요한 내용과 예측 가능한 문제의 답을 미리 노트 필기하면 문제의 정답을 좀 더 쉽게 찾을 수 있다.

2) 다양한 대화와 주제에 익숙해지자.

iBT TOEFL®은 실제 영어 사용 국가에서 학업을 할 수 있는 능력을 평가하는 TOEFL 본래의 목적에 충실하도록 변화한 만큼, 시험의 내용 또한 실제와 흡사하게 변화했다고 볼 수 있다. 대화의 내용이 좀 더 캠퍼스 상황으로 한정되었고, 대화와 강의의 길이가 길어졌으며, 주저하며 말하거나 대화 중간에 끼어든다거나 하는 자연스러운 청취 지문이 제시되고 있다. 발음에 있어서는 미국식 발음 외에 영국이나 호주식 발음도 가끔 청취 지문에 등장하여 다양한 언어가 사용되는 학업 상황을 좀 더 현실적으로 보여주고 있다.

3) 전체 내용을 이해한다.

iBT TOEFL®에서는 지문 전반의 내용을 이해하여 전체 주제를 찾거나(Main Idea Question) 또는 특정 정보의 상호 관계를 파악하는 문제(Connecting Content Question)가 많이 등장한다.

4) 억양이나 톤에 주의한다.

iBT TOEFL®에서 특히 눈에 띄는 문제 유형은 지문의 일부분을 다시 듣고 화자의 억양, 목소리 톤, 문맥상 전후 관계를 통해 정보에 대한 화자의 태도나 목적을 파악하는 문제 유형이다. 태도 파악 문제(Attitude Question)와 의도 파악 문제(Function Question)라고 불리는 이 문제 유형들은 지문의 의미 그 자체만으로 정답을 찾기보다는 특정 부분의 문맥상 의미를 파악하여 선택지에서 올바른 답을 골라야 한다.

3. Listening 영역의 문제 유형

iBT Listening 영역에서는 크게 5개의 문제 유형이 출제된다. 아래의 표는 Listening 영역의 문제를 유형별로 나누어 각 유형별 특징과 출제 문항 수를 표시해 놓은 것이다.

< iBT Listening 영역의 5가지 문제 유형>

주제 찾기 문제 Main Idea Question	강의나 대화의 목적 또는 전반적인 흐름을 묻는 문제 예) What is the conversation mainly about? 대화는 주로 무엇에 관한 것인가?
세부 사항 찾기 문제 Details Question	강의나 대화의 주요한 정보들에 관해 묻는 문제 예) What are the characteristics of ~? ~의 특징은 무엇인가?
의도 및 태도 파악 문제 Function & Attitude Question	화자가 특정 문장을 언급한 의도나 문장에 담긴 화자의 태도나 관점을 묻는 문제 예) Listen again to part of the conversation. Then answer the question. Why does the student say this: 대화의 일부를 다시 듣고 질문에 답하시오. 학생은 왜 이렇게 말하는가:
관계 파악 문제 Connecting Contents Question	강의나 대화에 주어진 정보들 간의 유기적 관계를 묻는 문제 (e.g. 인과, 비교, 추론하기, 결과 예측하기, 일반화하기) 예) Why does the professor say ~? 교수는 왜 ~라고 말하는가? In the conversation, the speakers discuss ~. Indicate in the table below ~. 대화에서 화자들은 ~에 대해 논의한다. ~인지 아래 표에 표시하시오.
추론 문제 Inference Question	강의나 대화를 통해 유추할 수 있는 것을 묻는 문제 예) What is the student most likely to do next? 학생이 다음에 무엇을 할 것 같은가?

4. 기존 시험과 개정 시험 간 Listening 영역 비교

	기존 iBT (2023년 7월 전)	개정 후 iBT (2023년 7월 이후)
지문 개수	대화 2~3개 강의 3~5개	대화 2개 강의 3개
지문당 문제 수	대화 각 5문제 강의 각 6문제	대화 각 5문제 강의 각 6문제
전체 시험 시간	41~57분	36분

- 지문 및 질문 유형은 기존과 동일하다.

PAGODA TOEFL

Actual Test

LISTENING

PART 01
Question Types

- Lesson 01   Main Idea
- Lesson 02   Details
- Lesson 03   Function & Attitude
- Lesson 04   Connecting Contents
- Lesson 05   Inference

01 Main Idea

- 지문의 중심 내용 혹은 요점을 묻는 문제 유형으로, 대화와 강의에 모두 출제된다.
- 지문당 한 문제씩 반드시 등장하는 유형으로, 맨 첫 번째 문제로 나오는 경우가 많다.
- 지문의 도입부에 주제가 제시되는 경우가 많지만 간혹 전반적인 내용을 이해해야 풀 수 있는 경우도 있다.
- 대화의 경우 학생이 교수 또는 직원과 어떤 문제나 상황에 대해 대화하는 지문이 대부분이다.
- 강의의 경우 교수가 특정 주제에 대한 예시를 들거나 정의를 설명한다.

📖 문제 유형

• What is the main [purpose/topic/idea] of the [conversation/lecture/talk/discussion]?	[대화/강의/담화/토론]의 [목적/주제/요지]는 무엇인가?
• What does the [speaker/professor] mainly talk about?	[화자/교수]는 주로 무엇에 관해 이야기하고 있는가?
• What is the [conversation/lecture/talk/discussion] mainly about?	[대화/강의/담화/토론]은 주로 무엇에 관한 것인가?
• What aspect of ~ does the professor mainly discuss?	교수는 주로 ~에 대한 어떤 면을 논의하고 있는가?
• Why does the student go to see the professor?	학생은 왜 교수를 찾아가는가?

💡 문제 풀이 전략

- 지문의 도입부에 대화나 강의 주제가 언급되는 경우가 많으므로 도입부에 집중한다.
- 도입부를 놓쳤거나 주제가 언급되지 않은 경우는 대화나 강의의 전반에 제시되는 예시와 설명을 종합하여 판단한다.
- 핵심어가 포함돼 있지만 너무 상세한 보기는 답이 아니다.
- 너무 일반적인 문장이나 너무 구체적인 문장은 답이 아니다.

🚨 피해야 할 오답 유형

- 지문에 아예 언급되지 않은 내용이나, 지문에 나온 단어를 썼지만 중심 내용이 아닌 보기들이 나오므로 유의한다.

핵심 유형 공략

Strategy 1 대화에서 용건을 말하는 초반에 집중하기

대화의 경우, 대화 초반에서 화자가 자신의 용건 및 문제가 무엇인지 교수 또는 교직원에게 이야기하므로 초반부를 놓치지 말아야 한다.

◐ 대화 전개 방식

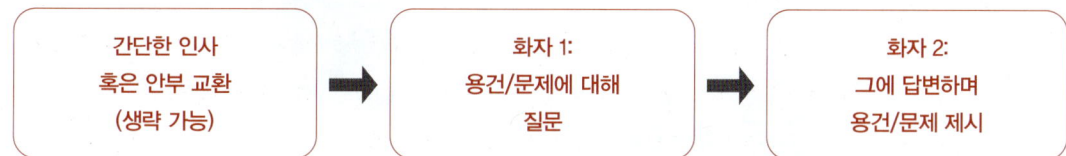

◐ 화자 1의 질문

How can I help you?	어떻게 도와드릴까요?
What can I do for you?	무엇을 해드릴까요?
What do you need?	무엇이 필요하신가요?
What do you want to talk about?	무엇에 대해 얘기하고 싶으신가요?

◐ 화자 2의 대답

The problem is ~.	(저의) 문제는 ~입니다.
I wanted to talk about ~.	~에 대해 얘기하고 싶었어요.
I came to ask you about ~.	~에 대해 여쭤보러 왔습니다.

Strategy 2 강의에서 주제를 이야기하는 초반에 집중하기

강의에서도 대화와 마찬가지로 대부분 도입부에서 교수가 자신이 설명하고자 하는 주제에 대해 이야기하므로 초반에 집중한다.

◐ 강의 전개 방식

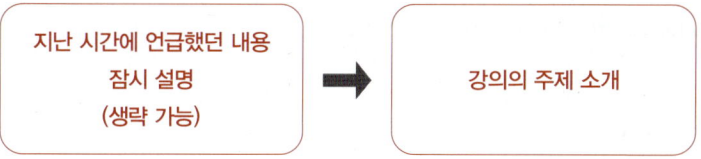

◐ 강의 주제 소개

Today, I want to talk about ~.	오늘은 ~에 대해 이야기하고자 합니다.
I'm going to discuss ~.	~을 논의할 것입니다.
Let's continue from the last time ~.	지난 시간에 이어 ~을 계속해 보겠습니다.
Now we are going to learn ~.	이제 ~을 배울 것입니다.

Sample Question 1

Listen to part of a conversation between a student and a housing officer.

What is the main reason that the student visited the woman?

Ⓐ To ask for a room change because the lock doesn't work well
Ⓑ To apply for a student loan because he doesn't have enough money for tuition
Ⓒ To report that his dorm room key is broken
Ⓓ To ask why the old key to his room doesn't work anymore

스크립트 및 정답

Listen to part of a conversation between a student and a housing officer.

Woman: Housing officer | Man: Student

- W: Yes, can I help you?
- M: I sure hope so. I just came back from winter vacation, and the key to my dorm room doesn't work. I don't know what the problem is.
- W: Okay. Let's see if we can sort out the problem. What is your name and your room number?
- M: Stan Perkins. And my room number is 233... in Beaumont Hall.
- W: Ah-ha... I think I see the problem. Well, Stan. They changed the lock on you because your tuition for this semester hasn't been paid yet. Once that is cleared up, I'll be able to issue you a key to the new lock. Sorry.
- M: It's not your fault, thanks. I guess I need to make some phone calls to clear this up. May I borrow your phone?

학생과 기숙사 관리인의 대화의 일부를 들으시오.

여: 기숙사 관리인 | 남: 학생

- 여: 네, 도와드릴까요?
- 남: 그래주시면 좋죠. 겨울 방학을 마치고 방금 돌아왔는데, 기숙사 방 열쇠가 작동하지 않아서요. 뭐가 문제인지 모르겠어요.
- 여: 네, 저희가 문제를 해결해드릴 수 있을지 어디 한번 봅시다. 학생 이름과 방 번호가 어떻게 되죠?
- 남: 스탠 퍼킨스입니다. 제 방은 233호... 보몬트홀에 있어요.
- 여: 아... 뭐가 문제인지 알겠어요. 음, 스탠. 학생의 이번 학기 등록금이 아직 납부되지 않아서 자물쇠를 바꿨던 거예요. 그게 해결되면 새 자물쇠에 맞는 열쇠를 드릴 수 있어요. 미안하네요.
- 남: 당신 잘못도 아닌데요. 고마워요. 그럼 제가 몇 군데 전화해서 이 문제를 해결해야겠군요. 전화 좀 빌릴 수 있을까요?

해석

Q. 학생이 여자를 찾아간 주된 이유는 무엇인가?

- Ⓐ 자물쇠가 제대로 작동하지 않아 방을 바꿔달라고 요청하려고
- Ⓑ 등록금을 낼 돈이 충분하지 않아서 학생 대출을 신청하려고
- Ⓒ 기숙사 방 열쇠가 고장 났다는 것을 신고하려고
- **Ⓓ 방의 예전 열쇠가 더 이상 작동되지 않는 이유를 물어보려고**

Sample Question 2

Listen to part of a lecture in an art class.

What is the lecture mainly about?

Ⓐ The historic importance that the two museums have in world art history
Ⓑ How different the two museums are in terms of the size of the collections they feature
Ⓒ The difference between the two museums in terms of the artistic periods they focus on
Ⓓ Why the Musée D'Orsay displays not only paintings but also sculptures and ceramics

 스크립트 및 정답

Listen to part of a lecture in an art class.

Man: Professor | Woman: Student

W: Professor Jenson, I know that the Musée D'Orsay is a very famous art museum in Paris... uh... second only to the Louvre. But I don't really know what the difference is between the collections featured in the two museums.

M: Let's see... Well, the primary difference between the two museums... besides the physical size of the two museum complexes... is that in the Louvre you can see works of art that span the many different artistic periods of mankind, okay? But, in the Musée D'Orsay you can see exhibits that focus only on the second half of the nineteenth century roughly between 1848 and 1905. There are a lot of Impressionist and Post-Impressionist works on display there. But... uh... the museum is not limited to paintings. You can find all different kinds of art there regardless of... uh... regardless of technique or means of expression.

W: I see. So the Musée D'Orsay does have sculpture and ceramics... in addition to paintings?

M: Right. But, besides some exceptions, the art was all created within the years I mentioned.

미술 강의의 일부를 들으시오.

남: 교수 | 여: 학생

여: 젠슨 교수님, 오르세 미술관은 파리에서 매우 유명한 미술관이라고 알고 있습니다... 어... 루브르 다음으로요. 하지만 그 두 미술관에 전시되어 있는 소장품들 간의 차이점이 뭔지는 잘 모르겠어요.

남: 봅시다... 음... 두 미술관 사이의 주된 차이점은... 두 미술관 단지의 물리적 크기를 제외하면... 루브르에서는 인류 예술에 있어 매우 다양한 시기에 걸친 예술 작품을 볼 수 있습니다. 알겠죠? 하지만 오르세 미술관에서는 대략 1848년에서 1905년 사이인 19세기 후반에만 초점을 둔 전시 작품들을 볼 수 있어요. 많은 인상파 및 후기 인상파 작품들이 그곳에 전시되어 있습니다. 하지만... 어... 그 미술관이 회화 작품에만 국한된 건 아니에요. 그곳에서는 표현 기법이나 표현 수단과는 무관하게... 어... 무관한 모든 종류의 다양한 예술 작품을 찾아볼 수 있죠.

여: 그렇군요. 그래서 오르세 미술관에는 그림뿐만 아니라... 조각이나 도예 작품도 있는 거군요?

남: 맞아요. 하지만 몇 가지 예외를 제외하면 이 작품들은 모두 제가 언급한 시기에 창작된 것들입니다.

해석

Q. 강의는 주로 무엇에 관한 것인가?

Ⓐ 두 미술관이 세계 미술사에서 차지하는 역사적 중요성
Ⓑ 두 미술관이 특징으로 삼는 소장품의 규모와 관련해 어떻게 다른지
Ⓒ 초점을 맞춘 예술 시대와 관련한 두 미술관의 차이점
Ⓓ 오르세 미술관이 왜 그림뿐만 아니라 조각과 도예 작품도 전시하는지

02 Details

- 대화나 강의의 중심 내용이 아닌 세부 사항을 묻는 유형이다.
- 출제 빈도가 가장 높은 유형으로, 지문당 2~3개의 문제가 출제된다.
- 정답이 두 개 이상인 경우도 있으므로 보기 전체를 꼼꼼히 살펴보는 것이 중요하다.
- 대화의 경우 학생이 교수 또는 교직원과 문제가 발생한 이유나 문제 해결 방법 등에 대한 세부 사항을 이야기한다.
- 강의의 경우 교수가 특정 주제와 관련해 직접 언급했던 세부 사항에 대해 자주 묻는다.

📖 문제 유형

- What does the [professor/employee] offer to do ~?   [교수/고용주]는 무엇을 해주겠다고 제시하는가?
- What are the two key features of ~?   ~의 두 가지 주요 특징은 무엇인가?
- What [is/are] the characteristic(s) of ~?   ~의 특징(들)은 무엇인가?
- What is the reason that ~?   ~하는 이유는 무엇인가?
- According to the professor, [what/why] is ~?   교수에 의하면, [~은 무엇인가/왜 ~인가]?
- What does the [student/professor] [say/talk] about ~?   [학생/교수]는 ~에 관해 무엇이라고 말하는가?

💡 문제 풀이 전략

- 대화 혹은 강의의 주제와 관련된 경우가 많다.
- 지문에 나온 단어가 포함된 보기가 항상 답인 것은 아니다.
- 대부분의 경우 패러프레이징(Paraphrasing)된 문장을 보기로 제시하기 때문에 동의어나 같은 의미를 나타내는 다른 표현을 익혀 둔다.
- 필기에 집중하다 보면 다른 세부 내용들을 놓칠 수 있으므로, 되도록 짧고 간단하게 자신이 알아볼 수 있는 기호나 약어를 사용하여 메모하는 것이 좋다.

피해야 할 오답 유형

- 지문에 아예 언급되지 않거나 반은 맞고 반은 틀린 내용의 보기 등이 제시될 수 있으므로 유의한다.

핵심 유형 공략

Strategy 1 | 메모를 하며 처음부터 끝까지 집중하기

세부 사항(Details) 문제에서는 다양한 문제가 출제되며, 주제(Main Idea) 문제처럼 정형화된 질문 유형이 아니므로 어떤 세부 사항을 묻는 문제가 출제될지 알 수 없다. 따라서 대화나 강의를 처음부터 끝까지 집중하여 듣는 것이 중요하며, 듣다가 중요하다고 생각되는 내용은 중간중간 메모하는 것이 좋다.

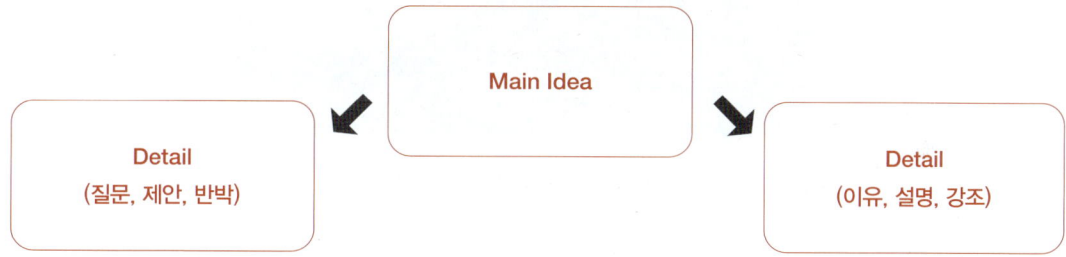

Strategy 2 | 노트테이킹(Note-Taking)은 이렇게 한다!

- 대화나 강의 중 질문이나 그 외의 기능어(Since, In fact, But 등)가 나오면 주의해 듣는다.
- 들리는 내용을 전부 메모하기보다는 주제와 연관된 세부 사항 위주로 메모한다.
- 필기에 집중하다 보면 다른 세부 내용들을 놓칠 수 있으므로 되도록 짧고 간단하게 적는다.

Strategy 3 | 패러프레이징(Paraphrasing)은 이렇게 한다!

- 패러프레이징이란 지문에서 언급했던 표현을 보기에서 그대로 한번 더 언급하는 것이 아니라 다른 말로 바꾸어 표현하는 것을 뜻한다.
- 많은 문제 유형에서 찾아볼 수 있으며, 세부 사항 문제에서 특히 자주 등장한다.
- 지문에 나온 표현이 패러프레이징 되지 않고 보기에 그대로 쓰였다면 오답일 가능성이 크므로 주의해야 한다.

Sample Question 1

Listen to part of a conversation between a student and an academic advisor.

According to the advisor, what is an advantage of making a career plan?

- Ⓐ It can lessen the students' stress concerning their graduation.
- Ⓑ It can help the students get a job after they graduate.
- Ⓒ It can teach the students how to write a good career plan paper.
- Ⓓ It can help the students when they apply for graduation.

스크립트 및 정답

Listen to part of a conversation between a student and an academic advisor.

Woman: Academic advisor | Man: Student

W: Nice to see you, Thomas. How can I help you today?

M: As an academic advisor working for the university, maybe you can explain this announcement to me. Why do they have to go out of their way to cause more stress and problems?

W: Announcement? What has gotten you so upset?

M: Did you see this announcement in the school newspaper?

W: No. What's it about?

M: It says here that starting next semester any student planning on applying for graduation is required to submit some kind of career plan, or they cannot graduate! What is the point in doing something like that?

W: Ah, yes. We have a meeting about that later in the week. But what it sounds like to me is that the university is looking for weaknesses to address in their programs. You know, they might be trying to see how they can better help students plan for their careers following graduation. I'm sure that you will find it to be more useful once we work out your career plan.

M: Okay, but why does it sound like we will be punished if we don't help them with their research into the issue? Why does the responsibility fall on us?

학생과 지도 교수의 대화의 일부를 들으시오.

여: 지도 교수 | 남: 학생

여: 만나서 반가워요, 토마스. 오늘은 뭘 도와줄까요?

남: 저희 대학의 지도 교수님이시니 제게 이 공고에 대해 설명해 주실 수 있을 것 같아서요. 그 사람들은 왜 굳이 스트레스와 문제를 더 만들어내는 걸까요?

여: 공고라고요? 뭐 때문에 그렇게 화가 난 거죠?

남: 학교 신문에 난 이 공고 보셨어요?

여: 아뇨, 뭐에 관한 건가요?

남: 다음 학기부터 졸업을 신청할 예정인 학생은 모두 진로 계획 같은 걸 반드시 제출해야 되고, 그렇지 않으면 졸업할 수 없다고 여기에 써 있어요! 대체 그렇게 하는 취지가 뭔가요?

여: 아, 맞아요. 이번 주말에 그 문제에 대한 회의가 잡혀 있어요. 그런데 내가 보기엔 대학이 그들의 프로그램 내에서 대처해야 할 취약점을 찾아내려고 하는 것 같군요. 그러니까, 대학 측에서 학생들이 졸업 후 진로 계획을 세우는 데 어떻게 더 나은 도움을 줄 수 있을지 알아보려는 걸 거예요. 일단 우리가 학생의 진로 계획서를 놓고 작업에 들어가면 그 편이 더 유용하다는 것을 분명히 알게 될 겁니다.

남: 그렇군요. 그런데 대학에서 그 문제를 조사하는 걸 도와주지 않으면 우리가 불이익을 받을 것처럼 들리는 이유는 뭐죠? 그 책임을 왜 우리가 부담해야 하는 건가요?

해석

Q. 지도 교수에 의하면, 진로 계획의 장점은 무엇인가?

Ⓐ 졸업과 관련된 학생들의 스트레스를 덜어줄 수 있다.
Ⓑ 학생들이 졸업 후 직업을 구하는 데 도움을 줄 수 있다.
Ⓒ 학생들에게 진로 계획서를 잘 쓰는 법을 가르쳐 줄 수 있다.
Ⓓ 학생들이 졸업을 신청할 때 도움을 줄 수 있다.

Sample Question 2

Listen to part of a lecture in an astronomy class.

According to the professor, which of the following is a characteristic of Drake's Equation?

- Ⓐ It compared America's and the former Soviet Union's space projects in a mathematical way.
- Ⓑ It proved the worldwide view which is shared by astronomers and the general public.
- Ⓒ It quantified the possibility that there is an advanced civilization somewhere in space.
- Ⓓ It succeeded in ascertaining the number of advanced civilizations in the entire universe.

스크립트 및 정답

Listen to part of a lecture in an astronomy class.

Man: Professor

M One of the most controversial topics among astronomers, both professional and amateur, as well as the general public, is whether or not extraterrestrial intelligence exists. For those who believe in extraterrestrial intelligence... such as myself... a mathematical formula known as Drake's Equation often... um... comes to the forefront when defending the idea. The equation is named after the astronomer Frank D. Drake, a pioneer in the search for signs of extraterrestrial intelligence. Basically, his equation is a... um... quantification of the probability that an advanced civilization exists somewhere in the universe. Okay, what this means is that depending on the assumptions about all of the equation's variables, the most typical of guesses claim that between 10,000 and 100,000 advanced civilizations exist... and that number is just for the Milky Way galaxy, not for the entire universe. Drake's theory is strong enough that the U.S. project called SETI... which stands for Search for Extraterrestrial Intelligence... has been underway for several years now, and SETI places much of its hopes on Drake's Equation. Some efforts to find extraterrestrial life were also underway in the former Soviet Union using the same mathematical equation.

천문학 강의의 일부를 들으시오.

남: 교수

일반인뿐만 아니라 프로와 아마추어 천문학자 사이에서 가장 논란이 되고 있는 주제 중 하나는 외계 생명체의 존재 여부입니다. 저처럼... 외계 생명체의 존재를 믿는 사람들에게... 드레이크 방정식이라고 알려진 수학 공식은... 음... 그 견해를 옹호하는 데 자주 전면에 부각되죠. 이 방정식은 외계 생명체의 흔적을 탐색한 개척자인 프랭크 D. 드레이크라는 천문학자의 이름을 따서 지은 것입니다. 기본적으로 그의 방정식은... 음... 선진 문명이 우주 어딘가에 존재한다는 확률을 수량화한 것입니다. 그러니까 이것이 의미하는 바는, 이 방정식의 모든 변수에 대한 가정에 따르면, 가장 전형적인 추측으로 1만에서 10만개의 선진 문명이 존재하고... 그 수는 전체 우주가 아닌 우리 은하계에만 해당하는 것이죠. 드레이크의 이론은 충분히 유력해서 SETI라 불리는... '외계 생명체 탐사'를 나타내는 미국의 프로젝트가... 현재 수년째 진행 중이며 SETI는 그 프로젝트의 희망을 대부분 드레이크 방정식에 걸고 있습니다. 외계 생명체를 찾으려는 노력은 구소련에서도 같은 수학 방정식을 이용해서 진행된 적이 있었습니다.

해석

Q. 교수에 의하면, 다음 중 어떤 것이 드레이크 방정식의 특징인가?

Ⓐ 미국과 구소련의 우주 프로젝트들을 수학적인 방식으로 비교했다.
Ⓑ 천문학자들과 일반 대중이 공유하는 범세계적인 견해를 증명했다.
Ⓒ 우주 어딘가에 선진 문명이 존재할 가능성을 수량화했다.
Ⓓ 전 우주에 존재하는 선진 문명의 수를 알아내는 데 성공했다.

03 Function & Attitude

- 의도 파악(Function) 유형이 화자의 말의 의도를 파악하는 데 중점을 두는 데 비해 태도 파악(Attitude) 유형은 화자의 감정과 태도를 제대로 파악했는지를 평가하는 문제이다.
- 대화나 강의에서 한 문제 정도 출제되는 질문 유형이다.
- 질문을 한 뒤 지문의 일부를 다시 들려주는 경우가 많다.
- 대화의 경우 화자가 한 말이 어떤 의미인지, 화자의 생각, 태도 또는 숨겨진 의도가 무엇인지를 묻는다. 특히 숨겨진 의도를 파악하려면 다시 들려주는 문장뿐만 아니라 지문의 전체 문맥을 파악하는 것이 중요하다.
- 강의의 경우 학생과 교수가 질문과 답을 주고받을 때 교수의 의견과 여담 등에서 자주 출제되며 교수가 학생들의 주의를 환기시키거나 자신이 앞서 했던 말을 번복할 때 나오기도 한다.

📕 문제 유형

의도 파악(Function)

- Listen again to part of the lecture. Then answer the question.
  Why does the professor say this:
  강의의 일부를 다시 듣고 질문에 답하시오.
  교수는 왜 이렇게 말하는가:

- What does the professor mean when he/she says this:
  교수는 다음과 같이 말하며 무엇을 의미하는가:

태도 파악(Attitude)

- What is the professor's attitude toward ~?
  ~에 대한 교수의 태도는 어떠한가?

- What does the professor feel by saying ~?
  ~라고 말할 때 교수는 어떤 감정을 느끼는가?

- What is the professor's opinion about ~?
  ~에 대한 교수의 의견은 무엇인가?

💡 문제 풀이 전략

- 구어체 표현이 자주 등장하므로 숙어나 관용어구 등을 알아 두면 좋다.
- 특정 문장만 듣고 직접 해석하여 답을 고르기보다는 해당 문장이 앞뒤의 문맥, 내용과 어떻게 연결되는지를 확인해야 한다. 즉, 지문의 문맥에 집중하는 것이 중요하다.
- 화자의 억양이 중요한 단서가 되므로 억양의 숨은 의미를 파악할 수 있어야 한다.
- 화자가 그 같은 말을 한 이유가 무엇인지 숙지하고 있어야 한다.
- 말투와 억양을 통해 화자의 감정이 드러나므로 이를 재빨리 파악하도록 한다.
- 어조와 문맥을 연결하여 화자의 감정을 알아차려야 한다.

🚨 피해야 할 오답 유형

- 지문에 아예 언급되지 않거나 문맥을 고려하지 않고 화자의 말을 잘못 해석한 보기들이 제시되므로 유의한다.

📖 핵심 유형 공략

Strategy 1 메모를 하며 처음부터 끝까지 집중하기

의도 및 태도 파악(Function & Attitude) 문제 유형은 주제(Main Idea) 문제 유형처럼 정형화된 질문 유형이 아니므로 대화나 강의 내용을 처음부터 끝까지 집중하여 듣는 것이 중요하며, 중요하다고 생각되는 부분은 메모하는 것이 좋다.

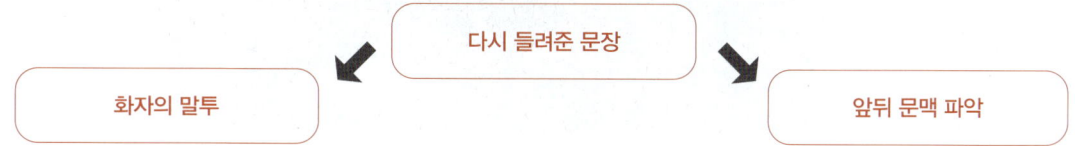

Strategy 2 전체 흐름에 주목하여 노트테이킹하기

- 대화나 강의의 세부적인 사항보다는 전체 흐름에 주목하며 필기한다.
- 의도 파악(Function) 문제는 화자가 특정한 말을 한 이유와 목적을 묻는 문제이므로 자신을 화자의 입장에 대입해보며 받아 적는다.
- 태도 파악(Attitude) 문제는 화자가 특정 주제나 상황에 대하여 어떻게 생각하고 있는지를 묻는 문제이므로 주요 내용에 대한 화자의 생각과 견해를 중심으로 메모한다.

Strategy 3 화자의 억양과 강세에 주의하기

문장을 다시 들을 때 화자의 말투는 문제를 이해하는 데 많은 도움이 된다. 화자의 말투를 통해 화자가 특정 주제나 사건 등에 어떠한 생각과 태도를 갖고 있는지 파악할 수 있다. 가령, 말투를 통해 화자가 만족하는지 불만스러워하는지, 혹은 긍정적인지 부정적인지를 파악할 수 있다.

Strategy 4 전후 상황 등 맥락을 반드시 정확히 파악하기

- 다시 들려준 문장만으로는 화자의 의도를 제대로 알아차리지 못할 수도 있다. 주어진 문장의 전후 상황을 고려하여 화자가 말하고자 하는 것을 정확히 파악하도록 한다.
- 다시 들려준 문장은 여러 가지 뜻으로 해석될 수 있으므로 앞뒤 문맥을 통해 상황에 맞는 답을 찾는 것이 중요하다.
- 자신을 화자의 상황에 대입하여 생각해보면 대화와 강의 내용 및 화자의 태도를 이해하는 데 도움이 된다.

Sample Question 1

TOEFL Listening

TOEFL Listening

Listen to part of a conversation between a student and an academic advisor.

Listen again to part of the conversation. Then answer the question.

Why does the employee say this:

Ⓐ Sophomores are not qualified to register for the class.
Ⓑ Professor Tatum does not allow sophomores to take the class.
Ⓒ The Holocaust is too heavy of an issue for sophomores to handle.
Ⓓ There are restrictions for sophomores to take the class.

 스크립트 및 정답

Listen to part of a conversation between a student and an academic advisor.

Woman: Academic advisor | Man: Student

W Hmm... It looks like we have a small problem here with your classes for next semester.
M What? Where? What's the problem?
W Well, you see here? This 'Overview of the Holocaust' class is an advanced history course.
M Yes, I know. I'm a history major and I plan on focusing on the Holocaust.
W Well, you are only a sophomore. You would need the signed consent of the professor teaching the course in order to register for it.
M I see. Professor Tatum is teaching it. He told me I could take it, but I guess he didn't know he'd have to sign for me to register. I can go by and get his signature after my three o'clock class. Would it be okay if I came back around four-thirty?

학생과 지도 교수의 대화의 일부를 들으시오.

여: 지도 교수 | 남: 학생

여 흠... 학생이 다음 학기에 듣는 수업들에 좀 문제가 있는 것 같네요.
남 네? 어디요? 뭐가 문제인 거죠?
여 여기 보여요? 이 '유대인 대학살 개관' 수업은 상급 역사 과정이에요.
남 네, 알아요. 저는 역사 전공이고 유대인 대학살에 집중해서 공부하려고 해요.
여 음, 학생은 겨우 2학년이에요. 이 수업에 등록하려면 수업 담당 교수님의 서명을 받은 동의서가 필요할 거예요.
남 그렇군요. 테이텀 교수님이 가르치시는 수업이에요. 저에게 이 수업을 들어도 된다고 하셨지만, 제가 등록하려면 서명을 해주셔야 한다는 걸 모르셨나 봐요. 3시 수업이 끝나고 잠깐 들러서 서명을 받을 수 있어요. 4시 30분쯤 다시 찾아와도 괜찮을까요?

해석

Q. 대화의 일부를 다시 듣고 질문에 답하시오.

> 남 네, 알아요. 저는 역사 전공이고 유대인 대학살에 집중해서 공부하려고 해요.
> 여 음, 학생은 겨우 2학년이에요.

직원은 왜 이렇게 말하는가:

> 여 음, 학생은 겨우 2학년이에요.

Ⓐ 2학년 학생들은 이 수업에 등록할 자격이 되지 않는다.
Ⓑ 테이텀 교수는 2학년 학생들이 수강하는 것을 허락하지 않는다.
Ⓒ 유대인 대학살은 2학년 학생들이 듣기에는 너무 무거운 주제다.
Ⓓ 2학년 학생들이 이 수업을 수강하는 데 제한이 있다.

Sample Question 2

Listen to part of a lecture in an architecture class.

How does the professor feel toward the student's initial answer?

Ⓐ He thinks the student answered without thinking hard.
Ⓑ He believes the student is ignorant.
Ⓒ He sees that the student has a brilliant idea.
Ⓓ He is a bit offended by the student's answer.

 **스크립트 및 정답**

Listen to part of a lecture in an architecture class.

Man: Professor | Woman: Student

M Wood continues to be the most common natural material used in construction, but the most common man-made material is... what?

W Plastic?

M Plastic for the construction of buildings?

W Oh, um... Concrete?

M That is better... Yes, concrete. Now, concrete is not a natural material, but the ingredients used to make concrete are. These include water and crushed rock, or gravel. Another ingredient is cement, which comes from powdered limestone, gypsum and clay... to name a few. When these components are mixed together, they form a fluid that can be poured into molds of any desired shape.

Oh... on a side note, people often use the terms "concrete" and "cement" interchangeably, which is incorrect. Cement as an ingredient in concrete, is a powdery substance that turns into a sticky, glue-like substance after it has been mixed with water. Then, given time it hardens into concrete. How much water is added to the cement determines how strong the cement will be, as well as how easily it can be shaped in molds. Less water means that the concrete will be stronger but not be as easy to shape, while the opposite is true if more water is used.

건축학 강의의 일부를 들으시오.

남: 교수 | 여: 학생

남 나무는 언제까지나 건축에서 가장 흔히 쓰이는 천연 자재이지만, 가장 흔히 쓰이는 인공 자재는... 무엇일까요?

여 플라스틱이요?

남 플라스틱으로 건물을 짓는다고요?

여 아, 음... 콘크리트요?

남 좀 낫군요... 네, 콘크리트입니다. 자, 콘크리트는 천연 자재가 아니지만, 콘크리트를 만드는데 쓰이는 재료들은 천연 자재입니다. 물과 잘게 부순 바위, 즉 자갈이 있죠. 또 다른 자재로는 시멘트가 있는데 이는 몇 가지 예를 들자면 석회 가루, 석고, 점토에서 생산되죠. 이런 요소들이 뒤섞이면 원하는 형태의 어떤 틀에도 부어넣을 수 있는 유동체가 됩니다.

아... 덧붙이자면, 사람들은 종종 "콘크리트"와 "시멘트"라는 용어를 혼용하는데, 이는 잘못된 겁니다. 콘크리트의 재료인 시멘트는, 물과 섞이고 나면 풀처럼 끈적거리는 성분으로 변하는 가루 물질입니다. 그리고 시간이 지나면 딱딱해져 콘크리트가 되죠. 물을 시멘트에 얼마나 넣느냐에 따라 틀에서 얼마나 모양이 쉽게 잡히는지 뿐만 아니라 시멘트가 얼마나 단단해지는지가 결정됩니다. 물을 적게 넣으면 콘크리트가 단단해지지만 모양을 만들기는 쉽지 않고, 물을 더 넣으면 그 반대가 됩니다.

해석

Q. 교수는 학생의 처음 답변에 대해 어떻게 생각하는가?

Ⓐ 학생이 깊이 생각하지 않고 답했다고 생각한다.
Ⓑ 학생이 무지하다고 본다.
Ⓒ 학생의 발상이 참신하다고 생각한다.
Ⓓ 학생의 답변에 약간 불쾌해하고 있다.

04 Connecting Contents

- 지문이 전체적으로 어떤 구조로 이루어져 있는지를 묻거나 교수나 학생의 발언이 이 지문에서 어떤 역할을 하는지를 파악하는 문제이다.
- 지문당 한 문제 정도가 출제되며, 아예 출제되지 않는 경우도 있다.
- 특정 문장이나 정보가 지문에서 어떤 역할을 하는지 묻거나 순서, 시간의 흐름, 예시에 대해 묻는 문제가 자주 출제된다.
- 대화의 경우 화자들의 대화를 통해 화자가 특정 행동이나 말을 한 목적을 유추할 수 있어야 한다.
- 강의의 경우 교수가 무언가를 언급한 후 그것을 언급한 이유를 묻는 문제가 자주 출제되므로 언급한 목적과 관련된 세부 사항을 주의 깊게 듣는다.
- 짝 맞추기나 순서 나열 등의 문제 유형이 간혹 출제될 때가 있다.

📖 문제 유형

• Why does the professor mention ~?	교수는 왜 ~를 언급하는가?
• [How/In what order] is the [lecture/discussion] organized?	[어떻게/어떤 순서로] [강의/토론]이 구성되어 있는가?
• How does the professor [begin/conclude] the [lecture/discussion]?	교수는 [강의/토론]을 어떻게 [시작하는가/끝마치는가]?
• In the [conversation/lecture], the speakers discuss ~. Indicate in the table below ~.	[대화/강의]에서 화자들은 ~에 대해 논의한다. ~인지 아래 표에 표시하시오.
• Put the following steps in order.	다음 단계들을 순서에 맞게 배열하시오.

💡 문제 풀이 전략

- 세부적인 사항에 집중하기보다는 각각의 큰 주제에 집중해야 한다.
- 각 문단이 어떻게 연결되어 있는지 파악하며 듣는다.
- 화자가 들려주는 강의가 어떤 흐름으로 진행되는지 파악해야 한다.
- 주제와 그다지 관련이 없는 이야기가 나왔다면 화자가 그 이야기를 언급한 이유를 추측할 수 있어야 한다.

🚨 피해야 할 오답 유형

- 대화나 강의에서 전혀 언급되지 않거나, 대화나 강의에 나온 단어를 포함하나 질문의 의도에 맞지 않은 내용의 보기가 제시되므로 주의한다.

핵심 유형 공략

Strategy 1 | '이유'와 관련된 세부 사항에 유의하기

관계 파악(Connecting Contents) 문제는 다양하게 출제가 되지만 대화의 경우 어느 정도 유추가 가능하다. 특히 학생이 특정 주제에 대해 이야기하는 이유 등을 묻는 질문이 출제되는 경우가 그렇다. 특정 단어나 주제를 언급한 이유를 묻는 질문이 많이 출제되기 때문에 세부 사항에 유의해야 한다.

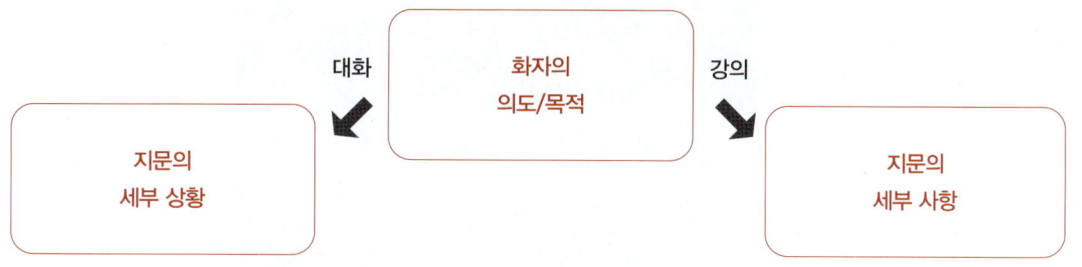

Strategy 2 | 대화에서 흔히 등장하는 상황

- 학생이 교수를 찾아온 상황: 강의 내용을 잘 이해하지 못한 경우, 과제에 대해 질문이 있는 경우, 프로젝트에 대해 문의하는 경우 등이 있다.
- 교수가 학생을 호출한 상황: 학생의 성적에 대해 묻는 경우, 학생이 현재 작업 중이거나 이미 완료한 프로젝트에 대해 질문하는 경우, 학생의 진로를 논의하는 경우 등이 있다.
- 학생이 다른 누군가와 대화하는 상황: 학생이 교직원, 도서관 사서 같은 다양한 인물과 기숙사 생활이나 수업 등록 등의 특정 주제에 대해 대화를 나누는 경우 등이 있다.

Strategy 3 | 강의 문제에서 주의해야 할 사항

강의에서는 대부분 교수가 무언가를 언급하는 이유를 묻는 유형이 출제된다. 간혹 교수가 해당 내용을 설명하는 목적이 무엇인지 묻는 문제가 출제되기도 한다. 이 경우는 강의의 세부 사항이 아닌 전체 내용에 대해 묻는 질문이라는 데 유의한다.

Strategy 4 | 노트테이킹은 이렇게 한다!

- 대화나 강의의 세부 사항과 전체 흐름을 모두 고려하여 필기한다.
- 화자의 목적과 의도에 대한 문제라는 점을 항상 염두에 둔다.

Sample Question 1

Listen to part of a conversation between a student and a professor.

Why does the professor mention "personality factors"?

Ⓐ To emphasize how important they are for taking this class
Ⓑ To tell the student that they play a crucial role in life
Ⓒ To show another specific method of dealing with stress
Ⓓ To explain how they influence one's intelligence

스크립트 및 정답

Listen to part of a conversation between a student and a professor.

Man: Professor | Woman: Student

M Hello, Maria. You said you wanted to ask a question about your assignment?

W Yes, Professor. I was having a hard time sorting out what explains an individual's ability to cope with different levels of stress.

M I see. Yes, it might be confusing at first. There are three different resources to which people resort when they encounter stress. The first of these resources is external support, such as friends and family. The second of these is made up of each individual's psychological resources, such as each person's educational background… um… intelligence, and several other relevant personality factors. As you can imagine, these vary to extreme degrees depending upon the person.

W Um… Personality factors such as what?

M Well… For instance, whether or not the person is introverted or extroverted. When a person moves to a new city or gets a new job, that personality trait will help determine how stressed out the person gets, right?

W And now I know the third one. They are the coping strategies a person uses to confront stress.

M You got it!

학생과 교수의 대화의 일부를 들으시오.

남: 교수 | 여: 학생

남 안녕하세요, 마리아. 과제와 관련해서 물어볼 것이 있다고 했죠?

여 네, 교수님. 다양한 수위의 스트레스를 극복하는 개인의 능력을 설명해줄 수 있는 게 무엇일지 분류하는 데 제가 애를 먹고 있었어서요.

남 그렇군요. 맞아요. 처음에는 헷갈릴 수 있어요. 사람들이 스트레스를 받을 때 의존하는 세 가지 다른 수단들이 있어요. 이 중 첫 번째는 가족이나 친구 같은 외부의 도움입니다. 두 번째는 개인의 정신적 자원, 예를 들면 개개인의 학력… 음… 지성, 그리고 이와 관련한 여러 가지 성격 요인들로 이루어져 있어요. 상상할 수 있듯이, 이들은 사람에 따라 극단적으로 다양하죠.

여 저… 성격 요인이라면 어떤 것이 있죠?

남 음… 어떤 사람이 내성적인지 외향적인지를 예로 들죠. 누군가 새 도시로 이사를 가거나 새 직업을 갖게 된다면, 그의 성격적 특징이 그가 얼마나 스트레스를 받느냐를 결정하게 될 겁니다, 그렇죠?

여 이제 세 번째가 뭔지 알겠어요. 개인이 스트레스에 대처하기 위해 사용하는 대응 전략들이에요.

남 바로 그거예요!

해석

Q. 교수는 왜 "성격 요인"을 언급하는가?

Ⓐ 이 수업을 듣는 데 그것이 얼마나 중요한지 강조하기 위해
Ⓑ 삶에서 그것이 매우 중대한 역할을 한다는 것을 말하기 위해
Ⓒ 스트레스를 다루는 또 하나의 구체적인 방법을 보여주기 위해
Ⓓ 그것이 개인의 지능에 어떻게 영향을 미치는지 설명하기 위해

Sample Question 2

Listen to part of a lecture in a history class.

Why does the professor mention the "new urban history"?

Ⓐ To explain how mankind's entire history was affected by it
Ⓑ To give a specific example that can create a certain topicality
Ⓒ To suggest how the historians' decision was influenced by it
Ⓓ To illustrate the importance of it and how it changes history

 **스크립트 및 정답**

Listen to part of a lecture in a history class.

Woman: Professor

W Historians should, of course, do their best to be true to the past. But, this class is designed to raise a very important question, and that is, which past is it we are doing our best to be true to? Seeing as there are so many aspects of mankind to examine, both positive and negative, scholars must make a choice. They have to decide which aspects deserve attention and which do not. Topicality becomes relevant when current social concerns affect which aspects are focused on by the scholars. In the past... oh... thirty years or so, there has been something of a broadening of the scope of historical inquiry. There are different reasons for this, but the biggest is due to the result of a relatively small minority of historians who are responding to the demands of topicality. A good example would be the "new urban history" that came out of the crisis in America's cities during the 1960s. This vein of history stresses social mobility, minority politics, and... um... inner city deprivation. This focus on minorities, especially African-Americans, gave rise to an increased interest in Africa... an issue of topicality.

역사 강의의 일부를 들으시오.

여: 교수

여 역사가들은 당연히 과거에 대해 진실하지 려는 노력을 해야 합니다. 하지만 이 수업에서는 매우 중요한 문제를 제기하려고 하는데, 그것은 바로 우리가 어떤 과거에 진실하기 위해 최선을 다하고 있는가입니다. 긍정적인 면과 부정적인 면을 모두 포함해 인류에는 검토해 보아야 할 매우 다양한 측면이 있기 때문에 학자들은 선택을 해야만 합니다. 그들은 주목할 가치가 있는 측면과 그렇지 않은 측면을 결정해야만 하죠. 현재의 사회적 관심사가 학자들이 어떤 측면에 초점을 맞춰야 할지에 영향을 줄 때 시의성이 중요해집니다. 지난... 어... 30여년 간, 역사적 탐구의 폭이 넓어지는 중요한 사건이 있었습니다. 이것에는 다양한 이유들이 있지만, 가장 큰 이유는 시의성의 요구에 응답하는 상대적으로 극소수였던 역사가들의 결실 덕분이었죠. 좋은 예로 1960년대 미국 도시들의 위기 상황에서 생겨난 "신도시사"가 있겠군요. 이 같은 역사의 경향은 사회적 유동성, 소수 집단의 정치 그리고... 음... 도심 지역의 쇠퇴를 강조합니다. 이렇게 소수 집단, 특히 미국 흑인에 초점을 두면서 아프리카에 대해 좀 더 큰 관심을 불러일으키게 됐는데... 이것이 시의성이라는 쟁점입니다.

해석

Q. 교수는 왜 "신도시사"를 언급하는가?

Ⓐ 이것이 전체 인류 역사에 얼마나 영향을 주었는지 설명하기 위해
Ⓑ 특정한 시의성을 이끌어 낼 수 있는 구체적인 예를 들기 위해
Ⓒ 그것이 역사학자들의 결정에 어떤 영향을 주었는지 시사하기 위해
Ⓓ 그것의 중요성과 그것이 역사를 어떻게 변화시키는지 보여주기 위해

05 Inference

- 지문에 언급되지 않은 내용을 추론하는 유형이다.
- 지문당 한 문제가 출제되거나 아예 출제되지 않는 경우도 있으며, 대화와 강의에서 모두 출제되는 문제 유형이다.
- 대화의 경우 화자들이 대화를 통해 말하고자 하는 내용과, 문제, 처해진 상황을 파악해야 한다.
- 강의의 경우 교수가 다음에 무엇을 할 것인지를 묻는 문제나, 교수의 설명을 통해 유추할 수 있는 정보 등을 묻는 문제가 출제되므로 정보를 종합할 수 있는 능력이 요구된다.

📖 문제 유형

• What can be inferred about the [man/woman]?	[남자/여자]에 대해 무엇을 추론할 수 있는가?
• What can be inferred from the professor's explanation about ~?	교수의 ~에 대한 설명으로부터 무엇을 추론할 수 있는가?
• What does the [student/professor] imply about ~?	[학생/교수]는 ~에 관해 무엇을 암시하는가?
• What can be concluded about ~?	~에 관해 어떤 결론을 내릴 수 있는가?
• What will the [student/professor] most likely do next?	[학생/교수]는 다음에 무엇을 할 것 같은가?

💡 문제 풀이 전략

- 문제를 들으면서 유추해야 할 내용과 추론 대상을 미리 짐작해 본다.
- 구체적인 정보를 종합해 보편적인 결론을 얻는 '일반화'와, 원인을 근거로 결과를 추리하는 '인과' 방식을 염두에 두고 듣는다.
- 화자나 주위 사람들이 향후에 일어날 일에 대해 이야기할 때는 특히 주의를 기울인다.
- 막연한 '추측'과 사실에 근거한 '추론'을 구분할 수 있어야 한다.
- 정답은 지문에 나온 표현과 전혀 다르게 패러프레이징 되어 제시될 수 있으므로 보기는 전부 꼼꼼히 살펴야 한다.

🚨 피해야 할 오답 유형

- 지문에 아예 언급되지 않거나 지문에서 언급된 내용을 다르게 추론하는 보기, 논리를 비약하는 보기 등이 오답으로 제시되므로 유의한다.

핵심 유형 공략

Strategy 1 추측이 아닌 사실에 기반한 추론하기

추론(Inference) 문제는 '추측'이 아닌 확신할 수 있는 '추론'에 대해 묻는 문제이므로 이 둘의 차이를 제대로 구분하는 것이 중요하다. 추론은 추측과 달리 사실에 기반을 두는 것으로, 대화나 강의를 들으면서 추론을 요구하는 대상이 무엇인지 미리 짐작해 보는 것이 도움이 된다.

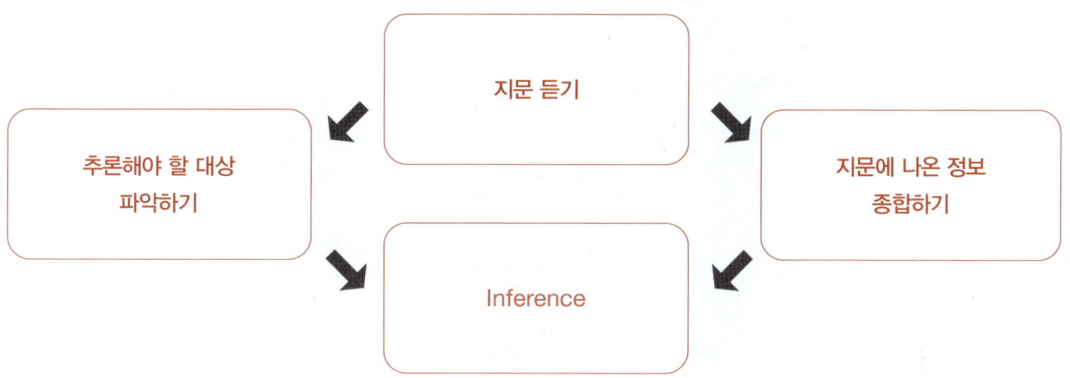

Strategy 2 추론해야 할 대상

- 지문의 핵심 문제나 주제: 일반적으로 이 두 가지에 대한 추론 문제가 주로 출제되긴 하지만 그렇다고 지문의 요점에만 초점을 맞춰 들으면 안 된다는 것을 기억한다.
- 교수/학생이 다음에 할 행동: 대화나 강의 지문을 들으며 전체적인 흐름을 파악하면 교수나 학생이 다음에 어떤 행동을 할지 유추할 수 있다. 가령, 학생이 교수와 무언가에 대해 이야기를 나누다 교수의 제안에 동의하는 경우, 학생이 교수의 제안을 받아들였으며 이를 실행할 것임을 유추할 수 있다.

Strategy 3 추론 시 주의해야 할 사항

추론(Inference) 문제는 높은 수준의 지식이나 추리력을 요구하는 문제가 아니라 지문을 이해하면 정답이 유추 가능한 수준의 문제이므로 너무 깊이 생각하지 않는 것이 좋다. 특히 지문에서 언급되었던 내용을 다른 관점에서 본다거나 패러프레이징하는 경우가 많으므로 주의한다.

Strategy 4 노트테이킹은 이렇게 한다!

- 대화나 강의의 세부적인 사항과 전체 흐름을 모두 고려하여 필기한다.
- 대화에서는 화자의 생각이나 문제점에 대한 반응을 요구하므로 이에 집중한다.
- 강의에서는 교수가 설명하는 강의의 주제와 그에 관련된 부주제에 대한 문제가 자주 출제된다.

Sample Question 1

Listen to part of a conversation between a student and a professor.

What can be inferred about the professor?

Ⓐ She is considering giving a perfect score to the student.
Ⓑ She thinks she should hire a new Teacher's Assistant.
Ⓒ She finds the student's behavior unusual and weird.
Ⓓ She thinks the student's attitude is praiseworthy.

 스크립트 및 정답

Listen to part of a conversation between a student and a professor.

Woman: Professor | Man: Student

W: Michael? Why are you waiting outside my office? Why didn't you knock?
M: Well, I didn't have an appointment and I didn't want to disturb you.
W: Please, come in and have a seat. How can I help you?
M: It's about the last test.
W: If I remember correctly, you aced it with a perfect score. Good job.
M: That's just it... I think the TA made a mistake. One of the multiple choice answers I gave was incorrect. So I didn't ace it, and you probably need to change it.
W: You want me to give you a lower grade? I must admit, this is a first for me... um... I applaud your honesty.
M: I know it is weird of me to bring it to your attention, but I believe that honest relationships in any situation bring about greater rewards in the end.

학생과 교수의 대화의 일부를 들으시오.

여: 교수 | 남: 학생

여: 마이클? 왜 내 연구실 밖에서 기다리고 있나요? 왜 노크를 하지 않았어요?
남: 음, 약속을 잡은 것도 아닌데다 교수님을 방해하고 싶지 않았거든요.
여: 어서 들어와 앉아요. 뭘 도와주면 될까요?
남: 지난번에 본 시험에 대한 건데요.
여: 내 기억이 맞는다면, 만점을 맞아서 A를 받지 않았나요? 잘했어요.
남: 바로 그것 때문인데요... 조교가 실수를 한 것 같습니다. 제가 풀었던 객관식 문제 하나가 답이 틀렸거든요. 그래서 만점을 받은 게 아니니 점수를 바꿔야 할 것 같아서요.
여: 점수를 더 낮춰 달라는 건가요? 솔직히 나로썬 이런 경우는 처음이군요... 음... 학생의 정직함을 칭찬하는 바예요.
남: 교수님께 이런 말씀을 드리는 게 이상하다는 건 알고 있지만, 저는 어떤 상황에서든 솔직한 관계가 나중에 더 큰 보상을 가져다 준다고 생각합니다.

해석

Q. 교수에 대해 무엇을 추론할 수 있는가?

Ⓐ 학생에게 만점을 주는 것을 고려하고 있다.
Ⓑ 새로운 조교를 구해야 한다고 생각한다.
Ⓒ 학생의 행동이 특이하고 이상하다고 생각한다.
Ⓓ 학생의 태도가 칭찬할 만하다고 생각한다.

Sample Question 2

Listen to part of a lecture in an engineering class.

What can be inferred from the professor's lecture about civil engineering?

Ⓐ It is a fairly new discipline to most people.
Ⓑ It has been established with the help of other disciplines.
Ⓒ It is most closely linked to mathematics.
Ⓓ It should not be counted as a scientific discipline.

스크립트 및 정답

Listen to part of a lecture in an engineering class.

Woman: Professor | Man: Student

W It appears that you have a fairly good idea about how civil engineering is a discipline that uses the various applications provided by physical and scientific principles. Now, can you tell me the basic source of advancements in civil engineering over the centuries?

M Sure... um... The advancement didn't really occur so much within the civil engineering discipline itself... I mean, most advancements were made, and are still being made, through civil engineering's close links to mathematics and physics.

W Excellent! I don't think I could have phrased it better myself. That is exactly right... Civil engineering does not stand on its own two feet. It is a discipline that is based upon a great collection of knowledge... mathematics and physics, as you said, but also mechanics, environmental science, geology, hydrology... and the list goes on and on. Okay... Another question for you. Before the term "civil engineer" was coined, what occupations were included in what we would now call civil engineering?

M In the past, well... any of the people involved in architectural design and construction... um... from the architects to the carpenters and stone masons, artisans in general. I suppose they would have been the original civil engineers.

공학 강의의 일부를 들으시오.

여: 교수 | 남: 학생

여 토목 공학이 어째서 물리 및 과학 법칙들을 아주 다양하게 응용하는 학문 분야인지에 대해 아주 잘 알고 있는 것 같군요. 그럼, 수 세기에 걸친 토목 공학 발전의 근본적인 원인에 대해 말해주겠어요?

남 네... 음... 토목 공학 분야 자체에서는 많은 발전이 이뤄지지 않았습니다... 제 말은, 대부분의 발전은 토목 공학의 수학 및 물리학의 밀접한 관계를 통해 이뤄진 것이며 여전히 그러하다는 것이죠.

여 훌륭해요! 나라도 그보다 더 잘 표현하진 못 했을 것 같군요. 정확히 맞아요... 토목 공학은 독자적으로는 존립할 수 없습니다. 이 분야는 학생이 말한 수학과 물리학뿐 아니라 기계학, 환경 과학, 지질학, 수문학 등... 끝없이 많은 여타 지식들의 집합체에 토대를 두고 있는 학문입니다. 좋아요... 질문을 하나 더 해 보죠. "토목 공학"이라는 용어가 만들어지기 전에는 우리가 현재 토목 공학이라고 부르는 것에 어떤 직업들이 포함돼 있었을까요?

남 과거에는, 음... 건축 설계와 건설 공사에 관여하는 모든 사람들이었죠... 음... 일반적으로 건축가부터 목수, 석공, 장인들이요. 그들이 최초의 토목 기사들이 아니었을까 합니다.

해석

Q. 교수의 토목 공학 강의에 대해 무엇을 추론할 수 있는가?

Ⓐ 대부분의 사람들에게 상당히 새로운 분야이다.
Ⓑ 다른 연구 분야의 조력으로 정립되었다.
Ⓒ 수학과 가장 밀접한 관계를 맺고 있다.
Ⓓ 과학의 한 분야로 간주되어서는 안 된다.

PART 02
Actual Tests

Actual Test 01

Actual Test 02

Actual Test 03

Actual Test 04

Actual Test 05

Actual Test 06

Actual Test 07

Actual Test 01

TOEFL Listening

Now put on your headset.

Click on **Continue** to go on.

TOEFL Listening

Changing the Volume

To change the volume, click on the **Volume** icon at the top of the screen. The volume control will appear. Move the volume indicator to the left or to the right to change the volume.

To close the volume control, click on the **Volume** icon again.

You will be able to change the volume during the test if you need to.

> You may now change the volume.
> When you are finished, click on **Continue**.

TOEFL Listening

Listening
Section Directions

This section measures your ability to understand conversations and lectures in English.

You will have 36 minutes to listen to the conversations and lectures and answer the questions. You will hear each conversation or lecture only one time.

After each conversation or lecture, you will answer questions about it. The questions typically ask about the main idea and supporting details. Some questions ask about the purpose of a speaker's statement or a speaker's attitude. Answer the questions based on what is stated or implied by the speakers.

You may take notes while you listen. You may use your notes to help you answer the questions. Your notes will not be scored.

In some questions, you will see this icon: 🎧 This means that you will hear, but not see, part of the question.

Some of the questions have special directions. These directions appear in a gray box on the screen.

Most questions are worth 1 point. If a question is worth more than 1 point, it will have special directions that indicate how many points you can receive.

You must answer each question. After you answer, click on **Next**. Then click on **OK** to confirm your answer and go on to the next question. After you click on **OK**, you cannot return to previous questions.

A clock at the top of the screen will show you how much time is remaining. The clock will not count down while you are listening. The clock will count down only while you are answering the questions.

Conversation 1

[1-5] Listen to part of a conversation between a student and a librarian.

1. What is the conversation mainly about?

   Ⓐ Finding out how to check out a book from the library
   Ⓑ Getting contact information of a particular book seller
   Ⓒ Finding out which books are sold at the book sale
   Ⓓ Deciding which books will be placed in storage

2. What does the woman say about the yearly book sale?

   Ⓐ It usually lasts for a whole year in the student library.
   Ⓑ It sells rare books that are out of print and expensive.
   Ⓒ It only sells donated books for charity purposes.
   Ⓓ It sells books that are donated by students and professors.

3. What are the criteria for deciding whether a book is put up for sale? Choose 2 answers.

   Ⓐ They have not been used for a long time.
   Ⓑ They are duplicate copies.
   Ⓒ They are old books.
   Ⓓ They exist in e-book form.

4. Why does the man mention volunteering?

   Ⓐ The student will have a higher chance of participating.
   Ⓑ The student is interested in the yearly book sale.
   Ⓒ The book sale is a popular school event.
   Ⓓ The library needs more volunteers for the book sale.

5. Listen again to part of the conversation. Then answer the question.

   Why does the man say this:

   Ⓐ To ask the student to buy it at the book sale at the end of the year
   Ⓑ To tell the student that it is too early to make a copy of the book
   Ⓒ To let the student know that she could search for it on the university's website
   Ⓓ To allow the student to scan the book at the university library office

Lecture 1

[1-6] Listen to part of a lecture in an ecology class. AT01_2

1. What is the talk mostly about?

   Ⓐ The history of the Colorado River and diverting its course
   Ⓑ The importance of the Colorado River to the people living around it
   Ⓒ The past water levels of the Colorado River and its future
   Ⓓ The people who use the water of the Colorado River for living

2. According to the professor, what is true about the Colorado River?

   Choose 2 answers.

   Ⓐ The trees that live around it give hundreds of years of information about it.
   Ⓑ Its power was great enough to create the Grand Canyon in Arizona.
   Ⓒ The first major diversion of it occurred at the end of the 19th century.
   Ⓓ Most of its precipitation falls on the eastern side of the Continental Divide.

3. According to the passage, what does the erratic flow of the river often lead to?

   Ⓐ Frequent droughts over hundreds of years
   Ⓑ A disaster caused by massive flooding
   Ⓒ A short period of sudden drought
   Ⓓ Unexpectedly heavy rainfall in the region

4. What can be inferred about the Colorado River?

   Ⓐ A substantial amount of its water is diverted to Nevada.
   Ⓑ Its water is expected to become more saline in 10 years.
   Ⓒ It is a vital source of water for Colorado and California.
   Ⓓ The first people who diverted it were various Native Americans.

5. Why does the professor mention the Hoover Dam?

   Ⓐ To indicate that it represented the start of building a series of dams for reservoirs
   Ⓑ To show how it contributed to the pollution of the water, making it murkier and bitterer
   Ⓒ To state that it was the first dam that successfully provided a stable water supply
   Ⓓ To explain how it led to the destruction of the ecosystem, especially the wetlands

6. Listen again to part of the lecture. Then answer the question.

   What does the professor mean when she says this:

   Ⓐ The professor thinks what the student said is not very creative.
   Ⓑ The professor is not sure what the student is trying to imply.
   Ⓒ The professor is trying to correct the student's statement.
   Ⓓ The professor knows that megaliter is not a commonly used word.

Lecture 2

[1-6] Listen to part of a lecture in a science class.

1. What is the lecture mainly about?

   Ⓐ The composition of various integuments
   Ⓑ The distinctions between nuts and seeds
   Ⓒ The culinary definitions of nuts and seeds
   Ⓓ The edible and inedible nuts and seeds

2. Which of the following is not mentioned in the lecture as an example of a true nut?

   Ⓐ Almond
   Ⓑ Chestnut
   Ⓒ Acorn
   Ⓓ Hazelnut

3. What does the professor mean when she says this:

   Ⓐ She thinks keeping calories in mind could benefit one's diet.
   Ⓑ She is expressing concern about the health issue regarding allergies.
   Ⓒ She suspects that nuts and seeds can be quite dangerous.
   Ⓓ She is explaining that consuming too much fat could be harmful.

4. Why does the professor mention a legume?

   Ⓐ To compare peanut seeds with walnut seeds
   Ⓑ To highlight interesting facts about the peanut
   Ⓒ To argue against the botanical definition of a drupe
   Ⓓ To illustrate a point about ground nuts and their name

5. What is true of both nuts and seeds?

   Ⓐ They have thick but soft integuments.
   Ⓑ They have fibrous, inedible endocarps.
   Ⓒ They contain many different nutrients.
   Ⓓ They are composed of 3 to 5 layers.

6. Why does the professor mention a coconut?

   Ⓐ To explain that it is a good source of energy for animals
   Ⓑ To tell the students that it is beneficial for one's health
   Ⓒ To give another example of a drupe with a misleading name
   Ⓓ To illustrate her point that it has an interesting looking exocarp

Conversation 2

[1-5] Listen to part of a conversation between a university employee and a student. AT01_4

Note-Taking

1. Why did the student go to the university book store?
   - Ⓐ To see if it carries a particular book
   - Ⓑ To request a refund for a damaged book
   - Ⓒ To get some documents printed
   - Ⓓ To complain about a book she purchased

2. What is indicated about the book in question? Choose 2 answers.
   - Ⓐ Some pages are wrongly printed.
   - Ⓑ The answer key is incorrect.
   - Ⓒ Pages are missing from it.
   - Ⓓ The pages are out of order.

3. Listen again to part of the conversation. Then answer the question. 🎧

   Why does the man say this: 🎧
   - Ⓐ To confirm that books have never been misprinted
   - Ⓑ To indicate that the computer database is not working
   - Ⓒ To state that corrupt files have not been uploaded before
   - Ⓓ To imply that the professor made a significant mistake

4. In the conversation, the speakers discuss the reasons why students cannot access the database outside of the library. Indicate in the table below whether each of the following is one of those reasons.

	Yes	No
Ⓐ It prevents students from selling the book.		
Ⓑ The professors want to profit from the sales.		
Ⓒ It makes it easier for students to do their homework.		
Ⓓ The students need to use their books in class.		

5. What will the student most likely do next?
   - Ⓐ Print out her homework assignments
   - Ⓑ Contact the professor of her class
   - Ⓒ Purchase a new copy of the book
   - Ⓓ Visit the university library computer lab

Lecture 3

[1-6] Listen to part of a lecture in a biology class.

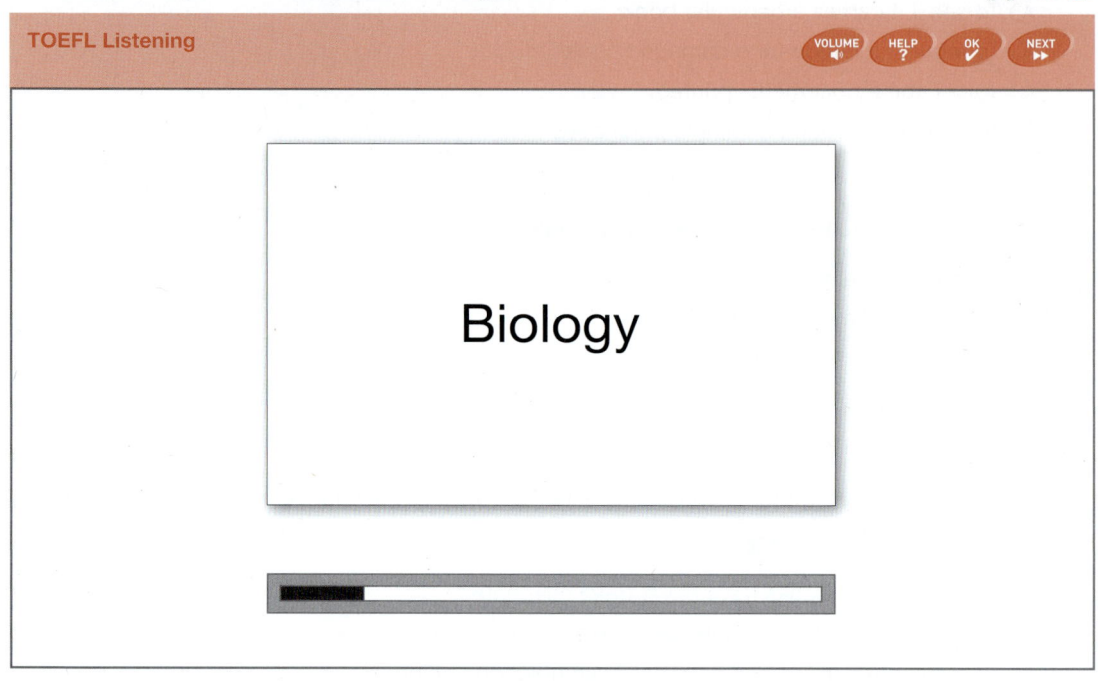

1. What is the main topic of the lecture?

   Ⓐ Different categories of camouflage and the animals that use them
   Ⓑ Three methods that animals use for camouflage and their weaknesses
   Ⓒ Some ways that animals practice camouflage and how they survive
   Ⓓ The most well-known examples of three categories of camouflage

2. According to the lecture, what are important factors that influence an animal's camouflage?

   Choose 2 answers.

   Ⓐ Temperature
   Ⓑ Resources
   Ⓒ Adaptation
   Ⓓ Surroundings
   Ⓔ Anatomy

3. Why does the professor mention natural habitat?

   Ⓐ To explain what kinds of advantages animals' natural habitats can provide
   Ⓑ To emphasize how difficult it is for animals to thrive outside of their natural habitat
   Ⓒ To talk about various animal behaviors according to their living environment
   Ⓓ To introduce the factor that animals utilize in concealing camouflage

4. What is true about disruptive camouflage?

   Ⓐ It provides predators with a misleading impression of the animal's body shape.
   Ⓑ It allows the animal a chance to survive by blending into the environment.
   Ⓒ It exaggerates the animal's body image and threatens away its predators.
   Ⓓ It causes a natural phenomenon that disturbs the predators.

5. What can be inferred about the animals that use adaptive camouflage?

   Ⓐ They tend to move from place to place to confuse their predators.
   Ⓑ Chromatophores can allow them to show different colors at the same time.
   Ⓒ They can change their body colors even though many of them are colorblind.
   Ⓓ Special color pigments are able to change their color to be similar to seawater.

6. What does the professor think about the mimic octopus?

   Ⓐ Its body is designed perfectly for living in the water.
   Ⓑ Other animals cannot compete with its superior skill.
   Ⓒ Its ability to copy so many animals must be difficult.
   Ⓓ Utilizing such camouflage will result in a lower chance of survival.

Actual Test 02

정답 및 해석 | p. 20

TOEFL Listening

Now put on your headset.

Click on **Continue** to go on.

TOEFL Listening

Changing the Volume

To change the volume, click on the **Volume** icon at the top of the screen. The volume control will appear. Move the volume indicator to the left or to the right to change the volume.

To close the volume control, click on the **Volume** icon again.

You will be able to change the volume during the test if you need to.

> You may now change the volume.
> When you are finished, click on **Continue**.

TOEFL Listening

Listening
Section Directions

This section measures your ability to understand conversations and lectures in English.

You will have 36 minutes to listen to the conversations and lectures and answer the questions. You will hear each conversation or lecture only one time.

After each conversation or lecture, you will answer questions about it. The questions typically ask about the main idea and supporting details. Some questions ask about the purpose of a speaker's statement or a speaker's attitude. Answer the questions based on what is stated or implied by the speakers.

You may take notes while you listen. You may use your notes to help you answer the questions. Your notes will not be scored.

In some questions, you will see this icon: 🎧 This means that you will hear, but not see, part of the question.

Some of the questions have special directions. These directions appear in a gray box on the screen.

Most questions are worth 1 point. If a question is worth more than 1 point, it will have special directions that indicate how many points you can receive.

You must answer each question. After you answer, click on **Next**. Then click on **OK** to confirm your answer and go on to the next question. After you click on **OK**, you cannot return to previous questions.

A clock at the top of the screen will show you how much time is remaining. The clock will not count down while you are listening. The clock will count down only while you are answering the questions.

Conversation 1

[1-5] Listen to part of a conversation between a student and a professor.

1. What is the conversation mainly about?
   Ⓐ How to obtain a faculty advisor
   Ⓑ The necessary steps for establishing a club
   Ⓒ Participating in different club activities
   Ⓓ How to find an old source from the library

2. Why does the woman mention a faculty advisor?
   Ⓐ To identify her role in the classic film club
   Ⓑ To clarify that the club already has one
   Ⓒ To explain the necessity of her visit to the professor
   Ⓓ To complain about the movie club's current one

3. According to the woman, what information did she get from the original charter?
   Ⓐ The names of the former club members
   Ⓑ Steps for organizing club meetings
   Ⓒ The contact information of university staff
   Ⓓ A list of films showing at the university

4. What does the man imply about the club the student is talking about?
   Ⓐ He does not understand the need for a movie club.
   Ⓑ He knows it will be hard to get the dean's permission.
   Ⓒ He cannot believe the club lasted for such a long time.
   Ⓓ He thinks the club will be successful in the future.

5. What is the professor's attitude toward the club's first meeting?
   Ⓐ He feels sorry that he has to miss the event.
   Ⓑ He thinks he should help the club get started.
   Ⓒ He is certain that he will attend the meeting.
   Ⓓ He is reluctant to be there since he is busy.

Lecture 1

[1-6] Listen to part of a lecture in an art class.

1. What does the professor mainly talk about?

    Ⓐ An upcoming class trip
    Ⓑ A comparison of impressionism and realism
    Ⓒ A modern artist's blending of genres
    Ⓓ The impact of realistic impressionism on modern art

2. According to the lecture, what is a commonality that impressionism and realism share?

    Ⓐ They are both movements that challenged perceptions of reality.
    Ⓑ They are both movements that started in the mid-19th century.
    Ⓒ They both changed the technique of their brushstrokes when compared to their predecessors.
    Ⓓ They both espoused a more subjective way of looking at the world.

3. According to the lecture, what is a feature of Frantzen's work "Summer Afternoon?"

    Ⓐ Brushstrokes that evoke a sense of movement
    Ⓑ Human figures dining on a blanket under a bright sun
    Ⓒ Darker colors that contrast with the brightness of the grass
    Ⓓ A lack of shadows that enhances the movement of the glittering light

4. Listen again to part of the lecture. Then answer the question. 🎧

    Why does the professor say this: 🎧

    Ⓐ She is implying that the students won't have any homework.
    Ⓑ She is disappointed that the students rarely come to class with their homework complete.
    Ⓒ She feels that the students should have sufficient information to draw some conclusions.
    Ⓓ She wonders if she has already given the students the same task in the past.

5. How does the professor organize the information in the lecture?

    Ⓐ By providing history first, then an example
    Ⓑ By providing a comparison first, then a synthesis
    Ⓒ By providing context first, then a variation
    Ⓓ By offering details, then a challenge

6. What will the class most likely do next?

    Ⓐ They will learn about another artist whose style is a mix of genres.
    Ⓑ They will discuss the movement's work, focusing on a French artist.
    Ⓒ They will dive into more examples of realistic impressionism.
    Ⓓ They will compare Frantzen's work with that of another artist.

Conversation 2

[1-5] Listen to part of a conversation between a student and a professor.

📋 Note-Taking

1. What are the speakers mainly discussing?
   - Ⓐ The importance of students being familiar with what they write
   - Ⓑ The story that the class discussed when the student was absent
   - Ⓒ The student's opinions about a story assigned for class discussion
   - Ⓓ The student's childhood memory and the theme of her paper

2. Why did the student miss the class?
   - Ⓐ She had to visit her sister who just had surgery.
   - Ⓑ She was ill and had to stay in the hospital for a few days.
   - Ⓒ She was enjoying Eudora Welty's stories too much.
   - Ⓓ She had to turn in a paper she had been working on.

3. Listen again to part of the conversation. Then answer the question. 🎧
   Why does the professor say this: 🎧
   - Ⓐ To persuade the student that the homework is simple
   - Ⓑ To tell the student that there was no homework
   - Ⓒ To ask the student to finish the homework right now
   - Ⓓ To show his surprise that the student did not read the book

4. Why does the student mention Welty's story *A Memory*?
   - Ⓐ To express the type of story she would rather read
   - Ⓑ To recommend a story for the professor to read later
   - Ⓒ To give an example from the assigned reading material
   - Ⓓ To compare it with interesting stories the class read earlier

5. According to the professor, what is true about Eudora Welty? Choose 2 answers.
   - Ⓐ She usually wrote about the things she had experienced.
   - Ⓑ She liked giving advice about how to become a writer.
   - Ⓒ She encouraged others to write about what they are familiar with.
   - Ⓓ She used myths and legends in her stories for themes and plots.

Lecture 2

[1-6] Listen to part of a lecture in a biology class.

1. What is the lecture mainly about?

   Ⓐ The history of preserving different coral species
   Ⓑ Reasons for and solutions to decreasing coral populations
   Ⓒ The lasting influence of antibiotics in the open ocean
   Ⓓ The characteristics of coral reefs and their habitats

2. According to the lecture, which of the following are benefits that coral reefs provide? **Choose 2 answers.**

   Ⓐ Purifying polluted ocean water
   Ⓑ Supporting diverse ocean species
   Ⓒ Protecting coastlines from storms
   Ⓓ Indirectly helping fish to grow

3. Why does the professor mention crown of thorns starfish?

   Ⓐ To give the students an example of a coral reef predator
   Ⓑ To compare the lives of starfish and coral reefs in general
   Ⓒ To explain how they help coral reefs to fight algae
   Ⓓ To emphasize that they are near extinction these days

4. Why does the professor say this: 🎧

   Ⓐ To indicate that finding the real cause is almost impossible
   Ⓑ To say that there are many different dangerous species
   Ⓒ To tell the students that getting rid of starfish was hard
   Ⓓ To emphasize that the main problem was elusive

5. According to the lecture, which of the following is true?

   Ⓐ Algae were releasing harmful toxins into the ocean.
   Ⓑ Bacteria were taking all the oxygen away from corals.
   Ⓒ Bacteria helped algae to release a large amount of sugar.
   Ⓓ Algae kept corals from getting enough nutrients for survival.

6. Why does the professor say using antibiotics to save the coral is problematic?

   Ⓐ Corals will spread at an unnecessarily rapid rate.
   Ⓑ Experiments using antibiotics often failed.
   Ⓒ The ocean is far different from a controlled environment.
   Ⓓ Antibiotics usually cause severe side effects.

Lecture 3

[1-6] Listen to part of a lecture in an astronomy class.

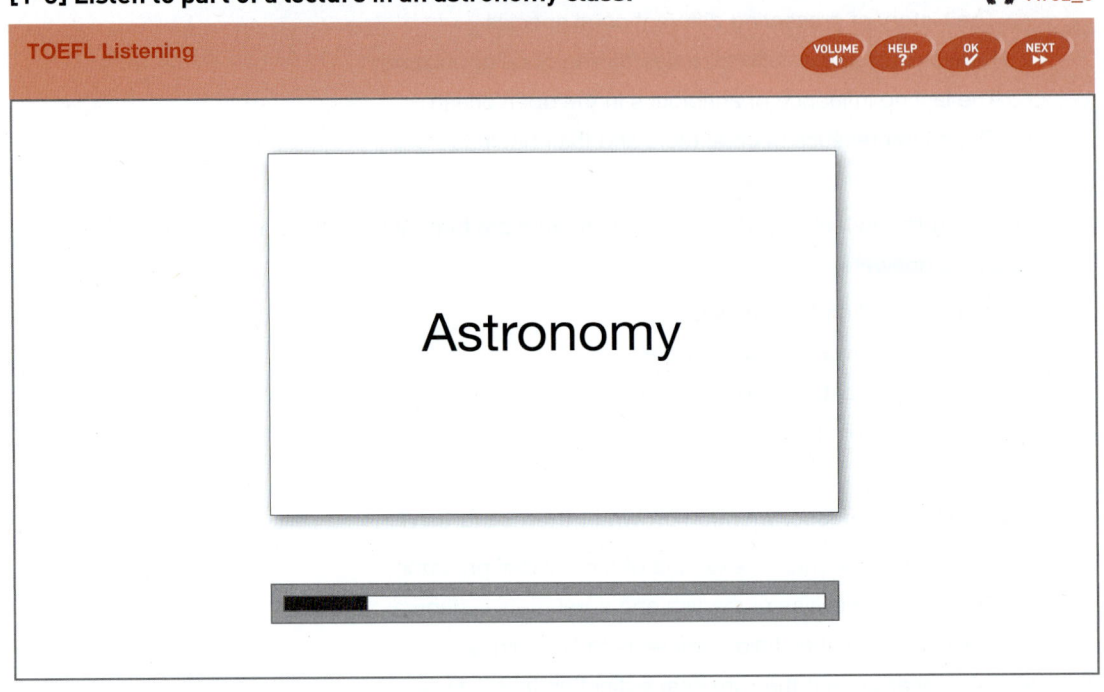

1. What is the lecture mainly about?
   - Ⓐ Characteristics of Uranus that make it an ice giant
   - Ⓑ Features that distinguish Uranus from other planets
   - Ⓒ The relationship between Uranus and Neptune
   - Ⓓ The difference between Uranus and other planets' axial tilts

2. What are the characteristics of Uranus? Choose 2 answers.
   - Ⓐ It contains more gas than Jupiter and Saturn do.
   - Ⓑ Its core and mantle composition are similar to those of Neptune.
   - Ⓒ It has a larger core and thicker mantle than Neptune.
   - Ⓓ Its temperature is the lowest out of the eight planets.
   - Ⓔ Its internal structure is composed of a thin mantle.

3. Why does Uranus have a uniform blue color?
   - Ⓐ It is mostly composed of hydrogen and helium.
   - Ⓑ It has a high content of methane in its atmosphere.
   - Ⓒ It has a ring system that reflects certain wavelengths.
   - Ⓓ It possesses a very thin atmosphere that absorbs sunlight.

4. What can be inferred about Uranus' axial tilt?
   - Ⓐ It is closer to horizontal than it is to vertical.
   - Ⓑ Its angle varies widely throughout its orbit.
   - Ⓒ It does not possess geographic poles.
   - Ⓓ It becomes nearly perpendicular every 42 years.

5. What is true about the atmosphere of Uranus?
   - Ⓐ It is motionless as the planet orbits the Sun very slowly.
   - Ⓑ Its wind blows most strongly at the center of its axis of rotation.
   - Ⓒ It is the most placid around the South and North poles.
   - Ⓓ Its winds move in the same direction as the planet's rotation at the equator.

6. Why does the professor mention future probes?
   - Ⓐ To explain that there are already many probes studying Uranus
   - Ⓑ To imply that Uranus has the potential to provide valuable resources
   - Ⓒ To emphasize that further research should be done regarding Uranus' weather
   - Ⓓ To tell the students that what we know about Uranus is very limited

Actual Test 03

정답 및 해석 | p. 37

TOEFL Listening

Now put on your headset.

Click on **Continue** to go on.

TOEFL Listening

Changing the Volume

To change the volume, click on the **Volume** icon at the top of the screen. The volume control will appear. Move the volume indicator to the left or to the right to change the volume.

To close the volume control, click on the **Volume** icon again.

You will be able to change the volume during the test if you need to.

> You may now change the volume.
> When you are finished, click on **Continue**.

TOEFL Listening

Listening
Section Directions

This section measures your ability to understand conversations and lectures in English.

You will have 36 minutes to listen to the conversations and lectures and answer the questions. You will hear each conversation or lecture only one time.

After each conversation or lecture, you will answer questions about it. The questions typically ask about the main idea and supporting details. Some questions ask about the purpose of a speaker's statement or a speaker's attitude. Answer the questions based on what is stated or implied by the speakers.

You may take notes while you listen. You may use your notes to help you answer the questions. Your notes will not be scored.

In some questions, you will see this icon: 🎧 This means that you will hear, but not see, part of the question.

Some of the questions have special directions. These directions appear in a gray box on the screen.

Most questions are worth 1 point. If a question is worth more than 1 point, it will have special directions that indicate how many points you can receive.

You must answer each question. After you answer, click on **Next**. Then click on **OK** to confirm your answer and go on to the next question. After you click on **OK**, you cannot return to previous questions.

A clock at the top of the screen will show you how much time is remaining. The clock will not count down while you are listening. The clock will count down only while you are answering the questions.

Conversation 1

[1-5] Listen to part of a conversation between a student and a housing officer.

📋 Note-Taking

1. What is the conversation mainly about?

    Ⓐ Filling out a complaint form about the student cafeteria's food
    Ⓑ Receiving permission to use a fully functional kitchen
    Ⓒ Trying to get a dormitory room that fits the student's needs
    Ⓓ Explaining the hardships that one could face living as a vegan

2. Listen again to part of the conversation. Then answer the question. 🎧
    Why does the student say this: 🎧

    Ⓐ To show his willingness to meet any requirements the university may have
    Ⓑ To indicate that he thinks the university policy is unfair
    Ⓒ To emphasize the importance of his dietary restrictions
    Ⓓ To show that he understands why he is not allowed to have premium accommodations

3. What is true about the policy regarding premium accommodations?

    Ⓐ They have more gas heaters and outlets in the kitchen for the residents.
    Ⓑ Students have to pay more money to use premium accommodations.
    Ⓒ Students can enjoy various vegetarian and vegan meal options there.
    Ⓓ They only accept students who are married or have children.

4. What can be inferred about the housing officer?

    Ⓐ She still has to follow dormitory regulations.
    Ⓑ She is unable to fix the broken kitchen appliances.
    Ⓒ She always immediately reports problems to her manager.
    Ⓓ She is usually able to solve problems right away.

5. What does the housing officer offer to do for the student?

    Ⓐ Have maintenance check out the shared kitchen as soon as possible
    Ⓑ Make an exception for him to live in the dormitory mentioned
    Ⓒ Tell the student's situation to her manager to see if there is any chance
    Ⓓ Assign a room in Granger Hall to the student and his sister

Lecture 1

[1-6] Listen to part of a lecture in a sociology class. 🎧 AT03_2

80 PART 02 Actual Tests

1. What is the lecture mainly about?
   - Ⓐ The impact that the Seabees had on the Levitt brothers
   - Ⓑ The difference between two styles of house designs
   - Ⓒ The legacy and influence of the Levitt brothers
   - Ⓓ The popularity of affordable housing communities

2. Why does the professor mention Henry Ford?
   - Ⓐ To compare the Levitt brothers' house building process to his car building method
   - Ⓑ To introduce a historical figure who had a heavy influence on the Levitt brothers
   - Ⓒ To explain why Henry Ford was the main competitor of the Levitt brothers
   - Ⓓ To emphasize the fact that building houses and cars are quite different

3. According to the professor, what was the ultimate goal of the Levitt brothers?
   - Ⓐ Influencing the house building trend in the United States
   - Ⓑ Helping American families to buy affordable houses
   - Ⓒ Launching new construction projects internationally
   - Ⓓ Having a town named after their family

4. Which of the following is true about the Cape Cod style?
   - Ⓐ Each house had its own unique appearance.
   - Ⓑ Its room layout followed the Ranch House style.
   - Ⓒ People often preferred it to apartments.
   - Ⓓ It was modeled after New England homes.

5. Which of the following are characteristics of the Ranch House? Choose 2 answers.
   - Ⓐ It was similar to traditional homes on Long Island.
   - Ⓑ It had a big window facing the backyard.
   - Ⓒ The kitchen and bathroom used separate plumbing.
   - Ⓓ The living room was located in the back of the house.

6. Listen again to part of the lecture. Then answer the question. 🎧
   Why does the professor say this: 🎧
   - Ⓐ To highlight the fact that the Levitt brothers succeeded in building affordable houses
   - Ⓑ To remind the students that today's mortgages are unbelievably high
   - Ⓒ To emphasize the dedication and commitment of the Levitt brothers
   - Ⓓ To indicate that it wasn't really possible to build houses at such a low price

Conversation 2

[1-5] Listen to part of a conversation between a professor and a student.

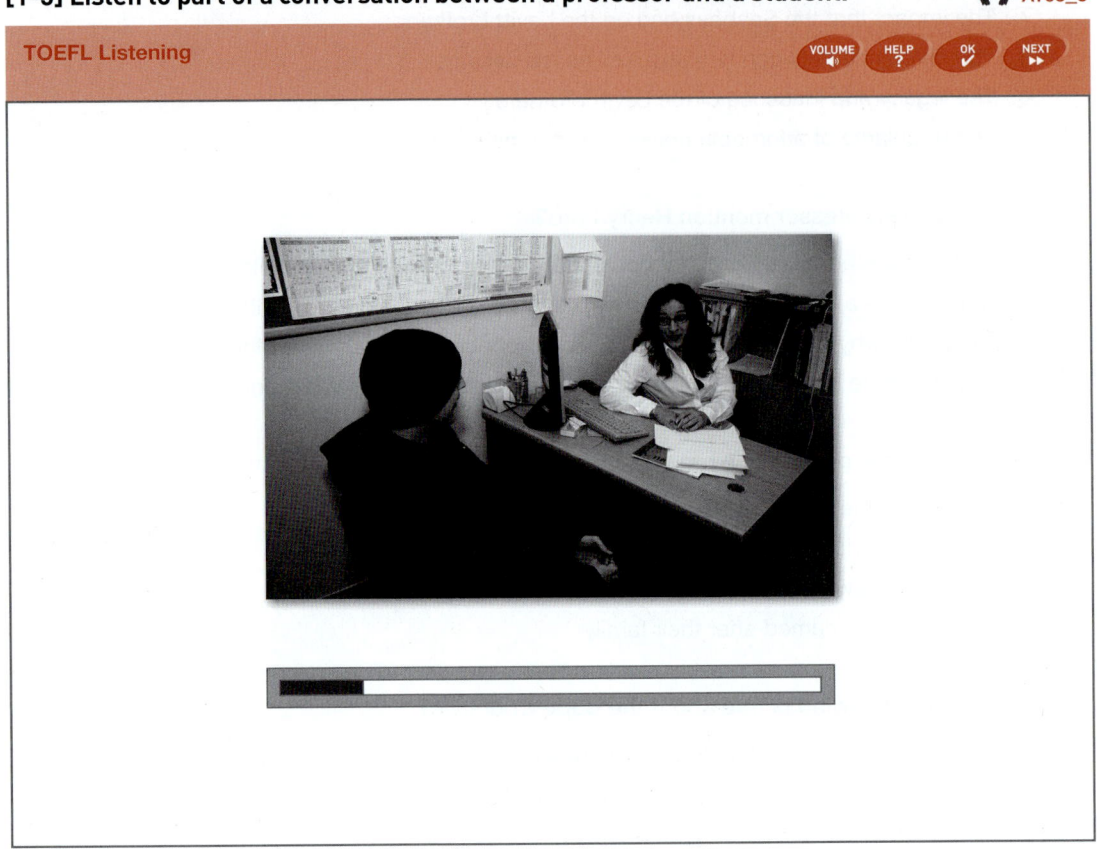

1. Why did the student want to talk to the professor?
    - Ⓐ He needed to ask the professor to allow him to participate in a field project.
    - Ⓑ He wanted to discuss how he should include research material in his paper.
    - Ⓒ He came to persuade the professor to give him more time for an assignment.
    - Ⓓ He felt worried that his paper would need to include some maps and charts.

2. What feature of his paper is the student concerned about?
    - Ⓐ The relevance of some of his sources
    - Ⓑ The data collected from his field project
    - Ⓒ The conciseness of his writing style
    - Ⓓ The number of pages the paper will have

3. What is the student's attitude toward the project the professor mentioned?
    - Ⓐ He is thrilled that he can research the topic he wanted to use for his paper.
    - Ⓑ He thinks it is rather boring compared to other types of historical projects.
    - Ⓒ He finds it to be very interesting, and is amazed that he could be a part of it.
    - Ⓓ He is uncertain if he would be the right candidate for such a big project.

4. According to the professor, what is true about the upcoming project that she mentioned?
    - Ⓐ It needs more donations from historians.
    - Ⓑ It requires 50 staff members to complete.
    - Ⓒ It will provide the student with housing.
    - Ⓓ It will begin during the winter vacation.

5. What is the student's next step for participating in the project?
    - Ⓐ He is going to do the required paperwork sometime next week.
    - Ⓑ He will start applying for housing to stay in during the winter vacation.
    - Ⓒ He is going to have a meeting with Judith regarding the project.
    - Ⓓ He will collect more information about Gerhard Foch and his work.

Lecture 2

[1-6] Listen to part of a lecture in a social science class. AT03_4

1. What is the lecture mainly about?

   Ⓐ The history of road paving
   Ⓑ The creation of tar and tarmac
   Ⓒ The lasting influence of John McAdam
   Ⓓ The characteristics of hot-mix asphalt

2. What does the professor say about corduroy roads?

   Ⓐ They were not usable during the rainy season.
   Ⓑ Logs were used to strengthen the ground.
   Ⓒ They were among the first asphalt-paved roads.
   Ⓓ They were commonly used in dry regions.

3. Why does the professor say this: 🎧

   Ⓐ To compare roads in regions with varied climates
   Ⓑ To emphasize that dry areas had more difficulties
   Ⓒ To show respect for people in drier areas for their road making efforts
   Ⓓ To discuss the difficulties of living in dry regions

4. What can be inferred about John Loudon McAdam's road building process?

   Ⓐ Large flat stones were put on the bottom for safety.
   Ⓑ Stones of different sizes were used without other binding material.
   Ⓒ Tar and gravel were combined together to resist rainwater.
   Ⓓ Wood and tar needed to be used for the base.

5. Why does the professor mention the Second World War?

   Ⓐ To give the students a historical example
   Ⓑ To contrast asphalt with tar use in the United States
   Ⓒ To explain how the use of tarmac became popular
   Ⓓ To illustrate a point about macadamisation

6. According to the lecture, which of the following is true?

   Ⓐ John McAdam invented tarmac and macadam.
   Ⓑ Hot-mix asphalt is not completely solid in hot weather.
   Ⓒ Asphalt gained wide popularity during World War II.
   Ⓓ Most roadways in the U.S. are paved with tarmac.

Lecture 3

[1-6] Listen to part of a lecture in an ecology class. 🎧 AT03_5

1. What is the lecture mainly about?

   Ⓐ The characteristics of various flora and fauna in the Amazon
   Ⓑ The comparison of the Amazon River ecosystem and those of other rivers
   Ⓒ The different types of speciation and their examples
   Ⓓ The process by which organisms develop symbiotic relationships

2. According to the lecture, how should speciation be defined?

   Ⓐ A way of discovering a new species in the forest
   Ⓑ A process that changes a species to a new one
   Ⓒ A method that a species uses for seasonal migration
   Ⓓ A method that animals use to survive environmental change

3. What does the professor mention as causes of speciation? Choose 2 answers.

   Ⓐ Large population
   Ⓑ Food chain
   Ⓒ Geographic obstacles
   Ⓓ Distance

4. Listen again to part of the lecture. Then answer the question. 🎧

   Why does the student say this: 🎧

   Ⓐ To express her confusion about the new topic the professor introduced
   Ⓑ To tell the professor that he has made a mistake about the lecture topic
   Ⓒ To show the professor that she studied the Amazon ecosystem thoroughly
   Ⓓ To point out that she has never heard of a tribe called the Attini before

5. According to the lecture, what can be inferred about sympatric speciation?

   Ⓐ It occurs when two different species compete for survival.
   Ⓑ It is a rare process which only happens to ant species.
   Ⓒ It does not require geographic barriers or distance.
   Ⓓ It shows that the environment is in danger because of human activities.

6. What is the professor's opinion about the symbiosis of leafcutter ants?

   Ⓐ He is certain that it ultimately is a doomed type of relationship.
   Ⓑ He believes that it can help the ants to find good leaves more easily.
   Ⓒ He doubts if it really is a necessary relationship for the ants.
   Ⓓ He thinks that it is a good strategy for both the ants and the fungus.

Actual Test 04

TOEFL Listening

Now put on your headset.

Click on **Continue** to go on.

TOEFL Listening

Changing the Volume

To change the volume, click on the **Volume** icon at the top of the screen. The volume control will appear. Move the volume indicator to the left or to the right to change the volume.

To close the volume control, click on the **Volume** icon again.

You will be able to change the volume during the test if you need to.

> You may now change the volume.
> When you are finished, click on **Continue**.

TOEFL Listening

Listening
Section Directions

This section measures your ability to understand conversations and lectures in English.

You will have 36 minutes to listen to the conversations and lectures and answer the questions. You will hear each conversation or lecture only one time.

After each conversation or lecture, you will answer questions about it. The questions typically ask about the main idea and supporting details. Some questions ask about the purpose of a speaker's statement or a speaker's attitude. Answer the questions based on what is stated or implied by the speakers.

You may take notes while you listen. You may use your notes to help you answer the questions. Your notes will not be scored.

In some questions, you will see this icon: 🎧 This means that you will hear, but not see, part of the question.

Some of the questions have special directions. These directions appear in a gray box on the screen.

Most questions are worth 1 point. If a question is worth more than 1 point, it will have special directions that indicate how many points you can receive.

You must answer each question. After you answer, click on **Next**. Then click on **OK** to confirm your answer and go on to the next question. After you click on **OK**, you cannot return to previous questions.

A clock at the top of the screen will show you how much time is remaining. The clock will not count down while you are listening. The clock will count down only while you are answering the questions.

Conversation 1

[1-5] Listen to part of a conversation between a student and an employee at the campus bookstore.

AT04_1

Note-Taking

1. What is the conversation mainly about?

    Ⓐ Organizing a student club meeting at the university bookstore
    Ⓑ Debating the controversy of Pluto being a dwarf planet
    Ⓒ Having t-shirts ordered for a student organization
    Ⓓ Designing the patterns of the astronomy club shirts

2. What is the employee's opinion about the astronomy club shirt?

    Ⓐ She thinks it is brilliantly designed.
    Ⓑ She is worried that it might be too complex.
    Ⓒ She believes it is worth the price.
    Ⓓ She thinks purple and black are necessary.

3. What does the student say about the planets in the solar system? Choose 2 answers.

    Ⓐ Pluto is excluded from the list of planets.
    Ⓑ Neptune is still considered a dwarf planet.
    Ⓒ Pluto is too small to be considered a planet.
    Ⓓ There are six main dwarf planets.

4. What is true about the club's shirt?

    Ⓐ It implies that astronomy majors should participate.
    Ⓑ It suggests that non-majors can join the club as well.
    Ⓒ It will be sold during the first astronomy club meeting.
    Ⓓ It helped to bring many non-major students to the club.

5. What will the student do next?

    Ⓐ Choose the colors to be included in the shirt pattern
    Ⓑ Call the club members to hear their opinions about the colors
    Ⓒ Follow the woman to design some sample patterns for the shirt
    Ⓓ Receive a copy of sample patterns to show to club members

Lecture 1

[1-5] Listen to part of a lecture in a biology class. 🎧 AT04_2

TOEFL Listening

Biology

TOEFL Listening

1. What is the lecture mainly about?
   - Ⓐ The characteristics of various plant pollinators
   - Ⓑ The relationships between plants and their pollinators
   - Ⓒ The effects of agriculture on pollination ecology
   - Ⓓ The destructive effects of some insects on pollination

2. What does the professor say is the ideal pollinator for a plant?
   - Ⓐ An animal that is able to fly from one flower to another
   - Ⓑ An animal that eats the pollen but not the nectar from the flower
   - Ⓒ An animal that can transfer a lot of pollen to another flower
   - Ⓓ An animal that is hungry and quick to leave after feeding

3. According to the professor, what are some features of a flowering plant that can affect how attractive it is to pollinators? Choose 2 answers.
   - Ⓐ Nectar
   - Ⓑ Size
   - Ⓒ Color
   - Ⓓ Location

4. According to the lecture, what can be inferred about the giant Amazon Water Lilies when they are red?
   - Ⓐ They are ready to attract beetles for pollination.
   - Ⓑ They have recently opened after releasing a beetle.
   - Ⓒ They are heating up and emitting odor to attract pollinators.
   - Ⓓ They are signaling that the plant has been fed upon.

5. Why does the professor mention agriculture?
   - Ⓐ To tell the students that he believes it is the most destructive type of disturbance
   - Ⓑ To give an example of one factor that can disrupt natural pollination ecology
   - Ⓒ To illustrate how pollination ecology is affected by agriculture in a positive way
   - Ⓓ To explain that it can provide new pollinators that could benefit the plants

6. Listen again to part of the lecture. Then answer the question. 🎧
   Why does the professor say this: 🎧
   - Ⓐ To show the student that bats usually prefer scent over colors
   - Ⓑ To explain a pollinator mostly attracted to the scent of a flower
   - Ⓒ To illustrate that the majority of plants attract pollinators in daytime
   - Ⓓ To tell the student that she has stated a common misconception

Conversation 2

[1-5] Listen to part of a conversation between a student and a professor.

Note-Taking

1. Why is the student talking to the professor?
   - Ⓐ To determine which subject would be the best to major in
   - Ⓑ To ask about the professor's experiences as a college student
   - Ⓒ To get advice about transferring to a different university
   - Ⓓ To decide which classes she needs to take the next semester

2. Which of these statements about the student is true?
   - Ⓐ She is a senior at Central University.
   - Ⓑ She is majoring in secondary education.
   - Ⓒ She wants to live on campus for a while.
   - Ⓓ She already took a few biology courses.

3. Why does the professor say this: 🎧
   - Ⓐ To suggest that the student should consider a different kind of change
   - Ⓑ To criticize the student for not looking for better options
   - Ⓒ To tell the student how brave she is for deciding to be a teacher
   - Ⓓ To give an example of his own poor decision-making in the past

4. What does the professor suggest the student do?
   - Ⓐ Transfer to Central University
   - Ⓑ Take more education courses
   - Ⓒ Change her major to chemistry
   - Ⓓ Visit her advisor for advice

5. What will most likely happen next?
   - Ⓐ The professor will sign the form that the student has filled out.
   - Ⓑ The student will go see her advisor to do some paperwork.
   - Ⓒ The student will move back to her hometown and change her major.
   - Ⓓ The advisor will come to give the student the form she needs.

Lecture 2

[1-6] Listen to part of a lecture in an ancient history class. 🎧 AT04_4

Ancient History

1. What is the lecture mainly about?
    Ⓐ The complex construction process of conduits
    Ⓑ The features of an ancient Roman technology
    Ⓒ The Roman Empire's need for water sources
    Ⓓ The difficulties of building and maintaining aqueducts

2. What is the professor's opinion about the Roman aqueducts?
    Ⓐ He doubts if it was necessary to build them with arches and bridges.
    Ⓑ He is amazed at how rapidly the water moved inside the conduits.
    Ⓒ He believes they contributed to the advancement of the empire.
    Ⓓ He thinks they put a limit on the population of the empire.

3. What aspect of aqueducts was NOT mentioned in the lecture?
    Ⓐ The amount of time they took to build
    Ⓑ Their aesthetic value
    Ⓒ How well constructed they were
    Ⓓ The great distances they covered

4. According to the professor, what were requirements for building an effective aqueduct?
    Choose 2 answers.
    Ⓐ A gradual degree of descent
    Ⓑ A water source located far from the city
    Ⓒ A water source near a mountain
    Ⓓ A downward route from the water source to the city

5. Why does the professor mention the size of ancient Rome's population?
    Ⓐ To explain why the Romans needed to transport so much water
    Ⓑ To point out that the water source had to come from a higher elevation
    Ⓒ To emphasize why water was so important for their survival
    Ⓓ To describe the various methods of bringing water into the city

6. What can be inferred from the professor's explanations about the aqueducts after the end of the empire?
    Ⓐ Their productivity is often praised by modern scientists.
    Ⓑ Some of them are still used in some parts of Rome.
    Ⓒ Many of them no longer can function as aqueducts.
    Ⓓ They need special care to provide service to people.

Lecture 3

[1-6] Listen to part of a lecture in an archaeology class. AT04_5

1. What is the lecture mainly about?
   - Ⓐ Different methods used for discovering Mayan relics
   - Ⓑ Reasons behind the disappearance of an ancient culture
   - Ⓒ Bill Saturno's discovery of an ancient settlement
   - Ⓓ Murals found in the ruins of the Mayan civilization

2. How did Bill Saturno discover the cave with ancient murals?
   - Ⓐ He had a map that was provided by NASA.
   - Ⓑ He accidentally entered it while taking a rest.
   - Ⓒ He was equipped with electromagnetic imaging technology.
   - Ⓓ He used a satellite to scan the surrounding area.

3. What significant role did NASA play in the discovery of Mayan ruins?
   - Ⓐ NASA granted Saturno access to its space satellites.
   - Ⓑ NASA provided Saturno with infrared images.
   - Ⓒ NASA allowed Saturno to use their facilities for research.
   - Ⓓ NASA gave Saturno a map from the ancient Mayans.

4. What do the shades of yellow in the infrared image represent?
   - Ⓐ Rainforest
   - Ⓑ Mountains
   - Ⓒ Ruins
   - Ⓓ Desert

5. What can be inferred about the discovery at San Bartolo?
   - Ⓐ The local people were aware of the location of the ancient ruins.
   - Ⓑ There are many ancient sites and ruins yet to be discovered.
   - Ⓒ The discovery could not have been made without NASA's help.
   - Ⓓ Saturno has found all of the Mayan ruins in Guatemala.

6. Listen again to part of the lecture. Then answer the question: 🎧
   Why does the professor say this: 🎧
   - Ⓐ To remind the student of what the scientists were dealing with
   - Ⓑ To indicate that the student misunderstood what she said
   - Ⓒ To illustrate what happened to the cities after the Maya abandoned them
   - Ⓓ To explain the differences between the two environments the pyramids are found in

Actual Test 05

정답 및 해석 | p. 73

TOEFL Listening

Now put on your headset.

Click on **Continue** to go on.

TOEFL Listening

Changing the Volume

To change the volume, click on the **Volume** icon at the top of the screen. The volume control will appear. Move the volume indicator to the left or to the right to change the volume.

To close the volume control, click on the **Volume** icon again.

You will be able to change the volume during the test if you need to.

> You may now change the volume.
> When you are finished, click on **Continue**.

TOEFL Listening

Listening
Section Directions

This section measures your ability to understand conversations and lectures in English.

You will have 36 minutes to listen to the conversations and lectures and answer the questions. You will hear each conversation or lecture only one time.

After each conversation or lecture, you will answer questions about it. The questions typically ask about the main idea and supporting details. Some questions ask about the purpose of a speaker's statement or a speaker's attitude. Answer the questions based on what is stated or implied by the speakers.

You may take notes while you listen. You may use your notes to help you answer the questions. Your notes will not be scored.

In some questions, you will see this icon:  This means that you will hear, but not see, part of the question.

Some of the questions have special directions. These directions appear in a gray box on the screen.

Most questions are worth 1 point. If a question is worth more than 1 point, it will have special directions that indicate how many points you can receive.

You must answer each question. After you answer, click on **Next**. Then click on **OK** to confirm your answer and go on to the next question. After you click on **OK**, you cannot return to previous questions.

A clock at the top of the screen will show you how much time is remaining. The clock will not count down while you are listening. The clock will count down only while you are answering the questions.

Conversation 1

[1-5] Listen to part of a conversation between a student and a professor.

📋 Note-Taking

1. Why did the woman go to see her professor?

   Ⓐ To ask a question about the topic that was discussed in class
   Ⓑ To question the connection between public relations and first impressions
   Ⓒ To request the professor's opinion about personal public relations
   Ⓓ To get guidance on a decision regarding the two internships she was offered

2. Why does the professor say this: 🎧

   Ⓐ To encourage the student to ask anything she wants to
   Ⓑ To suggest the student work harder to understand the topic
   Ⓒ To emphasize that criticizing someone can be hard at times
   Ⓓ To tell the student that he likes it when students criticize him

3. What point does the professor make when he discusses answering the telephone?

   Ⓐ People try to use personal public relations unconsciously in their daily lives.
   Ⓑ Public relations can only be applied by businesses and corporations.
   Ⓒ Personal public relations is a good way to improve a person's reputation.
   Ⓓ Public relations should be practiced every day to be developed further.

4. What does the professor imply about the internship position at Face Forward?

   Ⓐ It might not be able to provide the range of work experience the student wants.
   Ⓑ He already knows some students that have applied at the talent agency.
   Ⓒ It would be a better choice than interning at the online news service since it suits her.
   Ⓓ Even though it is a talent agency, it rarely deals with the entertainment industry.

5. What does the professor say about the online news service internship?
   Choose 2 answers.

   Ⓐ It is sponsored by the entertainment industry.
   Ⓑ It can provide experience in journalism.
   Ⓒ It has diverse sections including entertainment.
   Ⓓ It organizes various events related to journalism.

Lecture 1

[1-6] Listen to part of a lecture in an art history class. AT05_2

1. What is the lecture mainly about?
   - Ⓐ Some trivia regarding one of the most famous paintings of the Renaissance
   - Ⓑ A famous Renaissance artwork and the challenges it posed for its creator
   - Ⓒ Important characteristics of the Sistine Chapel and Michelangelo's painting
   - Ⓓ The difficulties that discouraged Michelangelo from painting frescoes

2. What is the main reason that made Michelangelo hesitate when taking the commission?
   - Ⓐ He usually preferred taking on stable projects from the government.
   - Ⓑ He didn't consider himself a better painter than his contemporaries.
   - Ⓒ He wanted to be able to work on other projects at the same time.
   - Ⓓ He viewed himself as more of a sculptor than a painter.

3. Why does the professor mention a geometric design?
   - Ⓐ To describe a popular style of art in churches during the Renaissance period in Italy
   - Ⓑ To explain how Michelangelo's style changed over the course of his work
   - Ⓒ To tell the students about the original design that was on the ceiling of the chapel
   - Ⓓ To show the power Michelangelo had over the subject matter for the commission

4. What were the problems with painting frescoes? Choose 2 answers.
   - Ⓐ The artist was not able to fix errors since the plaster dries quickly.
   - Ⓑ The plaster dried quickly and started to break apart after painting.
   - Ⓒ It required too much water, which tended to obscure the painting.
   - Ⓓ Painters needed an assistant who could wet the plaster.
   - Ⓔ Laying out a new plaster every day required a lot of work.

5. Which method did Michelangelo use to paint on the 20-meter-high ceiling?
   - Ⓐ He designed a floor that was supported by several beams.
   - Ⓑ He constructed a temporary platform that stood on the ground.
   - Ⓒ He devised a large scaffold that was held up by thick ropes.
   - Ⓓ He sat on a little wooden board that hung from the ceiling.

6. What can be inferred about the influence of the commission on Michelangelo?
   - Ⓐ It brought him many more opportunities to paint frescoes.
   - Ⓑ It did not bring him the fame and praise he expected.
   - Ⓒ It ended up having a lasting effect on Michelangelo's health.
   - Ⓓ It eventually opened up the path to Michelangelo becoming a poet.

Lecture 2

[1-6] Listen to part of a lecture in a botany class. 🎧 AT05_3

1. What is the main topic of the lecture?
   - Ⓐ The downfall of the hemp industry
   - Ⓑ The versatility of hemp
   - Ⓒ The best uses for hemp fibers
   - Ⓓ The resurgence of the hemp industry

2. According to the lecture, hemp fiber is superior to cotton because of its
   - Ⓐ Low density
   - Ⓑ Moisture absorption
   - Ⓒ Water repellent qualities
   - Ⓓ Hygienic properties

3. According to the lecture, hemp can be found in all of the following EXCEPT
   - Ⓐ Hardware
   - Ⓑ Bedsheets
   - Ⓒ Clothing and apparel
   - Ⓓ Backpacks

4. What is the professor's attitude toward hemp?
   - Ⓐ He is against marijuana use.
   - Ⓑ He believes the timber industry did a big disservice to America's consumers.
   - Ⓒ He is a proponent of hemp's usefulness.
   - Ⓓ He believes hemp is intriguing but has no place in today's society.

5. According to the lecture, why did hemp fall out of use?
   - Ⓐ The cotton industry wielded significant political lobbying power.
   - Ⓑ Propaganda was aimed at associating hemp with marijuana.
   - Ⓒ Consumers preferred the use of timber as a construction material for homes.
   - Ⓓ Children feared the effects of wearing clothes made from hemp.

6. What will the class most likely do next?
   - Ⓐ The class will learn about newer applications of hemp in the context of sustainability.
   - Ⓑ The class will learn about other sustainable plant fibers.
   - Ⓒ The class will enter a discussion on the materials taught.
   - Ⓓ The professor will answer any questions.

Conversation 2

[1-5] Listen to part of a conversation between a student and a radio station manager. AT05_4

Note-Taking

1. Why does the student come to the radio station?

   Ⓐ To complain about the quality of the music played by the radio station
   Ⓑ To suggest some new content for the radio show's program
   Ⓒ To check if his club could be promoted on the show
   Ⓓ To look to become an engineering manager at the radio station

2. Why does the student mention 80s music?

   Ⓐ It is the reason why he likes listening to the woman's radio show.
   Ⓑ It gave him the reason and determination for joining the radio station.
   Ⓒ It inspired him when he was trying to solve his club advertising matter.
   Ⓓ It is what gave him the idea of establishing the Foreign Film Club.

3. According to the student, what is true about the club?

   Ⓐ It was made to discuss foreign music with other students.
   Ⓑ Its meeting location will be posted on the student bulletin board.
   Ⓒ It needs to have a certain number of people to receive approval.
   Ⓓ It is looking for a new managerial staff to advertise a movie.

4. What did the board of directors make a new university policy?

   Ⓐ All student organizations have to recruit at least 50 new members.
   Ⓑ New student organizations need to post their advertisements on the bulletin board.
   Ⓒ Only organizations with the university's permission could post their fliers.
   Ⓓ The university will require all organizations to advertise themselves.

5. What will the student most likely do next?

   Ⓐ Approve the club's plans for advertising
   Ⓑ Become a guest on the woman's radio show
   Ⓒ Realize his hopes of creating an official club
   Ⓓ Look for some people to attend an event

Lecture 3

[1-6] Listen to part of a lecture in an engineering class. AT05_5

1. What is the main idea of the lecture?

    Ⓐ The effect of the wind on buildings and the application of CFD
    Ⓑ The history of famous tall buildings and the way they were constructed
    Ⓒ The development of CFD and its application over time
    Ⓓ The role that nearby structures play on the construction of buildings

2. Why does the professor mention the elevator?

    Ⓐ To explain how it helped with building skyscrapers at the beginning of the 20th century
    Ⓑ To elaborate on how it changed the living environments of upper- and lower-class people
    Ⓒ To show its influence on the construction and exterior design of a building
    Ⓓ To talk about the development of construction technology over time

3. What can be inferred about reinforced concrete?

    Ⓐ It increased the chance of collapse since it made the walls thinner.
    Ⓑ It allowed more space inside the building with its wrought iron beams.
    Ⓒ It caused buildings to be more vulnerable to the wind than before.
    Ⓓ It increased costs for the construction of skyscrapers.

4. What makes analyzing lateral loading difficult?

    Ⓐ Modern buildings' tall and slender structures
    Ⓑ Wind constantly blowing from the same direction
    Ⓒ The negative pressure that buildings experience
    Ⓓ The many variables such as geography and weather

5. According to the lecture, which of the following are true about CFD? Choose 2 answers.

    Ⓐ It is mostly used for airplanes and other types of vehicles nowadays.
    Ⓑ It predicts a building's reactions to different burdening conditions.
    Ⓒ It was first used on a building after the completion of the Empire State Building.
    Ⓓ Its first full-scale use was for the World Trade Center, completed in 1970.
    Ⓔ It is so complex that it is difficult to obtain trustworthy data from it.

6. What problem does the Burj Khalifa have that is different from other buildings?

    Ⓐ The wind pattern most affects the middle part of the building.
    Ⓑ The lateral loading of the building is much more severe than that of other buildings.
    Ⓒ The difference between the lateral loading at the top and the bottom is huge.
    Ⓓ The construction was more complicated due to the orientation of its surfaces.

Actual Test 06

정답 및 해석 | p. 91

TOEFL Listening

Now put on your headset.

Click on **Continue** to go on.

TOEFL Listening

Changing the Volume

To change the volume, click on the **Volume** icon at the top of the screen. The volume control will appear. Move the volume indicator to the left or to the right to change the volume.

To close the volume control, click on the **Volume** icon again.

You will be able to change the volume during the test if you need to.

> You may now change the volume.
> When you are finished, click on **Continue**.

Listening
Section Directions

This section measures your ability to understand conversations and lectures in English.

You will have 36 minutes to listen to the conversations and lectures and answer the questions. You will hear each conversation or lecture only one time.

After each conversation or lecture, you will answer questions about it. The questions typically ask about the main idea and supporting details. Some questions ask about the purpose of a speaker's statement or a speaker's attitude. Answer the questions based on what is stated or implied by the speakers.

You may take notes while you listen. You may use your notes to help you answer the questions. Your notes will not be scored.

In some questions, you will see this icon: 🎧 This means that you will hear, but not see, part of the question.

Some of the questions have special directions. These directions appear in a gray box on the screen.

Most questions are worth 1 point. If a question is worth more than 1 point, it will have special directions that indicate how many points you can receive.

You must answer each question. After you answer, click on **Next**. Then click on **OK** to confirm your answer and go on to the next question. After you click on **OK**, you cannot return to previous questions.

A clock at the top of the screen will show you how much time is remaining. The clock will not count down while you are listening. The clock will count down only while you are answering the questions.

Conversation 1

[1-5] Listen to part of a conversation between two professors.

1. What is the conversation mainly about?
   - Ⓐ Receiving more funding from the school for upcoming excavations
   - Ⓑ Persuading students to get more firsthand experience in the field
   - Ⓒ A recent research trip the woman went on with her students
   - Ⓓ Interesting samples the woman brought with her from an excavation site

2. What is true about the woman's recent excavation?
   - Ⓐ They spent many days in the forest wondering where to excavate.
   - Ⓑ Bad weather conditions prevented her team from excavating further.
   - Ⓒ A storm eventually washed away the ruins that her team was studying.
   - Ⓓ It took more time than she had expected since she was short of staff.

3. According to the lecture, what can be inferred about excavations in rainforests?
   - Ⓐ Weather conditions play an important role.
   - Ⓑ Excavation teams often get lost in the forest.
   - Ⓒ Temples are usually found on high ground.
   - Ⓓ Using satellite imagery is very difficult.

4. Why does the woman say this: 🎧
   - Ⓐ To indicate that students need to participate directly in the field
   - Ⓑ To state that her students wouldn't enjoy actual field work that much
   - Ⓒ To explain why she tries to encourage her students to travel as much as they can
   - Ⓓ To express her disappointment that her students do not appreciate what they study

5. What does the man say about budget cuts?
   - Ⓐ He expects there to be more budget cuts in the future.
   - Ⓑ The board of directors values the archaeology department.
   - Ⓒ They limited the number of students excavation teams could take.
   - Ⓓ Because of them, professors are trying to research abroad more.

Lecture 1

[1-6] Listen to part of a lecture in an earth science class.

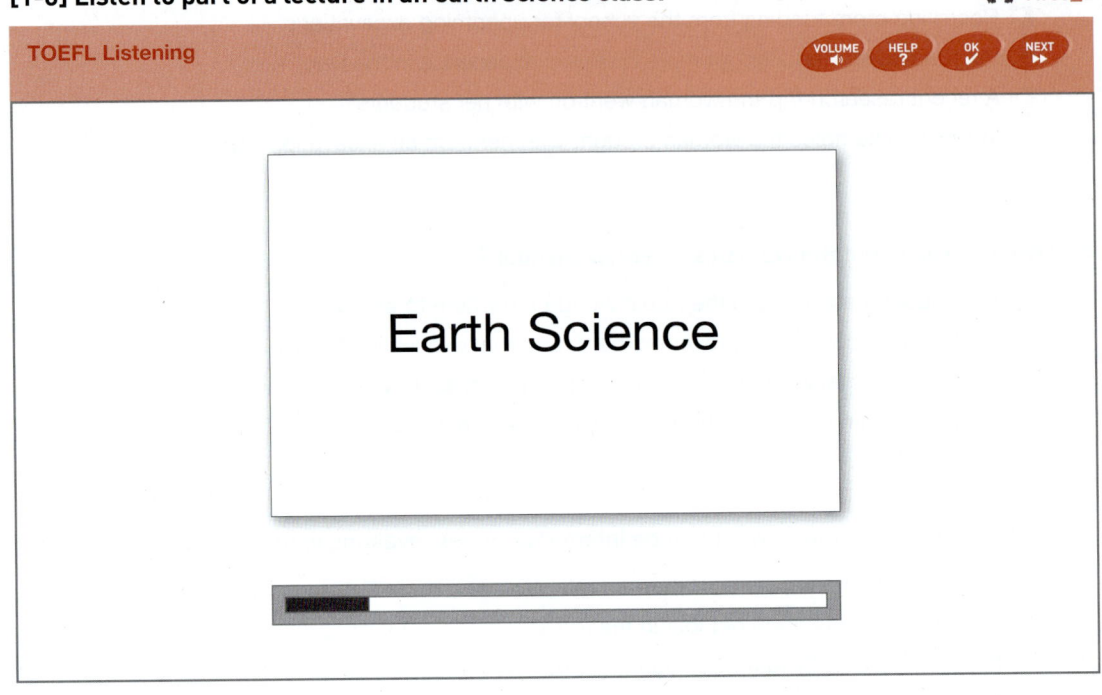

1. What is the lecture mainly about?
   - Ⓐ A method used for discovering Earth's climatic history
   - Ⓑ Stalagmites that are formed in different climates
   - Ⓒ Types of cave structures found on different continents
   - Ⓓ The impact of the Mandate of Heaven on Chinese society

2. Which of the following are characteristics of stalagmites? Choose 2 answers.
   - Ⓐ They are usually formed during a period of heavy rainfall.
   - Ⓑ They are useful for determining past amounts of rainfall.
   - Ⓒ Minerals like calcium carbonate in the water make them grow.
   - Ⓓ They are dangerous because of their radioactive nature.

3. According to the professor, what information did the Wanxiang Cave in China reveal?
   - Ⓐ The climate of the region dating back for 2,000 years
   - Ⓑ Records written about four droughts in the last 2,000 years
   - Ⓒ The size that stalagmites can reach inside of a cave
   - Ⓓ The origin of the philosophy of the Mandate of Heaven

4. Why is uranium important to the study described?
   - Ⓐ It leaves a residue when it decays, which forms stalagmites.
   - Ⓑ It helps in detecting stalagmites underground.
   - Ⓒ It is what keeps the stalagmites in caves intact.
   - Ⓓ It allows stalagmite layers to be accurately dated.

5. Why does the professor mention the Mandate of Heaven?
   - Ⓐ To explain how the climate of Gansu Province affected the whole of China
   - Ⓑ To show that climate changes in China coincided with its political situation
   - Ⓒ To compare different methods of determining the amount of rainfall
   - Ⓓ To point out that severe drought in the region was a common thing

6. What can be inferred about studying caves in order to determine the amount of rainfall?
   - Ⓐ It revealed that the Sun is the sole factor for the growth of stalagmites.
   - Ⓑ It provides more accurate results than analyzing tree rings and ice cores.
   - Ⓒ It showed that some countries would be unable to utilize this method.
   - Ⓓ It supports the evidence that the amount of rainfall depends on stalagmites.

Lecture 2

[1-6] Listen to part of a lecture in a zoology class. 🎧 AT06_3

1. What is the main topic of the lecture?
   - Ⓐ The differences between horns and antlers
   - Ⓑ The reasons that animals grow horns and antlers
   - Ⓒ The various animals that have horns and antlers
   - Ⓓ The energy investment that horns and antlers require

2. Listen again to part of the lecture. Then answer the question. 🎧
   Why does the professor say this: 🎧
   - Ⓐ To indicate that she is disappointed with the student's answer
   - Ⓑ To point out that the student made an error in his answer
   - Ⓒ To show that the student failed to answer the question
   - Ⓓ To inform the student that he gave more detail than she expected

3. The speakers list the characteristics of horns and antlers. Indicate which characteristic belongs to which bodily structure.

	Horns	Antlers
Ⓐ Common on male animals		
Ⓑ Shed and regrown every year		
Ⓒ Have a keratin sheath over bone		
Ⓓ Usually have a branched structure		
Ⓔ Signify the health of the animal		

4. Why does the professor mention the horned owl?
   - Ⓐ To provide an example of a misleadingly named organism
   - Ⓑ To illustrate that even birds sometimes grow horns
   - Ⓒ To indicate an animal that preys on chameleons
   - Ⓓ To emphasize how common horns are in nature

5. According to the professor, what is the characteristic of the horns of Jackson's chameleons?
   - Ⓐ They are used to defend against predators.
   - Ⓑ They are not able to inflict actual damage.
   - Ⓒ They are structurally the same as bovids'.
   - Ⓓ They grow from the top of their heads.

6. What can be inferred about dung beetles?
   - Ⓐ Their horns have bone cores like mammal horns.
   - Ⓑ Most species are very large for beetles.
   - Ⓒ Their horns are not used to compete for mates.
   - Ⓓ Female dung beetles do not typically protect their nests.

Conversation 2

[1-5] Listen to part of a conversation between two students.

Note-Taking

1. What is the conversation mainly about?

    Ⓐ The students feeling overworked from their schedules
    Ⓑ The students' plans for the next semester
    Ⓒ Difficult classes they are both signed up for
    Ⓓ How they are planning for graduate school

2. Why has the male student registered for 18 credits next semester?

    Ⓐ He is preparing for graduate school.
    Ⓑ His teaching seminar takes up six credits.
    Ⓒ He couldn't take a full course load last semester.
    Ⓓ He has to attend school from home.

3. What is the female student's attitude toward her education?

    Ⓐ She feels she can get the same quality of education at a cheaper institution.
    Ⓑ She wonders if the education at the university is worth the high tuition.
    Ⓒ She finds her degree to be increasingly unaffordable.
    Ⓓ She is frustrated with the unresponsiveness of some of her professors.

4. How will publishing the female student's work benefit her? Choose 2 answers.

    Ⓐ It will open many doors for her in her aspirations to join the teaching profession.
    Ⓑ Her work will be presented at a literature conference.
    Ⓒ Her work can potentially be used toward her senior thesis.
    Ⓓ She can use the publication in her graduate school applications.
    Ⓔ The publication can be counted for course credit.

5. What will the female student most likely do next?

    Ⓐ She will consult with Dr. Davis about a collaboration.
    Ⓑ She will go to the community college she is registered at.
    Ⓒ She will prepare for her senior thesis.
    Ⓓ She will persuade Mike to take classes at a different college.

Lecture 3

[1-6] Listen to part of a lecture in a social science class. 🎧 AT06_5

1. What is the main idea of the lecture?

   Ⓐ How newspapers in the U.S. developed over time
   Ⓑ Why U.S. newspapers were able to succeed overseas
   Ⓒ How newspapers gained popularity in the 18th century
   Ⓓ Why U.S. citizens started reading newspapers

2. Why does the professor mention *Publick Occurrences Both Foreign and Domestick*?

   Ⓐ To compare the characteristics of it with the first daily newspaper
   Ⓑ To distinguish it from the other daily newspapers at the time
   Ⓒ To compare Benjamin Harris's experience with Benjamin Towne's
   Ⓓ To highlight the importance of the first American newspaper

3. What is a key feature of *The Pennsylvania Evening Post* mentioned in the lecture?

   Ⓐ It published editorial articles for the first time.
   Ⓑ It was the first American daily newspaper.
   Ⓒ It contained detailed stories about crimes.
   Ⓓ It was unable to survive against harsh competition.

4. What does the professor mean when she says this: 🎧

   Ⓐ She believes that muck-raking is not different from public service.
   Ⓑ She feels annoyed because muck-raking is so undervalued these days.
   Ⓒ She wants to explain that muck-raking had a positive impact at first.
   Ⓓ She knows that the students do not appreciate muck-raking at all.

5. According to the lecture, what is true about William Randolph Hearst?

   Ⓐ He devoted most of his newspaper to opinion pieces.
   Ⓑ He was heavily criticized for his reports on the fighting.
   Ⓒ He contributed to the development of yellow journalism.
   Ⓓ He was responsible for the Spanish American War.

6. According to the professor, what can be inferred about the future of newspapers?

   Ⓐ They will start competing with TV news.
   Ⓑ They will focus more on foreign issues.
   Ⓒ They will try to print more editions.
   Ⓓ They will eventually cease publication.

Actual Test 07

정답 및 해석 | p. 110

TOEFL Listening

Now put on your headset.

Click on **Continue** to go on.

TOEFL Listening

Changing the Volume

To change the volume, click on the **Volume** icon at the top of the screen. The volume control will appear. Move the volume indicator to the left or to the right to change the volume.

To close the volume control, click on the **Volume** icon again.

You will be able to change the volume during the test if you need to.

> You may now change the volume.
> When you are finished, click on **Continue**.

Listening
Section Directions

This section measures your ability to understand conversations and lectures in English.

You will have 36 minutes to listen to the conversations and lectures and answer the questions. You will hear each conversation or lecture only one time.

After each conversation or lecture, you will answer questions about it. The questions typically ask about the main idea and supporting details. Some questions ask about the purpose of a speaker's statement or a speaker's attitude. Answer the questions based on what is stated or implied by the speakers.

You may take notes while you listen. You may use your notes to help you answer the questions. Your notes will not be scored.

In some questions, you will see this icon: 🎧 This means that you will hear, but not see, part of the question.

Some of the questions have special directions. These directions appear in a gray box on the screen.

Most questions are worth 1 point. If a question is worth more than 1 point, it will have special directions that indicate how many points you can receive.

You must answer each question. After you answer, click on **Next**. Then click on **OK** to confirm your answer and go on to the next question. After you click on **OK**, you cannot return to previous questions.

A clock at the top of the screen will show you how much time is remaining. The clock will not count down while you are listening. The clock will count down only while you are answering the questions.

Conversation 1

[1-5] Listen to part of a conversation between a student and a library employee.

Note-Taking

1. Why does the student meet with the employee?

    Ⓐ The student needs help finding resources for a final paper for a psychology class.
    Ⓑ The student needs help locating sources for a literature review.
    Ⓒ The student doesn't know where to find the rare books collection.
    Ⓓ The student is unfamiliar with writing psychology reviews.

2. What is the topic that the student is trying to write on?

    Ⓐ Contemporary psychoanalysis
    Ⓑ Self-psychology
    Ⓒ Relational psychotherapy
    Ⓓ Melanie Klein

3. What errors has the student committed? Choose 2 answers.

    Ⓐ He couldn't find the writing books in the reserved books section.
    Ⓑ He tried to touch rare books without the required specialized gloves.
    Ⓒ He didn't understand what Dr. Meyer meant when he mentioned books on reserve.
    Ⓓ He thought the rare books collection was located within the reserved books area.
    Ⓔ He didn't realize that psychology journals now come in electronic form.

4. Listen again to part of the conversation. Then answer the question.

    Why does the employee say this: 🎧

    Ⓐ The employee is also relieved that she got the chance to explain the location of the psychology section.
    Ⓑ The employee is sympathizing with the student's panic regarding the project.
    Ⓒ The employee realizes how fortunate it is that the topic of reserved books came up.
    Ⓓ The employee is pointing out the location of a psychology journal.

5. What will the student most likely do next?

    Ⓐ Read an original edition of a book by Melanie Klein
    Ⓑ Obtain a new ID card
    Ⓒ Search for articles by Heinz Kohut
    Ⓓ Search the psychology books on reserve

Lecture 1

[1-6] Listen to part of a lecture in a geology class.

AT07_2

1. What is the lecture mainly about?

    Ⓐ Volcanic activity contributing to the formation of water on Earth
    Ⓑ The different atmospheric structures of Earth and Mars
    Ⓒ The Late-Heavy Bombardment period on Earth, the Moon and Mars
    Ⓓ Theories regarding the process of water formation on Earth

2. Why does the professor say this: 🎧

    Ⓐ To tell the students to focus on some other interesting points
    Ⓑ To request different opinions from as many students as possible
    Ⓒ To prepare to introduce the topic of the lecture to students
    Ⓓ To indicate that no one really knows the answers to her questions

3. What can be inferred about the volcanic theory?

    Ⓐ It is the main source for the formation of water on the Earth's surface after all.
    Ⓑ It is questionable since volcanoes could not generate enough greenhouse gases.
    Ⓒ It is flawed because the concentration of deuterium was higher after the volcanic activity.
    Ⓓ It is significant since it produced various gases for more than 200 million years.

4. Why does the professor mention deuterium?

    Ⓐ To provide evidence of how meteors burn up when they enter the Earth's atmosphere
    Ⓑ To show how volcanoes erupted and emitted various gases, including greenhouse gases
    Ⓒ To explain that the comet theory cannot be the main reason for water formation
    Ⓓ To point out that deuterium had a significant impact on the formation of the ocean

5. What connection does the professor make between comets and meteors?

    Ⓐ Meteors contributed more to the formation of water on the planet than comets did.
    Ⓑ The theory of meteors depositing water on Earth has been discredited by the comets theory.
    Ⓒ They both had significant influence on the formation of oceans and land masses.
    Ⓓ Meteorites and comets hitting the Earth's surface eventually led to volcanic eruptions.

6. According to the professor, what is true about the Late Heavy Bombardment?
    Choose 2 answers.

    Ⓐ It set the stage for creating life on Earth.
    Ⓑ It activated volcanoes all over the globe.
    Ⓒ It produced greenhouse gases.
    Ⓓ It lasted more than a billion years.

Lecture 2

[1-6] Listen to part of a lecture in a history class.

1. What is the main topic of the lecture?

   Ⓐ The influence of the Hurrians on their neighboring cultures
   Ⓑ Hurrian religion and its influence on Greek religion
   Ⓒ Recent research and excavations regarding the Hurrians
   Ⓓ The discovery of the location of the Hurrians' central city

2. According to the lecture, what is true about the Hurrians? Choose 2 answers.

   Ⓐ They dominated the Middle East by 2000 BCE.
   Ⓑ They spoke a different language from their neighbors.
   Ⓒ They started using a cuneiform writing system around 2000 BCE.
   Ⓓ They had a great influence on the Assyrians in particular.

3. What resulted from the Hurrians' small-scale urbanization?

   Ⓐ It helped with determining when they began settlements.
   Ⓑ It led to higher levels of migration to other countries.
   Ⓒ It increased the attacks from their enemies in general.
   Ⓓ It made studying their culture and cities rather difficult.

4. Why does the professor mention Khabur ware and Nuzi ware?

   Ⓐ To support the opinion that they were widely used for decoration
   Ⓑ To describe their influence on their contemporaries
   Ⓒ To introduce another benefit of making pottery
   Ⓓ To emphasize the skillful pottery making of the Hurrians

5. What can be inferred about the religion of the Hurrians?

   Ⓐ It was recognized throughout the region, affecting certain cultures.
   Ⓑ It spread very quickly to other countries, becoming their state religion.
   Ⓒ It helped Egyptians shape the concept of their own gods and religion.
   Ⓓ It ended up disappearing with the rise of the new religion of the Hittites.

6. Listen again to part of the lecture. Then answer the question.

   Why does the professor say this:

   Ⓐ To start a discussion regarding the Hurrians' political influence
   Ⓑ To show the student that he is the one who is in charge
   Ⓒ To indicate that he was just about to discuss the Hurrian kingdom
   Ⓓ To tell the student not to rush to the next topic so fast

Conversation 2

[1-5] Listen to part of a conversation between a student and a university staff.

📋 Note-Taking

1. Why did the man come to the woman's counter?

    Ⓐ To change his major from biology to another subject
    Ⓑ To complain about the university's tuition application system
    Ⓒ To see if he can find help to pay for his tuition and textbooks
    Ⓓ To get information about elective courses that he should take

2. Why does the man mention new editions and older editions?

    Ⓐ To explain the process of buying books from an online store
    Ⓑ To point out that using older editions does not always work
    Ⓒ To tell the woman that they both cost almost the same
    Ⓓ To show how both of them could be used in classes

3. Why does the man not want to apply for a student loan?

    Ⓐ He has to take more elective courses to apply for it.
    Ⓑ It usually takes a very long time to pay back completely.
    Ⓒ The deadline for the application process has already passed.
    Ⓓ Biology majors are rarely given student loans.

4. What does the woman recommend the man do?

    Ⓐ Get a job that would pay him more than his current one
    Ⓑ Ask his academic advisor for help with his schedule
    Ⓒ Try to look for other locations to major in biology
    Ⓓ Find another part-time job at the library

5. Why does the woman say this: 🎧

    Ⓐ To praise the man for trying to take so many classes
    Ⓑ To see if the man can really handle this situation
    Ⓒ To imply that the man doesn't know what he is doing
    Ⓓ To indicate that the current schedule would be too hard to manage

Lecture 3

[1-6] Listen to part of a lecture in an art history class.

1. What is the lecture mainly about?
    Ⓐ The artistic value of the Chauvet cave paintings
    Ⓑ The techniques used by the Chauvet cave painters
    Ⓒ An analysis of the Chauvet cave painting's subjects
    Ⓓ The similarities between the Chauvet and Lascaux cave paintings

2. According to the lecture, which of the following is NOT something that painters of the Lascaux cave painting used to paint?
    Ⓐ Paint brushes made of animal hair
    Ⓑ Their own fingers
    Ⓒ Plant material
    Ⓓ Bones of small animals

3. According to the lecture, how did the painters of the Chauvet cave use the surfaces of the cave walls to their advantage?
    Ⓐ They used the contours of the walls to make shapes of animals.
    Ⓑ They used the uneven surfaces to add dimensionality to the figures.
    Ⓒ They used shading and perspective to make the animal paintings realistic.
    Ⓓ They incorporated the color of the cave itself into the depicted scenes.

4. According to the lecture, what might the abstract symbols on the Chauvet paintings indicate? Choose 2 answers.
    Ⓐ Identities of animals
    Ⓑ Indicators that aided in hunting
    Ⓒ Religious or spiritual symbols
    Ⓓ A basic written language
    Ⓔ Sorcery practices

5. How does the professor organize the lecture?
    Ⓐ By different elements of the painting, in no meaningful order
    Ⓑ From an earlier cave painting to a slightly newer one
    Ⓒ From concrete features of the cave painting to more abstract ones
    Ⓓ From more-obvious to less-obvious components of the painting

6. What will the class most likely do next?
    Ⓐ They will move on to another important element of the paintings.
    Ⓑ They will continue the discussion on emotional depictions.
    Ⓒ They will discuss more examples of dynamism in the cave paintings.
    Ⓓ They will study the role of animals in the cave paintings' depicted scenes.

PAGODA TOEFL

Actual Test

LISTENING

PAGODA TOEFL Actual Test Listening

3rd Edition

파고다교육그룹 언어교육연구소 저

해설서

TOEFL® is a registered trademark of Educational Testing Service (ETS).
This publication is not endorsed or approved by ETS.

PAGODA Books

PAGODA TOEFL
Actual Test Listening

3rd Edition

파고다교육그룹 언어교육연구소 저

해설서

PAGODA Books

Actual Test 01

본서 | P. 52

Conversation 1	1. Ⓒ	2. Ⓓ	3. Ⓐ, Ⓑ	4. Ⓑ	5. Ⓑ	
Lecture 1	1. Ⓐ	2. Ⓑ, Ⓒ	3. Ⓑ	4. Ⓒ	5. Ⓐ	6. Ⓓ
Lecture 2	1. Ⓑ	2. Ⓐ	3. Ⓓ	4. Ⓑ	5. Ⓒ	6. Ⓒ
Conversation 2	1. Ⓓ	2. Ⓐ, Ⓒ	3. Ⓒ	4. Yes – Ⓐ, Ⓓ / No – Ⓑ, Ⓒ	5. Ⓓ	
Lecture 3	1. Ⓐ	2. Ⓓ, Ⓔ	3. Ⓓ	4. Ⓐ	5. Ⓑ	6. Ⓑ

● 내가 맞은 문제 유형의 개수를 적어 보고 어느 유형에 취약한지 확인해 봅시다.

문제 유형	맞은 개수
Main Idea	5
Detail	9
Connecting Contents	6
Function & Attitude	5
Inference	3
Total	28

Conversation 1

[1-5] Listen to part of a conversation between a student and a librarian.

Man: Librarian | Woman: Student

M: Hello, were you able to find everything you needed?

W: Yes, and no… There is a book that I've checked out many times. The first time that I located it was two years ago for a paper I was writing. Since then I've checked it out many times, and I've noticed that I am the only person that has done so for a long time.

M: Really? What book might that be?

W: This one right here.

M: *Ancient Celtic Jewelry*… That is a fairly obscure topic, isn't it? Let me bring up its check-out history. Oh, that is unusual. We actually have two copies of this book, but no one has checked out either copy other than you and Professor MacMillan in the last four years.

W: Professor MacMillan is the instructor I had when I wrote that paper.

M: Oh, so you're majoring in jewelry making?

W: Yes, I am. And that's why I have a question for you. I heard that the library has a book sale every spring, when professors, students, and local bookstores donate old books. My friend also told me that old books from this library sometimes are included in the sale…

M: That is true. If we have more than one copy and they are unpopular, then they may be included in the yearly book sale. However, there is no way to guarantee that it will happen to any particular book. And there is no way for a patron to request that a book be included. Despite our yearly sale, this is not actually a bookstore. I hope you understand.

W: Yes, I do. But, that's where I have run into another problem. I've tried to find this book at every bookstore I could find — both brick-and-mortar stores and online book vendors. It has gone out of print, and no one seems to have a copy.

M: That is very unfortunate, but I think you would actually find the same is true for many of the books in our collection. It is the nature of academic publications. They rarely gain widespread popularity, and it rarely lasts long if they do.

W: I see.
M: But, I know someone who may be able to help you. If you contact this bookstore, they will try to track down even books that are out of print. Here's the address and the phone number. You should ask for Michelle.
W: Really? Thank you so much!
M: You're welcome. But, don't get your hopes up too high. She is good at what she does, but it may still be impossible to find.
W: Ok. I guess if she fails, then I could just make a lot of photocopies.
M: That is an option, but I doubt that these pictures would reproduce well.
W: You're probably right. I could use a scanner.
M: You could also volunteer to help at the book sale. You wouldn't be able to select the book to be included, but our volunteers get first choice from the books that are included in the sale. If it makes it in, you would have a very strong chance of getting it. So, why don't you hold off on trying to reproduce it for a while?
W: Ok, I will. Thank you for your help!

여: 그렇군요.
남: 하지만 학생에게 도움이 될 수도 있는 사람을 알고 있어요. 이 서점에 연락하면 이미 절판된 책들도 찾아봐 줄 겁니다. 여기 주소랑 전화번호예요. 미쉘을 바꿔달라고 하면 돼요.

여: 그래요? 정말 감사합니다!
남: 천만에요. 하지만 너무 큰 기대는 하지 말아요. 그녀가 자기 일을 능숙하게 해내긴 하지만 여전히 못 찾을 수도 있으니까요.

여: 네. 못 찾아낸다면 그냥 복사를 많이 하는 수밖에는 없겠네요.
남: 그것도 한 가지 방법이지만 이 사진들이 잘 나올지는 모르겠네요.

여: 그러게요. 스캐너를 사용해 봐야겠어요.
남: 도서 할인 행사에서 자원봉사를 할 수도 있어요. 그 책이 할인에 포함되도록 할 수는 없겠지만, 자원봉사자에게는 할인에 포함된 책을 1순위로 구입할 수 있는 선택권이 주어져요. 만일 이 책이 할인에 포함된다면, 학생이 이 책을 구입하게 될 가능성이 매우 높죠. 그러니 책 복사는 잠시 보류하는 게 어때요?

여: 네, 그럴게요. 도와주셔서 감사합니다!

어휘

notice v 알아차리다 | **obscure** adj 난해한 | **unusual** adj 특이한 | **local** adj 지역의 | **donate** v 기부하다 | **guarantee** v 보장하다 | **patron** n 후원자 | **brick-and-mortar** n 소매 | **vendor** n 판매 회사 | **publication** n 출판물 | **widespread** adj 광범위한 | **popularity** n 인기 | **reproduce** v 복사하다

1. Main Idea
What is the conversation mainly about?
- (A) Finding out how to check out a book from the library
- (B) Getting contact information of a particular book seller
- **(C) Finding out which books are sold at the book sale**
- (D) Deciding which books will be placed in storage

2. Detail
What does the woman say about the yearly book sale?
- (A) It usually lasts for a whole year in the student library.
- (B) It sells rare books that are out of print and expensive.
- (C) It only sells donated books for charity purposes.
- **(D) It sells books that are donated by students and professors.**

1.
이 대화는 주로 무엇에 관한 것인가?
- (A) 도서관에서 책을 어떻게 대출하는지 알아보기
- (B) 특정 도서 판매자의 연락처 받기
- **(C) 도서 할인 행사에 어떤 책들이 판매되는지 알아보기**
- (D) 어떤 책들을 창고에 보관할지 결정하기

2.
여자는 연례 도서 할인 행사에 대해 뭐라고 하는가?
- (A) 학생 도서관에서 보통 1년 내내 계속된다.
- (B) 절판된 값비싼 희귀 서적들을 판매한다.
- (C) 자선 목적으로 기부된 책들만 판매한다.
- **(D) 학생들과 교수들이 기부한 책들을 판매한다.**

3. **Detail**
What are the criteria for deciding whether a book is put up for sale? Choose 2 answers.
- Ⓐ **They have not been used for a long time.**
- Ⓑ **They are duplicate copies.**
- Ⓒ They are old books.
- Ⓓ They exist in e-book form.

4. **Connecting Contents**
Why does the man mention volunteering?
- Ⓐ The student will have a higher chance of participating.
- Ⓑ **The student is interested in the yearly book sale.**
- Ⓒ The book sale is a popular school event.
- Ⓓ The library needs more volunteers for the book sale.

5. **Function & Attitude**
Listen again to part of the conversation. Then answer the question.

> Ⓜ You could also volunteer to help at the book sale. You wouldn't be able to select the book to be included, but our volunteers get first choice from the books that are included in the sale. If it makes it in, you would have a very strong chance of getting it. So, why don't you hold off on trying to reproduce it for a while?

Why does the man say this:

> Ⓜ So, why don't you hold off on trying to reproduce it for a while?

- Ⓐ To ask the student to buy it at the book sale at the end of the year
- Ⓑ **To tell the student that it is too early to make a copy of the book**
- Ⓒ To let the student know that she could search for it on the university's website
- Ⓓ To allow the student to scan the book at the university library office

---

3.
책이 할인에 포함되는지를 결정하는 기준은 무엇인가? 두 개를 고르시오.
- Ⓐ 오랜 기간 동안 사용되지 않았다.
- Ⓑ 2권 이상 있다.
- Ⓒ 오래된 책이다.
- Ⓓ 전자책 형태이다.

4.
남자가 자원봉사를 언급하는 이유는 무엇인가?
- Ⓐ 학생이 참여하게 될 가능성이 더 높을 것이다.
- Ⓑ 학생은 연례 도서 할인 행사에 관심이 있다.
- Ⓒ 도서 할인 행사는 인기 있는 교내 행사이다.
- Ⓓ 도서관은 도서 할인 행사에 더 많은 자원봉사자를 필요로 한다.

5.
대화의 일부를 다시 듣고 질문에 답하시오.

> 🎧 도서 할인 행사에서 자원봉사를 할 수도 있어요. 그 책이 할인에 포함되도록 할 수는 없지만, 자원봉사자에게는 할인에 포함된 책을 1순위로 구입할 수 있는 선택권이 주어져요. 만일 이 책이 할인에 포함된다면, 학생이 이 책을 구입하게 될 가능성이 매우 높죠. 그러니 책 복사는 잠시 보류하는 게 어때요?

남자는 왜 이렇게 말하는가:

> 🎧 그러니 책 복사는 잠시 보류하는 게 어때요?

- Ⓐ 학생에게 그 책을 연말 도서 할인 행사 때 사라고 당부하기 위해
- Ⓑ 학생에게 책을 복사하는 게 아직은 너무 이르다고 말하기 위해
- Ⓒ 대학 웹사이트에서 검색 가능하다는 것을 학생에게 알려주기 위해
- Ⓓ 학생이 그 책을 대학교 도서관 사무실에서 스캔하는 것을 허가하기 위해

Lecture 1

[1-6] Listen to part of a lecture in an ecology class.

Man: Student | Woman: Professor

W: Today we will continue our discussion of the environmental impact of dams by looking at the history of the Colorado River. For nearly six million years, the mighty Colorado River ran its course from the heights of the Rocky Mountains about 2,334 kilometers to a lush delta where it emptied into the Gulf of California. The awesome power of this river can be seen along its course through northern Arizona, where it carved out the Grand Canyon. For thousands of years, the only people who relied upon its water were various Native American tribes. The first people who began diverting water from the river were Mormon settlers, but their influence was minor compared to what began happening at the end of the nineteenth century.

In the 1880s, the first major diversion of water from the Colorado River began near its headwaters in Colorado. 80 percent of Colorado's precipitation falls on the western side of the Continental Divide, while the majority of its population has always lived to the eastern side, so they decided to build the Grand Ditch. Completed in 1936, it supplied about 21,800 megaliters of water per year. Yes?

M: Professor, how much water is that? I'm not familiar with that term... megaliter...

W: That isn't surprising. Most people never need to deal with such large volumes. A megaliter is one million liters. So, this ditch supplied about 21.8 billion liters of water... which is a lot of water, but it is only a fraction of what the Colorado River Basin supplies. Many more canals, tunnels and dams were constructed to divert the river's water over the years. But, they encountered a problem. The further downriver you are, the more silt is suspended in the water. This supply of silt is what created the massive delta, much like the one where the Mississippi River empties into the Gulf of Mexico — also known as the state of Louisiana. On top of that, the flow of the river is actually quite erratic, and it would often flood. When people tried to divert water downstream, it often ended in disaster. The Alamo Canal was dug in 1900, but in 1905, massive flooding destroyed the head of the canal, and the river's entire flow coursed into the valley, creating the Salton Sea before they managed to return it to its course. This and other events spurred increased dam building, which in turn led to the need to share the water evenly. You see, seven states rely on the Colorado River to supply water for agriculture, drinking, and power. In 1922, the water was divided up under the Colorado River Compact. First, they divided the river course into the Upper and Lower Basin. Then, they allocated the water according to population and usage. Nevada, which had few people and thought it had enough groundwater for growth, received the smallest portion at 4 percent. Colorado and California both received over 50 percent of the Upper and Lower Basin portions respectively. The percentages total up to about 18.5 trillion liters of water. How did they arrive at such a number? They averaged out 20 years of data on flow rates for the river and its many tributaries. Unfortunately, for them, those 20 years turned out to be the wettest period in over 400 years. When precipitation returned to normal, droughts put their water supply in jeopardy.

This is when they began building massive dams to create reservoirs that could supply their needs, and forever altered the river. The first was the Hoover Dam, which was completed in 1935 and created Lake Mead. These dams were very successful, and they provided both stable water supplies and hydro-electric power. However, every time a new dam was added, the flow of the river was reduced. These dams lower the temperature of the water and prevent silt from flowing downstream. This makes the water more saline, that is, saltier, which is bad for the environment. More importantly, the water flow has been reduced so much that the lush wetlands of the delta have all but disappeared, and the water never reaches the ocean most years.

어휘

impact n 영향 | **dam** n 댐 | **lush** adj 비옥한 | **delta** n 삼각주 | **rely** v 의지하다 | **divert** v 방향을 바꾸게 하다 | **headwater** n 상류 | **precipitation** n 강수 | **familiar with** ~에 익숙한 | **supply** v 공급하다 | **fraction** n 일부 | **canal** n 수로 | **construct** v 건설하다 | **encounter** v 맞닥뜨리다 | **silt** n 유사 | **erratic** adj 불규칙한 | **spur** v 박차를 가하다 | **evenly** adv 균일하게, 균등하게 | **agriculture** n 농업 | **compact** n 조약, 협정 | **allocate** v 분배하다, 할당하다 | **usage** n 사용 | **groundwater** n 지하수 | **respectively** adv 각각 | **tributary** n 지류 | **drought** n 가뭄 | **jeopardy** n 위험 | **reservoir** n 저수지 | **alter** v 바꾸다, 변화시키다 | **successful** adj 성공적인 | **stable** adj 안정적인 | **hydro-electric** adj 수력 전력의 | **flow** v 흐르다 | **saline** adj 염분이 있는 | **wetland** n 습지

1. **Main Idea**

What is the talk mostly about?

Ⓐ **The history of the Colorado River and diverting its course**
Ⓑ The importance of the Colorado River to the people living around it
Ⓒ The past water levels of the Colorado River and its future
Ⓓ The people who use the water of the Colorado River for living

2. **Detail**

According to the professor, what is true about the Colorado River? Choose 2 answers.

Ⓐ The trees that live around it give hundreds of years of information about it.
Ⓑ **Its power was great enough to create the Grand Canyon in Arizona.**
Ⓒ **The first major diversion of it occurred at the end of the 19th century.**
Ⓓ Most of its precipitation falls on the eastern side of the Continental Divide.

3. **Detail**

According to the passage, what does the erratic flow of the river often lead to?

Ⓐ Frequent droughts over hundreds of years
Ⓑ **A disaster caused by massive flooding**
Ⓒ A short period of sudden drought
Ⓓ Unexpectedly heavy rainfall in the region

4. **Inference**

What can be inferred about the Colorado River?

Ⓐ A substantial amount of its water is diverted to Nevada.
Ⓑ Its water is expected to become more saline in 10 years.
Ⓒ **It is a vital source of water for Colorado and California.**
Ⓓ The first people who diverted it were various Native Americans.

5. **Connecting Contents**

Why does the professor mention the Hoover Dam?

Ⓐ **To indicate that it represented the start of building a series of dams for reservoirs**
Ⓑ To show how it contributed to the pollution of the water, making it murkier and bitterer

1.
강의는 주로 무엇에 대한 것인가?

Ⓐ 콜로라도강의 역사와 강의 흐름 바꾸기
Ⓑ 콜로라도강 부근 거주민들에게 있어 강의 중요성
Ⓒ 콜로라도강의 과거 수위와 강의 미래
Ⓓ 생계를 위해 콜로라도강의 물을 이용하는 사람들

2.
교수에 의하면, 콜로라도강에 대해 옳은 것은 무엇인가?
두 개를 고르시오.

Ⓐ 강 주변의 나무들이 강에 대한 수백 년의 정보를 전해 준다.
Ⓑ 강의 힘은 애리조나에 그랜드캐니언을 만들어 낼 정도로 강력했다.
Ⓒ 최초의 주요한 강 흐름 전환은 19세기 말에 일어났다.
Ⓓ 강의 대부분의 강수량은 록키산맥 분수계의 동쪽에 내린다.

3.
지문에 의하면 강의 불규칙한 흐름은 종종 무엇으로 이어지는가?

Ⓐ 수백 년에 걸친 빈번한 가뭄
Ⓑ 거대한 홍수로 인한 참사
Ⓒ 짧은 기간의 갑작스러운 가뭄
Ⓓ 예기치 않게 그 지역에 내리는 폭우

4.
콜로라도강에 대해 무엇을 추론할 수 있는가?

Ⓐ 강물의 상당량이 네바다주로 유입된다.
Ⓑ 10년 내에 강이 더 많은 염분을 함유할 것으로 보인다.
Ⓒ 콜로라도와 캘리포니아주의 필수적인 수원이다.
Ⓓ 강의 흐름을 처음으로 바꾼 이들은 다양한 북미 원주민 부족들이었다.

5.
교수는 왜 후버댐을 언급하는가?

Ⓐ 저수지를 위한 댐 건설의 시발점을 대변했다는 것을 알리려고
Ⓑ 물을 더 탁하고 쓰게 만듦으로써 어떻게 오염의 원인이 되었는지 보이려고

Ⓒ To state that it was the first dam that successfully provided a stable water supply
Ⓓ To explain how it led to the destruction of the ecosystem, especially the wetlands

6. Function & Attitude

Listen again to part of the lecture. Then answer the question.

> Ⓜ Professor, how much water is that? I'm not familiar with that term… megaliter…
> Ⓦ That isn't surprising.

What does the professor mean when she says this:

> Ⓦ That isn't surprising.

Ⓐ The professor thinks what the student said is not very creative.
Ⓑ The professor is not sure what the student is trying to imply.
Ⓒ The professor is trying to correct the student's statement.
Ⓓ **The professor knows that megaliter is not a commonly used word.**

Ⓒ 안정적인 물 공급에 성공한 최초의 댐이었다는 것을 말하려고
Ⓓ 생태계, 특히 습지의 파괴로 어떻게 이어졌는지 설명하려고

6.

강의의 일부를 다시 듣고 질문에 답하시오.

> 남 교수님, 그게 얼마큼의 양인가요? 메가리터라는 단어에 익숙하지 않아서요…
> 여 놀라운 일은 아니에요.

교수는 다음과 같이 말하며 무엇을 의미하는가:

> 여 놀라운 일은 아니에요.

Ⓐ 학생이 말한 것이 그다지 창의적이지 않다고 생각한다.
Ⓑ 학생이 무엇을 암시하려는 것인지 모르겠다.
Ⓒ 학생이 한 말을 바로잡으려 하고 있다.
Ⓓ **메가리터가 흔히 사용되는 단어가 아니라는 것을 안다.**

Lecture 2

🎧 AT01_3

[1-6] Listen to part of a lecture in a science class.

Man: Student | Woman: Professor

Ⓦ As I am sure you all recall, Maria asked an interesting and difficult question at the end of class on Monday. What is the difference between a nut and a seed? The answer to this question is very complicated, so please pay attention. We will be approaching this from a botanical perspective and not a culinary one. In cooking, there are many things that we call nuts, and their names actually contain the word nut, but strictly speaking, they are not nuts. These include walnuts and peanuts. In fact, almost all of the things we call nuts in the kitchen fall under one of three categories in science: seeds, drupes, and true nuts.
So, let's start with seeds. When flowering plants, conifers and many other land plants reproduce, the ovary of the plant forms a thick outer skin layer after it is fertilized called its integument. This

과학 강의의 일부를 들으시오.

남자: 학생 | 여자: 교수

여 여러분 모두 기억하겠지만, 마리아가 월요일 수업이 끝날 때 흥미로우면서도 어려운 질문을 하나 했었어요. 견과와 씨앗의 차이가 무엇인가? 이 질문에 대한 답은 매우 복잡하니 집중해 주세요. 우리는 요리가 아닌 식물학적인 관점에서 이 문제에 접근하려고 합니다. 요리에는 우리가 견과류라고 부르는 많은 것들이 있고, 사실상 그것들의 이름 자체에도 nut라는 말이 들어가지만 엄밀히 말해서 그것들은 견과류가 아닙니다. 여기에는 호두와 땅콩이 포함됩니다. 사실, 우리가 주방에서 견과류라고 부르는 거의 모든 것들은 과학적으로는 씨앗, 핵과, 진짜 견과, 이렇게 세 가지 범주에 해당됩니다.

자, 씨앗부터 시작해 봅시다. 꽃을 피우는 식물, 침엽수, 그리고 많은 다른 육상 식물들이 번식할 때, 식물의 씨방은 수정을 한 후에 외피라고 불리는 두꺼운 외부 표피층을 만듭니다. 이러한 표피는 얇고 꽤 부드

skin may be thin and fairly soft or very hard and sometimes quite thick. If the seed is edible, we call the meat inside of the integument its kernel. Keep that word in mind, it will come up again. Outside of the integument may be a pericarp.

Broadly speaking, all of the things we call fruits contain a seed, but they are distinguished by how the layers of the pericarp form. In a fruit, it forms into three layers. The endocarp may contain one or more seeds within it. Outside of the endocarp, we find the thick, fleshy mesocarp. That is the part we are interested in when we eat fruit. Then on the outside we find the exocarp, or skin of the fruit.

With a drupe, like a peach, the kernel is contained within a very hard endocarp that is often referred to as a pit or a stone — for obvious reasons.

Now, if you take a walnut straight from a tree, you will find that it is actually a drupe. It has a tough exocarp surrounding a fibrous, inedible mesocarp. Inside of that, we find its extremely hard endocarp, what we usually think of as the nut's shell. But, the part we eat is only the kernel, or the seed of the drupe. Other nuts that fall into this category are pecans and almonds.

In a true nut, the layers of the pericarp are fused into one hard outer shell that does not open along a natural seam. Contained inside is the kernel. Nuts that fall into this category include chestnuts, acorns, and hazelnuts.

M Why does walnut have 'nut' in its name if it is a drupe and not a nut?

W That is actually a pretty common situation. Take the coconut for instance. Much like walnuts, by the time coconuts reach the store, all that remains is the endocarp with the kernel within. Most people probably wouldn't recognize a coconut that had just been harvested. It has a thick green exocarp that covers a very thick and fibrous mesocarp; both of which are usually removed before they are sold. The water inside the kernel is fairly unique for seeds, and is quite nutritious.

Speaking of nutrition, seeds of all kinds are a great source of nutrients. They contain large amounts of protein, vitamins, minerals, and fat, while nuts contain all of these plus high levels of vitamin B and fiber. They play an important role in the diets of humans and animals alike. Many animals such as squirrels and some birds store nuts away in trees or buried underground to help them survive the colder weather from late fall to early spring, when there is very little available food. However, while nutritious, humans should keep their fat content in mind. The oils contained in nuts are mostly healthy types of fat, but even healthy fats should be eaten in moderation.

M Professor, what about peanuts? You mentioned them, and you said they are not a true nut, so what are they?

W Yes, I did, didn't I? Well, the peanut is a seed, but it is not a nut nor is it a drupe. It is actually a legume, making it closer to a bean or a pea. After a flower on a peanut plant is fertilized, its stem will grow until it reaches the soil. After the ovary is buried under the soil, it will develop into a peanut. They have a hard outer shell, but the seeds are separate from it, much like peas in a pod. This is why they are sometimes called ground nuts, but only the ground part is accurate.

있긴 하지만, 인간은 견과의 지방 함유량을 염두에 두어야 합니다. 견과에 함유되어 있는 기름은 대부분 건강한 종류의 지방이지만 건강에 좋은 지방이라 할지라도 적당히 섭취해야 합니다.

교수님, 땅콩은 어떤가요? 땅콩을 언급하시고 진짜 견과가 아니라고 하셨는데, 그럼 그것들은 뭔가요?

아, 그렇다고 했죠? 음, 땅콩은 씨앗이지만 견과나 핵과는 아닙니다. 그것은 사실 두과 작물이며, 콩이나 완두콩에 더 가깝지요. 땅콩 식물의 꽃이 수정을 한 후 그 줄기는 땅에 도달할 때까지 자라게 됩니다. 씨방이 땅 속에 묻히고 나면, 그것이 땅콩으로 크는 것입니다. 그것은 딱딱한 외피를 가지고 있지만, 씨앗은 꼬투리에 들어있는 완두콩처럼 외피와 분리가 됩니다. 이것이 땅콩이 때때로 '땅의 견과(ground nut)'라고 불리는 이유이지만, 오직 땅을 일컫는 부분만 정확하죠.

어휘

recall v 기억해 내다 | **nut** n 견과 | **seed** n 씨앗 | **complicated** adj 복잡한 | **approach** v 접근하다 | **botanical** adj 식물학의 | **perspective** n 관점 | **culinary** adj 요리의 | **strictly** adv 엄격히 | **walnut** n 호두 | **peanut** n 땅콩 | **drupe** n 핵과 | **conifer** n 침엽수 | **reproduce** v 번식하다 | **ovary** n 씨방 | **fertilize** v 수정하다 | **integument** n 외피 | **edible** adj 먹을 수 있는 | **kernel** n 알맹이 | **pericarp** n 과피 | **broadly** adv 널리, 광범위하게 | **distinguish** v 구분하다 | **endocarp** n 내과피 | **mesocarp** n 중과피 | **exocarp** n 외과피 | **tough** adj 단단한 | **fibrous** adj 섬유로 된 | **pecan** n 피칸 | **fuse** v 녹다, 융화하다 | **chestnut** n 밤 | **acorn** n 도토리 | **hazelnut** n 개암 | **recognize** v 알아차리다, 식별하다 | **nutrient** n 영양소 | **protein** n 단백질 | **fat** n 지방 | **content** n 함유량 | **moderation** n 적당함, 절제 | **legume** n 두과 작물 | **accurate** adj 정확한

---

1. Main Idea

What is the lecture mainly about?

Ⓐ The composition of various integuments
Ⓑ The distinctions between nuts and seeds
Ⓒ The culinary definitions of nuts and seeds
Ⓓ The edible and inedible nuts and seeds

2. Detail

Which of the following is not mentioned in the lecture as an example of a true nut?

Ⓐ Almond
Ⓑ Chestnut
Ⓒ Acorn
Ⓓ Hazelnut

1.

이 강의의 주제는 무엇인가?

Ⓐ 다양한 외피의 구성
Ⓑ 견과와 씨앗의 차이점
Ⓒ 음식으로서의 견과 및 씨앗의 정의
Ⓓ 식용 및 비식용 견과와 씨앗

2.

다음 중 강의에서 진짜 견과의 예로 언급되지 않은 것은 무엇인가?

Ⓐ 아몬드
Ⓑ 밤
Ⓒ 도토리
Ⓓ 개암

3. Function & Attitude

What does the professor mean when she says this:

> W However, while nutritious, humans should keep their fat content in mind.

Ⓐ She thinks keeping calories in mind could benefit one's diet.
Ⓑ She is expressing concern about the health issue regarding allergies.
Ⓒ She suspects that nuts and seeds can be quite dangerous.
Ⓓ **She is explaining that consuming too much fat could be harmful.**

4. Connecting Contents

Why does the professor mention a legume?

Ⓐ To compare peanut seeds with walnut seeds
Ⓑ **To highlight interesting facts about the peanut**
Ⓒ To argue against the botanical definition of a drupe
Ⓓ To illustrate a point about ground nuts and their name

5. Detail

What is true of both nuts and seeds?

Ⓐ They have thick but soft integuments.
Ⓑ They have fibrous, inedible endocarps.
Ⓒ **They contain many different nutrients.**
Ⓓ They are composed of 3 to 5 layers.

6. Connecting Contents

Why does the professor mention a coconut?

Ⓐ To explain that it is a good source of energy for animals
Ⓑ To tell the students that it is beneficial for one's health
Ⓒ **To give another example of a drupe with a misleading name**
Ⓓ To illustrate her point that it has an interesting looking exocarp

---

3.
교수는 다음과 같이 말하며 무엇을 의미하는가:

> 예 그러나 영양가가 있긴 하지만, 인간은 견과의 지방 함유량을 염두에 두어야 합니다.

Ⓐ 칼로리를 신경 쓰는 것이 식단에 도움이 된다고 생각한다.
Ⓑ 알레르기와 관련된 건강상의 쟁점에 대해 우려를 표현하고 있다.
Ⓒ 견과와 씨앗이 꽤 위험할 수 있다고 의심한다.
Ⓓ 너무 많은 지방을 섭취하는 것이 해로울 수 있다는 것을 설명하고 있다.

4.
교수는 왜 두과 작물을 언급하는가?

Ⓐ 땅콩 씨앗을 호두 씨앗과 비교하기 위해서
Ⓑ 땅콩에 대한 흥미로운 사실들을 강조하기 위해서
Ⓒ 핵과의 식물학적 정의에 반대하는 주장을 하기 위해서
Ⓓ 땅의 견과와 그 이름에 대한 핵심을 설명하기 위해서

5.
견과와 씨앗에 모두 해당되는 것은 무엇인가?

Ⓐ 두껍지만 부드러운 외피가 있다.
Ⓑ 섬유질이면서 먹을 수 없는 내과피가 있다.
Ⓒ 다양한 영양소를 함유하고 있다.
Ⓓ 3~5개의 층으로 구성되어 있다.

6.
교수는 왜 코코넛을 언급하는가?

Ⓐ 그것이 동물에게 좋은 에너지 공급원이라는 것을 설명하기 위해
Ⓑ 그것이 건강에 이롭다는 것을 학생들에게 말해주기 위해
Ⓒ 오해를 일으키는 이름을 가진 핵과의 또 다른 예를 제시하기 위해
Ⓓ 그것이 신기하게 생긴 외과피를 가지고 있다는 자신의 의견을 입증하기 위해

Conversation 2

[1-5] Listen to part of a conversation between a university employee and a student.

Man: Employee | Woman: Student

W: Excuse me, do you have a moment?
M: Uh, sure, how can I help you?
W: I bought this workbook here the other day, but I didn't open it until I was in class yesterday. And well… just look at the pages.
M: Oh my, these pages are upside down.
W: Yes, they are, and some pages are missing entirely.
M: Wow, are any of the other workbooks like this?
W: Yes, every book my classmates bought is like this.
M: All of them were printed wrong? We are going to have to reprint the books. All of the students that bought this workbook will have to be notified. Which professor wrote this book?
W: Professor Abelard wrote it. He is the dean of the French department.
M: Really? Hold on. Let me check something. We keep a database of all the books that we print for professors.
W: Can students access that database?
M: Um, yes. You can, but only from the university library computer labs. That is what you will need to do until we get new copies of the book printed.
W: I see. How long will that take?
M: Um, I don't know… About a week, maybe?
W: That long? We have an exam this week on material that is included in the book.
M: Unless that material is on missing pages, that shouldn't be a problem.
W: I think that some of it is. They cannot reprint the books any sooner than that?
M: No, the university press is very busy. There are print orders from many professors and student organizations that have already been scheduled.
W: Yeah, ok, I get that. But, shouldn't this take priority over some of those?
M: Yes, it should, but that is a decision for the press manager to make.
W: I see. What were you going to check?
M: I was going to check the database version of the workbook to see if the master copy is intact. OK, here it is… Oh, no… This has never happened before.
W: What's wrong?

대학교 직원과 학생의 대화의 일부를 들으시오.

남자: 직원 | 여자: 학생

여: 실례합니다. 잠시 시간 괜찮으세요?
남: 아, 네. 어떻게 도와 드릴까요?
여: 저번에 여기서 이 워크북을 샀지만 어제 수업이 있기 전까지는 열어 보지 않았거든요. 그리고 음… 이 페이지들을 보세요.
남: 오 이런, 페이지들이 거꾸로네요.
여: 네, 그리고 일부 페이지는 완전히 빠져 있어요.
남: 세상에, 다른 워크북들도 혹시 이런가요?
여: 네, 저와 수업을 같이 듣는 학생들의 모든 책이 이래요.
남: 전부 잘못 인쇄되었다고요? 책을 재인쇄해야겠군요. 이 워크북을 구매한 학생들에게 공지를 하고요. 어떤 교수님이 이 책을 쓰셨죠?
여: 알베라드 교수님이 쓰셨어요. 프랑스어학과의 학장님이세요.
남: 정말이요? 잠시만요. 확인 좀 해볼게요. 교수님들을 위해 인쇄하는 모든 책들의 데이터베이스를 보관하고 있거든요.
여: 학생들이 그 데이터베이스에 접근할 수 있나요?
남: 음, 네. 할 수 있지만 대학교 도서관 컴퓨터실에서만 할 수 있어요. 우리가 책의 새 제본을 받을 때까지 학생이 해야 할 것이죠.
여: 그렇군요. 얼마나 걸리나요?
남: 음, 모르겠어요… 아마 한 주 정도요?
여: 그렇게나 오래요? 이 책에 포함된 내용에 관해 이번 주에 시험이 있는데요.
남: 그 내용이 빠진 페이지에 있지 않는 한 문제는 없을 거예요.
여: 일부는 그런 것 같아요. 그보다 더 빨리 책을 재인쇄할 수는 없나요?
남: 안 돼요. 대학교 인쇄소가 아주 바쁘거든요. 이미 예정된 교수님과 학생 단체의 인쇄 주문이 많아요.
여: 음, 네, 알아요. 하지만 이 문제가 일부 주문보다는 더 우선 사항이 되어야 하지 않을까요?
남: 네, 그래야 하지만 그건 인쇄소 매니저가 내릴 결정이에요.
여: 알겠습니다. 무엇을 확인하려고 하셨던 거죠?
남: 마스터 복사본이 손상되지 않았는지 보려고 워크북의 데이터베이스 버전을 확인하려고 했어요. 아, 여기 있네요… 아, 이런… 이런 일은 한 번도 일어난 적이 없는데.
여: 뭐가 문제인가요?

| M | The master copy is in shambles as well. I am going to have to notify Professor Abelard. He has to provide us an intact copy of the file before we can do the reprint.
| W | So that could take even longer than you said?
| M | I'm afraid so.
| W | Then, I guess Professor Abelard is going to have to adjust his exams to compensate for the delay.
| M | Not necessarily. If we can upload the intact version to the database soon, then you can still go to the library to do your workbook assignments.
| W | That isn't fair. I mean, there are only so many computers in the library labs, and there are four sessions of this course this semester. Plus, we will have to compete with all of the other students on campus to use those computers.
| M | That does present a problem.
| W | I don't understand why every student needs to have a copy of the workbook. If the database exists, why do students have to go to the library to use it?
| M | Well, there are a few reasons for that. You need to have your workbook in class, right? You need to check your homework, and you sometimes use it in class as well.
| W | Yeah, but we could just print out the pages we need…
| M | That's another reason! Think about it. If any student could just print out pages from workbooks whenever they want to, then what would stop them from making copies of the book and selling them to other students?
| W | Uh, that actually is a very good point. I guess I'd better get over to the library soon, then.
| M | Yes, and I need to call Professor Abelard. Thank you for bringing this to our attention!

어휘

entirely adv 완전히 | **reprint** v 다시 인쇄하다 | **notify** v 공지하다 | **access** v 접근하다, 이용하다 | **press** n 인쇄소 | **order** n 주문 | **organization** n 조직, 단체 | **priority** n 우선 순위 | **decision** n 결정 | **intact** adj 온전한, 손상되지 않은 | **shambles** n 난장판 | **adjust** v 조정하다 | **compensate** v 보상하다 | **delay** n 지연 | **necessarily** adv 어쩔 수 없이, 필연적으로 | **assignment** n 과제 | **compete** v 경쟁하다

1. Main Idea
Why did the student go to the university book store?

A To see if it carries a particular book
B To request a refund for a damaged book
C To get some documents printed
D To complain about a book she purchased

2. Detail
What is indicated about the book in question?

Choose 2 answers.

A Some pages are wrongly printed.
B The answer key is incorrect.
C Pages are missing from it.
D The pages are out of order.

3. Function & Attitude
Listen again to part of the conversation. Then answer the question.

> M I was going to check the database version of the workbook to see if the master copy is intact. OK, here it is… Oh, no… This has never happened before.
> W What's wrong?

Why does the man say this:

> M This has never happened before.

A To confirm that books have never been misprinted
B To indicate that the computer database is not working
C To state that corrupt files have not been uploaded before
D To imply that the professor made a significant mistake

4. Connecting Contents
In the conversation, the speakers discuss the reasons why students cannot access the database outside of the library. Indicate in the table below whether each of the following is one of those reasons.

	Yes	No
A It prevents students from selling the book.	✓	
B The professors want to profit from the sales.		✓
C It makes it easier for students to do their homework.		✓
D The students need to use their books in class.	✓	

1.
학생은 왜 대학교 서점에 갔는가?

A 서점이 특정한 책을 판매하는지 보려고
B 손상된 책의 환불을 요청하려고
C 어떤 문서를 인쇄하려고
D 자신이 구매한 책에 관해 불만을 제기하려고

2.
문제가 된 책에 관해 무엇을 알 수 있는가?

두 개를 고르시오.

A 일부 페이지가 잘못 인쇄되었다.
B 답이 틀렸다.
C 페이지가 빠져 있다.
D 페이지 순서가 잘못되었다.

3.
대화의 일부를 다시 듣고 질문에 답하시오.

> 남 마스터 복사본이 손상되지 않았는지 보려고 워크북의 데이터베이스 버전을 확인하려고 했어요. 아, 여기 있네요… 아, 이런… 이런 일은 한 번도 일어난 적이 없는데.
> 여 뭐가 문제인가요?

남자는 왜 이렇게 말하는가:

> 남 이런 일은 한 번도 일어난 적이 없는데.

A 책이 지금까지 한 번도 잘못 인쇄된 적이 없다는 것을 확실히 하려고
B 컴퓨터 데이터베이스가 작동하지 않는다고 가리키려고
C 잘못된 파일이 전에는 업로드된 적이 없었다고 말하려고
D 교수가 큰 실수를 했다고 암시하려고

4.
대화에서 화자들은 학생들이 도서관 외부에서 데이터베이스를 이용할 수 없는 이유를 논의하고 있다. 아래의 테이블에 각 내용이 이유에 해당하는지 표시하시오.

	네	아니오
A 학생들이 책을 판매하는 것을 막는다.	✓	
B 교수들은 책 판매로 수익을 올리고 싶어 한다.		✓
C 학생들이 과제를 하기 더 쉽게 해 준다.		✓
D 학생들이 수업 시간에 책을 사용해야 한다.	✓	

5. Inference

What will the student most likely do next?

Ⓐ Print out her homework assignments
Ⓑ Contact the professor of her class
Ⓒ Purchase a new copy of the book
Ⓓ Visit the university library computer lab

5.

학생은 다음에 무엇을 할 것 같은가?

Ⓐ 수업 과제를 프린트한다
Ⓑ 수업 교수님에게 연락한다
Ⓒ 새 책을 구입한다
Ⓓ 대학교 도서관 컴퓨터실을 방문한다

Lecture 3

 AT01_5

[1-6] Listen to part of a lecture in a biology class.

Man: Professor

Most animal species have developed some form of natural camouflage. Although particular types of camouflage can vary widely, they all serve the same ultimate purpose. Camouflage makes the organism difficult to see so it can either catch food or avoid becoming food for another organism.

The type of camouflage that an organism develops depends upon several factors. The most important factor is, of course, the organism's environment. The easiest way to hide is to blend into one's surroundings, and many types of camouflage depend upon looking like elements in the animal's natural habitat. For this reason, many animals use something in their habitat as a "model" for their camouflage.

The animal's physiology and behavior are also important in determining what kind of concealment will be the most effective. Different animals have different skin coverings, and fur, feathers, and scales all provide different means for concealment. How an animal usually behaves can be equally important as solitary animals tend to use very different techniques from those that travel in large groups.

Also, since the underlying purpose of camouflage is to hide from other organisms, the physiology and behavior of an organism's prey or predators is just as important. Only adaptations that help an animal survive will be passed on, so the camouflage that an animal develops must provide it with an advantage. After all, if an animal's main predator is color-blind, exactly matching the colors in its habitat would be pointless.

생물학 강의의 일부를 들으시오.

남자: 교수

대부분의 종들은 자연적인 위장의 형태를 발달시켰습니다. 특정 유형의 위장은 매우 다양할 수 있지만 모든 위장의 궁극적인 목적은 같죠. 위장은 생물을 식별하기 어렵게 만들어서 그 생물이 먹이를 포획하거나 혹은 다른 생물의 먹이가 되는 것을 피할 수 있도록 해줍니다.

생물이 발달시킨 위장의 종류는 몇 가지 요인에 달려있습니다. 가장 중요한 요인은 물론 그 생물이 살고 있는 환경이에요. 숨기 가장 쉬운 방법은 주변에 섞이는 것이고, 많은 유형의 위장이 동물의 자연 서식지에 있는 요소들과 닮게 보이는 데 의존합니다. 이런 이유로 많은 동물들이 자신들의 서식지에서 위장을 위한 "본보기"로 무언가를 사용합니다.

동물의 생리학과 행동 또한 어떤 유형의 은폐가 가장 효과적일지 결정하는 데 중요합니다. 여러 다른 동물들이 다양한 피부막을 갖고 있고 털, 깃털, 그리고 비늘은 모두 은폐를 위한 다양한 수단을 제공합니다. 혼자 사는 동물들은 크게 무리 지어 이동하는 동물들과는 매우 다른 위장 방법을 사용하는 경향이 있기 때문에, 동물이 보통 어떻게 행동하는지도 마찬가지로 중요합니다.

또한 위장의 근본적인 목적은 다른 생물들로부터 숨는 것이기 때문에 생물의 먹잇감이나 포식자의 생리학과 행동 역시 마찬가지로 중요합니다. 동물이 생존하도록 돕는 적응만이 후세에 전해질 것이기에 동물이 개발하는 위장은 동물에게 이점을 제공해주죠. 어쨌든 어떤 동물의 주된 포식자가 색맹이라면, 서식지에 있는 색깔에 자신의 색을 맞추는 것은 쓸데없는 일이 될 겁니다.

The different types of camouflage can be placed into one of three main categories: concealing, disruptive, and adaptive. The majority of animals use concealing camouflage that allows them to blend into their background. Many animals have bodies that are mostly one uniform color that makes them difficult to see when in their natural habitat. Lions live in grasslands, so their bodies are a yellowish-tan color that is similar to the dry grasses that surround them. Similarly, many aquatic creatures like sharks and other fish have grayish-blue coloring that lets them blend into the softly lit water. Other animals take their concealment to the extreme and they actually look like objects in their habitat. For example, many types of mantis insects look remarkably like leaves.

Some animals use disruptive camouflage that breaks up their outline instead of trying to match the background. Tigers, zebras, and many other animals use stripes of contrasting colors to break up their outline. When another animal tries to watch them as they move, it is very difficult to keep track of their movement and location.

The true masters of camouflage, however, are those organisms that use adaptive camouflage. As these animals move through their habitat, the background changes and their coloration alters to match it. This adaptation is exemplified by cephalopods like cuttlefish and octopuses. These animals are not only able to change color, but can also change the texture of their skin and overall shape to blend in with the background or to imitate objects on the sea floor. These animals have special skin cells that contain pigments called chromatophores. Each of these cells contains one color of pigment, and the animals can expand or contract them to change their overall body color. When gliding over a sandy sea bottom, a cuttlefish can make its skin mottled with color to match the small stones below it, or it can create larger blotches of color to mimic larger objects like seashells or stones. Its brilliant mimicry is even more impressive when you take into account the fact that cuttlefish cannot see color. Their entire world is just shades of grey, but they can perceive such minute differences in shade that they are able to use their chromatophores to rapidly blend into new surroundings in a variety of colors.

서로 다른 위장의 유형은 세 개의 주된 카테고리로 분류될 수 있습니다: 은폐, 혼란, 적응이죠. 대다수의 동물들은 자신을 배경으로 섞여들도록 만들어주는 은폐 위장술을 사용합니다. 많은 동물들은 자연 서식지에 있을 때 이들을 보기 어렵게 만들어주는 하나의 통일된 색으로 된 몸을 갖고 있죠. 사자는 초원에서 살기 때문에 이들의 몸은 이들을 둘러싼 마른 풀과 비슷한 색인 노랗게 그을린 듯한 색입니다. 마찬가지로, 상어나 다른 물고기들과 같은 수중 생물들은 흐릿하게 햇빛을 받은 물에 그들이 잘 섞여들도록 해주는 푸른 회색을 띱니다. 다른 동물들은 극단적으로 은폐를 해서 실제로 그들 서식지의 물체처럼 보입니다. 예를 들어, 몇몇 사마귀 종들은 나뭇잎과 정말로 흡사해 보입니다.

어떤 동물들은 배경에 자신을 맞추려고 하는 대신 몸의 윤곽을 흐트러트리는 혼란 위장술을 사용합니다. 호랑이, 얼룩말, 그리고 다른 많은 동물들이 몸의 윤곽을 모호하게 만들기 위해 대비색의 줄무늬를 이용합니다. 다른 동물이 이들이 움직일 때 보려고 하면, 움직임이나 위치를 지속적으로 파악하기가 매우 어렵죠.

그러나 위장의 명수는 적응 위장을 하는 생물들입니다. 이 동물들이 자신의 서식지에서 이동할 때 배경이 변하고 이들의 몸 색깔 또한 그에 맞춰 변화하죠. 이 적응은 갑오징어나 문어와 같은 두족류 동물들의 전형적인 예입니다. 이 동물들은 배경에 섞여들거나 해저에 있는 물체를 흉내내기 위해 색을 바꿀 수 있을 뿐만 아니라 피부의 질감과 전체적인 모양 또한 바꿀 수 있어요. 이 동물들은 색소 세포라고 불리는 색소를 가진 특별한 피부 조직을 갖고 있습니다. 이 조직 하나하나가 특정한 색상을 갖고 있으며 동물들은 전체적인 몸의 색을 변화시키기 위해 이 조직들을 확장하거나 수축할 수 있어요. 모래로 덮인 해저를 미끄러지듯 헤엄칠 때 갑오징어는 자신 아래에 있는 작은 돌들과 비슷하게 보이도록 피부를 얼룩덜룩하게 만들 수 있고 또는 조개 껍데기나 돌과 같은 더 큰 물체를 흉내내기 위해 더 큰 얼룩 색깔들을 만들어낼 수도 있죠. 이 생물의 뛰어난 흉내내기는 갑오징어가 색맹이라는 사실을 알면 훨씬 더 굉장해 보입니다. 갑오징어의 모든 세계는 그저 서로 다른 색조의 회색으로만 이루어져 있지만, 색조들 사이의 미세한 차이마저 인식할 수 있어서 여러 색으로 이루어진 새로운 환경에 빠르게 녹아드는 것이 가능하도록 색소 세포를 이용할 수 있어요.

The appropriately-named mimic octopus carries its camouflage even further. Not only does it use its chromatorphores to blend in with its background, it can also copy the shapes and textures of other animals and objects. These masters of disguise can perfectly copy other predator species to discourage animals from attacking them. They can also seemingly transform into an algae-covered rock or a frond of coral and disappear almost instantly. There are many organisms that disguise themselves as other animals to avoid or frighten away predators, but they usually only mimic one animal. No other species has as many disguises as the mimic octopus.

알맞게 이름 붙여진 흉내 문어는 위장을 더 높은 수준으로 끌고 갑니다. 배경에 섞여들기 위해 색조 세포를 이용할 뿐만 아니라 다른 동물과 물체의 모양과 질감 역시 흉내 낼 수 있죠. 이 위장의 달인들은 동물들이 그들을 공격하는 것을 저지하기 위해 다른 포식자 종들을 완벽하게 흉내 낼 수 있습니다. 또한 겉보기에 조류로 덮인 바위나 산호의 엽상체로 변할 수 있고 거의 순식간에 사라지기도 하죠. 포식자들을 피하거나 겁을 줘서 쫓아버리기 위해 스스로 위장을 하는 생물들은 많지만, 그들은 보통 한 동물만을 흉내 냅니다. 흉내 문어만큼 많은 위장을 하는 종은 없죠.

어휘

camouflage n 위장 | **particular** adj 특정한 | **vary** v 각기 다르다 | **widely** adv 널리, 폭넓게 | **serve** v 쓰일 수 있다, 기여하다 | **ultimate** adj 궁극적인 | **purpose** n 목적 | **avoid** v 피하다 | **blend** v 섞다 | **surroundings** n 환경 | **element** n 요소 | **habitat** n 서식지 | **physiology** n 생리학 | **concealment** n 은폐 | **effective** adj 효과적인 | **covering** n 어떤 것을 덮는 막, 층 | **fur** n 털 | **feather** n 깃털 | **scale** n 비늘 | **behave** v 행동하다 | **solitary** adj 혼자 하는 | **underlying** adj 근원적인 | **predator** n 포식자 | **adaptation** n 적응 | **color-blind** adj 색맹의 | **matching** adj 어울리는 | **pointless** adj 무의미한 | **disruptive** adj 혼란의, 분열의, 지장을 주는 | **adaptive** adj 적응할 수 있는 | **uniform** adj 균일한, 한결같은 | **grassland** n 풀밭, 초원 | **aquatic** adj 물가에서 사는, 수생의 | **mantis** n 사마귀 | **outline** n 윤곽 | **stripe** n 줄무늬 | **contrasting** adj 대조적인 | **location** n 위치 | **master** n 명수, 달인 | **coloration** n 천연색 | **alter** v 변하다, 달라지다 | **exemplify** v 전형적인 예가 되다 | **cephalopod** n 두족류 동물 | **cuttlefish** n 갑오징어 | **octopus** n 문어 | **texture** n 감촉, 질감 | **overall** adj 전반적인 | **imitate** v 흉내 내다 | **pigment** n 색소 | **chromatophore** n 색소 세포 | **expand** v 확장하다 | **contract** v 수축하다 | **glide** v 미끄러지듯 가다 | **mottled** adj 얼룩덜룩한 | **blotch** n 얼룩, 반점 | **mimic** v 흉내를 내다 | **seashell** n 조개껍데기 | **impressive** adj 인상적인 | **take into account** ~을 고려하다 | **entire** adj 전체의 | **shade** n 그늘 | **perceive** v 인지하다 | **minute** adj 극미한 | **rapidly** adv 급속히 | **appropriately** adv 적당하게, 알맞게 | **disguise** n 변장, 위장 | **transform** v 변형하다 | **frond** n 엽상체 | **coral** n 산호 | **instantly** adv 순식간에 | **frighten** v 겁주다

---

1. **Main Idea**
What is the main topic of the lecture?
Ⓐ **Different categories of camouflage and the animals that use them**
Ⓑ Three methods that animals use for camouflage and their weaknesses
Ⓒ Some ways that animals practice camouflage and how they survive
Ⓓ The most well-known examples of three categories of camouflage

2. **Detail**
According to the lecture, what are important factors that influence an animal's camouflage? Choose 2 answers.
Ⓐ Temperature
Ⓑ Resources
Ⓒ Adaptation
Ⓓ **Surroundings**
Ⓔ **Anatomy**

1.
강의의 주제는 무엇인가?
Ⓐ 위장의 서로 다른 유형과 그것들을 이용하는 동물들
Ⓑ 위장을 위해 동물들이 이용하는 세 가지 방법과 이들의 약점들
Ⓒ 동물들이 위장을 실행하는 방법들과 그들이 어떻게 생존하는지
Ⓓ 세 가지 위장 카테고리들의 가장 잘 알려진 예시들

2.
강의에 의하면, 동물의 위장에 영향을 미치는 중요한 요인은 무엇인가? 두 개를 고르시오.
Ⓐ 온도
Ⓑ 자원
Ⓒ 적응
Ⓓ 주변 환경
Ⓔ 몸 구조

3. **Connecting Contents**
Why does the professor mention natural habitat?

Ⓐ To explain what kinds of advantages animals' natural habitats can provide
Ⓑ To emphasize how difficult it is for animals to thrive outside of their natural habitat
Ⓒ To talk about various animal behaviors according to their living environment
Ⓓ **To introduce the factor that animals utilize in concealing camouflage**

4. **Detail**
What is true about disruptive camouflage?

Ⓐ **It provides predators with a misleading impression of the animal's body shape.**
Ⓑ It allows the animal a chance to survive by blending into the environment.
Ⓒ It exaggerates the animal's body image and threatens away its predators.
Ⓓ It causes a natural phenomenon that disturbs the predators.

5. **Inference**
What can be inferred about the animals that use adaptive camouflage?

Ⓐ They tend to move from place to place to confuse their predators.
Ⓑ **Chromatophores can allow them to show different colors at the same time.**
Ⓒ They can change their body colors even though many of them are colorblind.
Ⓓ Special color pigments are able to change their color to be similar to seawater.

6. **Function & Attitude**
What does the professor think about the mimic octopus?

Ⓐ Its body is designed perfectly for living in the water.
Ⓑ **Other animals cannot compete with its superior skill.**
Ⓒ Its ability to copy so many animals must be difficult.
Ⓓ Utilizing such camouflage will result in a lower chance of survival.

3.
교수는 왜 자연 서식지를 언급하는가?

Ⓐ 동물들의 자연 서식지가 이들에게 어떤 종류의 이점을 주는지를 설명하려고
Ⓑ 자연 서식지 바깥에서 번성한다는 것이 동물들에게 있어 얼마나 어려운지를 강조하려고
Ⓒ 생활 환경에 따른 다양한 동물들의 행동에 대해 이야기하려고
Ⓓ 은폐 위장에서 동물들이 이용하는 요소를 소개하려고

4.
혼란 위장에 대해 옳은 것은 무엇인가?

Ⓐ 포식자에게 동물의 몸 형태에 대한 그릇된 인상을 준다.
Ⓑ 환경에 섞여들게 함으로써 동물에게 생존의 기회를 준다.
Ⓒ 동물의 몸 이미지를 과장해서 포식자를 겁을 주어 쫓아버린다.
Ⓓ 포식자들을 방해하는 자연적 현상을 일으킨다.

5.
적응 위장을 이용하는 동물들에 대해 무엇을 추론할 수 있는가?

Ⓐ 포식자들을 혼란스럽게 하기 위해 이곳저곳으로 옮겨 다니는 경향이 있다.
Ⓑ 색소 세포가 이들로 하여금 동시에 다른 색들을 나타내도록 해줄 수 있다.
Ⓒ 다수가 색맹임에도 자신의 몸 색깔을 바꿀 수 있다.
Ⓓ 특별한 색소가 이들의 몸을 해수와 비슷한 색으로 바뀌게 해줄 수 있다.

6.
교수는 흉내 문어에 대해 어떻게 생각하는가?

Ⓐ 이들의 몸은 물속에서 살기에 완벽하게 만들어져 있다.
Ⓑ 다른 동물들은 이들의 우월한 기술을 따라올 수 없다.
Ⓒ 많은 생물들을 따라 하는 능력은 분명 어려울 것이다.
Ⓓ 그러한 위장을 이용하는 것은 생존의 확률을 더 낮출 것이다.

Actual Test 02

본서 | P. 64

Conversation 1	1. Ⓑ	2. Ⓒ	3. Ⓐ	4. Ⓒ	5. Ⓒ	
Lecture 1	1. Ⓒ	2. Ⓐ	3. Ⓐ	4. Ⓒ	5. Ⓑ	6. Ⓓ
Conversation 2	1. Ⓒ	2. Ⓐ	3. Ⓑ	4. Ⓒ	5. Ⓐ, Ⓓ	
Lecture 2	1. Ⓑ	2. Ⓑ, Ⓒ	3. Ⓐ	4. Ⓓ	5. Ⓑ	6. Ⓒ
Lecture 3	1. Ⓑ	2. Ⓑ, Ⓓ	3. Ⓑ	4. Ⓐ	5. Ⓒ	6. Ⓓ

● 내가 맞은 문제 유형의 개수를 적어 보고 어느 유형에 취약한지 확인해 봅시다.

문제 유형	맞은 개수
Main Idea	5
Detail	12
Connecting Contents	4
Function & Attitude	4
Inference	3
Total	28

Conversation 1

[1-5] Listen to part of a conversation between a student and a professor.

Man: Professor | Woman: Student

W: Excuse me, Professor DeWitt? Can I speak with you for a minute?

M: Of course, young lady. Have we met before?

W: No, not that I know of, sir. My name is Laura Alvarez, and I'm a sophomore history major.

M: History major, huh? Well, that explains why our paths haven't crossed before, since I teach geology. What can I help you with Ms. Alvarez? I take it you haven't come to ask me to be your advisor.

W: No, not to ask you to be my advisor. Some of my friends and I want to revive an old club that used to exist on this campus. We are all interested in classic films, and we already meet about once a week to watch them together. We want to become an official club so we can use an auditorium to view them. Then we learned that such a club had already existed.

M: Yes, indeed it did. Which I guess explains why you came to talk to me. You are aware that I was one of the founding members of that club?

W: Yes, I viewed the original charter and compared the names to university alumni. How is it that you ended up teaching at the same university you graduated from?

M: Actually, I only returned here a few years ago. I taught at a few other colleges first. But, I guess that I really always wanted to return here at some point. It seems you know more about me than I do about you. What kind of help were you looking for?

W: As you know, all clubs need to have a faculty advisor. And, we were hoping that you would be able to fill that position for us.

M: I'm flattered, but why didn't you go to one of the drama professors? They seem a more likely choice than me even if I was in the original club.

W: Some of the other members tried to, but they were all too busy with classes and theater productions. Since you are a film lover like us, I suggested that we ask you, and they sent me to do so personally.

M: I accept. Have you already filled out the basic application form?

W: Yes, I have a copy of it with me.

M: May I see that? Ok… You already have your officers appointed… and you have more than the minimum number of members. Have you written out your club constitution?

W: Yes, sort of. We mostly just updated the original one that you and your friends wrote twenty years ago.

M: Updated? How so?

W: Well, there are new regulations and requirements that have been put into effect since the club disbanded five years ago.

M: It lasted for that long? Wow, I had no idea. I guess you just need my signature then, right?

W: Yes. Everyone will be so pleased that you've agreed to be our faculty advisor.

M: Have you decided what film you will be showing for the first official club meeting?

W: We have. It's the same movie that was shown at your first official meeting. We were hoping you could attend.

M: Two questions — how do you know what we showed, and where did you manage to get a copy of that film?

W: Well, the club kept very accurate records, so finding out which film was shown was pretty easy. However, actually finding the film was much more difficult. So, will you be joining us?

M: I wouldn't miss it.

어휘

sophomore n 2학년 | geology n 지질학 | revive v 부활시키다 | exist v 존재하다 | auditorium n 강당 | founding member n 창립 회원 | charter n 인가서 | alumnus n 졸업생 (복수는 alumni) | faculty n 교수진 | flattered adj 우쭐해 하는 | production n 제작, 연출 | personally adv 개인적으로 | appoint v 임명하다, 지명하다 | regulation n 규정 | requirement n 요건 | disband v 해산하다

---

1. **Main Idea**

What is the conversation mainly about?

Ⓐ How to obtain a faculty advisor
Ⓑ The necessary steps for establishing a club
Ⓒ Participating in different club activities
Ⓓ How to find an old source from the library

1.

대화는 주로 무엇에 관한 것인가?

Ⓐ 지도 교수를 구하는 방법
Ⓑ 동아리를 설립하기 위해 필요한 단계들
Ⓒ 다양한 동아리 활동에 참여하는 것
Ⓓ 도서관에서 오래된 자료를 찾는 방법

2. Connecting Contents

Why does the woman mention a faculty advisor?

Ⓐ To identify her role in the classic film club
Ⓑ To clarify that the club already has one
Ⓒ **To explain the necessity of her visit to the professor**
Ⓓ To complain about the movie club's current one

3. Detail

According to the woman, what information did she get from the original charter?

Ⓐ **The names of the former club members**
Ⓑ Steps for organizing club meetings
Ⓒ The contact information of university staff
Ⓓ A list of films showing at the university

4. Inference

What does the man imply about the club the student is talking about?

Ⓐ He does not understand the need for a movie club.
Ⓑ He knows it will be hard to get the dean's permission.
Ⓒ **He cannot believe the club lasted for such a long time.**
Ⓓ He thinks the club will be successful in the future.

5. Function & Attitude

What is the professor's attitude toward the club's first meeting?

Ⓐ He feels sorry that he has to miss the event.
Ⓑ He thinks he should help the club get started.
Ⓒ **He is certain that he will attend the meeting.**
Ⓓ He is reluctant to be there since he is busy.

Lecture 1

AT02_2

[1-6] Listen to part of a lecture in an art class.

Woman: Professor | Man: Student

W Okay class, take your seats. I hope you've all read my email on the exhibit at the Mendoza Gallery. In case you haven't, the gallery is displaying work by Rose Frantzen, who I've been encouraging all of you to look up, as she is someone that will come up in our classes on several occasions. Frantzen's work is definitely modern, and she calls her genre realistic impressionism. Now, all of you should sense immediately that this is a mix of genres.

Let me jog your memory. What is impressionism? We see it emerge in the mid-19th century. The brushstrokes are often small, and when put together, they give the viewer the bare impression of form. Often, the colors are unblended, and there is an emphasis on light. Basically, the point is to argue that we don't really understand what the real world is. In the end, the world is the way we perceive it. So that's a quick recap of impressionism. Can someone remind me what realism is?

M I feel like realism is sort of the opposite of impressionism. It tries to depict the world as accurately as possible. If my memory serves me right, it was a reaction to the bourgeois art that was popular at the time. Realist artists used more everyday sights as their subjects, like farmers and urban landscapes. You know, sights more familiar to the working-class.

W Very good, Toby! As you described very well, realism wanted to take the focus away from grandiose kings and lords dressed in their finery, things that didn't reflect the reality of the majority, and instead, to the common people, often highlighted their struggles. In this way, they brought the focus to something more quote-unquote "real." So I want to put these together for you by going back to Frantzen, who stylized her genre as realistic impressionism. Take a look at one of her pieces here. This is her 2008 work called "Summer Afternoon." Look at it. Doesn't it feel like a portal to a tranquil countryside scene? It invites viewers to join in on the warmth and peace of a lazy summer day.

I first want to point out the lush landscape. There is such a striking blend of colors—lush greens, golden yellows, and serene blues. They evoke the vibrant hues of a sun-drenched countryside. I'm sure many of you can sense movement in the brushstrokes. Frantzen is making the viewer sense life in something still. But what truly sets this piece apart is Frantzen's adept handling of light and shadow. The sunlight filters through the canopy of trees, casting dappled patterns on the ground below. These interplays of light and shadow create a dynamic visual rhythm, and... how should I put this... draws the viewer's eye deeper into the scene's depth and dimension.

And yet, it's not just the landscape that captivates us—it's the human element that breathes life into the painting. In the foreground, you can see a group of figures lounging leisurely on a blanket, their relaxed postures and content expressions mirroring the relaxed pace of the afternoon. Frantzen's portrayal of these individuals is remarkably nuanced, with each figure exuding a distinct sense of personality and presence.

I feel like I've done all the homework for you! I'm hoping you can do the rest on your own. What is Frantzen's realistic impressionism as seen in this painting? The style, brushstrokes, and focus on lighting all evoke impressionistic art, but the real focus on humans, their completely imaginable way of spending an afternoon, and their relatable emotions, take their cue from realism. I want to place her work side by side with that of Montse Valdés, which, as we'll see in a second, has some resemblances but also obvious differences. Give me a moment as I get my slides ready.

그리고 풍경만이 우리를 사로잡는 것은 아닙니다—이 그림에 생명을 불어넣는 것은 인간의 요소입니다. 전경에서 보시면, 인물들이 담요 위에 느긋하게 누워 있는 모습을 볼 수 있습니다. 그들의 편안한 자세와 만족스러운 표정은 오후의 여유로운 속도를 그대로 반영하고 있습니다. 프란첸이 묘사한 이 인물들은 매우 세밀하게 표현되어, 각각의 인물이 독특한 성격과 존재감을 발산합니다.

마치 제가 여러분을 대신해 모든 숙제를 해준 기분이네요! 나머지는 여러분이 스스로 해보길 바랍니다. 이 그림에서 프란첸의 사실적 인상주의는 무엇인가요? 스타일, 붓질, 그리고 조명에 대한 집중은 인상주의적 예술을 떠올리게 하지만, 인간에 대한 진정한 초점, 그들의 상상 가능한 오후를 보내는 방식, 그리고 그들의 공감할 수 있는 감정은 사실주의에서 영감을 받았습니다. 이제 그녀의 작품을 몬세 발데스의 작품과 나란히 놓아보려고 하는데요, 곧 보게 되겠지만, 비슷한 점도 있지만 분명한 차이도 있습니다. 슬라이드를 준비할 테니 잠시만 기다려 주세요.

어휘

exhibit n 전시회 | **display** v 전시하다 | **genre** n 장르 | **realistic** adj 현실적인 | **impressionism** n 인상주의 | **brushstroke** n 붓질 | **unblended** adj 혼합되지 않은 | **emphasis** n 강조 | **perceive** v 인지하다 | **recap** n 요약 | **realism** n 사실주의 | **depict** v 묘사하다 | **bourgeois** adj 부르주아의 | **grandiose** adj 웅장한 | **finery** n 화려한 옷 | **stylize** v 양식화하다 | **portal** n 입구, 문 | **tranquil** adj 고요한 | **landscape** n 풍경 | **serene** adj 차분한 | **evoke** v 불러일으키다 | **vibrant** adj 활기찬 | **hue** n 색조 | **canopy** n 지붕 모양으로 우거진 것 | **interplay** n 상호작용 | **dynamic** adj 역동적인 | **rhythm** n 리듬 | **dimension** n 차원 | **foreground** n 전경 | **leisurely** adv 느긋하게 | **posture** n 자세 | **content** adj 만족한 | **nuance** n 미묘한 차이 | **exude** v 발산하다 | **distinct** adj 뚜렷한 | **imaginable** adj 상상할 수 있는 | **relatable** adj 공감할 수 있는 | **resemblance** n 유사성 | **obvious** adj 명백한

1. Main Idea

What does the professor mainly talk about?

Ⓐ An upcoming class trip
Ⓑ A comparison of impressionism and realism
Ⓒ A modern artist's blending of genres
Ⓓ The impact of realistic impressionism on modern art

1.

교수는 주로 무엇에 대해 이야기하는가?

Ⓐ 다가오는 수학여행
Ⓑ 인상주의와 사실주의의 비교
Ⓒ 현대 예술가의 장르 혼합
Ⓓ 현대 미술에 미친 사실적 인상주의의 영향

2. Detail

According to the lecture, what is a commonality that impressionism and realism share?

- (A) **They are both movements that challenged perceptions of reality.**
- (B) They are both movements that started in the mid-19th century.
- (C) They both changed the technique of their brushstrokes when compared to their predecessors.
- (D) They both espoused a more subjective way of looking at the world.

3. Detail

According to the lecture, what is a feature of Frantzen's work "Summer Afternoon?"

- (A) **Brushstrokes that evoke a sense of movement**
- (B) Human figures dining on a blanket under a bright sun
- (C) Darker colors that contrast with the brightness of the grass
- (D) A lack of shadows that enhances the movement of the glittering light

4. Function & Attitude

Listen again to part of the lecture. Then answer the question.

> W: Frantzen's portrayal of these individuals is remarkably nuanced, with each figure exuding a distinct sense of personality and presence. I feel like I've done all the homework for you!

Why does the professor say this:

> W: I feel like I've done all the homework for you!

- (A) She is implying that the students won't have any homework.
- (B) She is disappointed that the students rarely come to class with their homework complete.
- (C) **She feels that the students should have sufficient information to draw some conclusions.**
- (D) She wonders if she has already given the students the same task in the past.

5. Detail

How does the professor organize the information in the lecture?

- (A) By providing history first, then an example
- (B) **By providing a comparison first, then a synthesis**
- (C) By providing context first, then a variation
- (D) By offering details, then a challenge

2.

강의에 따르면, 인상주의와 사실주의의 공통점은 무엇인가?

- (A) 두 운동 모두 현실에 대한 인식에 도전한 운동이다.
- (B) 두 운동 모두 19세기 중반에 시작되었다.
- (C) 두 운동 모두 이전 작가들과 비교해 붓질 기법을 변화시켰다.
- (D) 두 운동 모두 세상을 바라보는 더 주관적인 방식을 옹호했다.

3.

강의에 따르면, 프란첸의 작품 "여름 오후"의 특징은 무엇인가?

- (A) 움직임의 느낌을 자아내는 붓질
- (B) 밝은 태양 아래 담요 위에서 식사하는 인물들
- (C) 잔디의 밝기와 대조를 이루는 더 어두운 색상
- (D) 반짝이는 빛의 움직임을 강조하는 그림자의 부재

4.

강의의 일부를 다시 들으시오. 그리고 질문에 답하시오.

> C1: 프란첸이 묘사한 이 인물들은 매우 세밀하게 표현되어, 각각의 인물이 독특한 성격과 존재감을 발산합니다. 마치 제가 여러분을 대신해 모든 숙제를 해준 기분이네요!

교수는 왜 이렇게 말하는가:

> C1: 마치 제가 여러분을 대신해 모든 숙제를 해준 기분이네요!

- (A) 학생들에게 과제가 없을 것임을 암시하고 있다.
- (B) 학생들이 과제를 거의 완성하지 않고 수업에 오는 것에 실망하고 있다.
- (C) 학생들이 결론을 내릴 수 있는 충분한 정보를 가지고 있다고 느끼고 있다.
- (D) 과거에 이미 학생들에게 같은 과제를 준 적이 있는지 궁금해하고 있다.

5.

교수는 강의에서 정보를 어떻게 구성하는가?

- (A) 역사를 먼저 설명한 다음 예제를 제공함
- (B) 먼저 비교를 한 다음, 정보의 종합을 제공함
- (C) 맥락을 먼저 제공한 다음 변형을 제공함
- (D) 세부 사항을 제공한 다음 도전 과제를 제시함

6. Inference

What will the class most likely do next?

Ⓐ They will learn about another artist whose style is a mix of genres.
Ⓑ They will discuss the movement's work, focusing on a French artist.
Ⓒ They will dive into more examples of realistic impressionism.
Ⓓ They will compare Frantzen's work with that of another artist.

Conversation 2

 AT02_3

[1-5] Listen to part of a conversation between a student and a professor.

Man: Professor | **Woman:** Student

🆆 Good afternoon, professor. You wanted to see me?

🅼 Yes, indeed I did, Miranda. We missed you in class on Monday.

🆆 Oh, yeah, sorry about that. I had to go back to my hometown over the weekend. My sister was in the hospital. I didn't get back until last night.

🅼 I'm sorry to hear that. Is she alright?

🆆 Yes, she had to take out her tonsils. She is expected to make a full recovery.

🅼 That's good. Mine were taken out when I was younger as well.

🆆 Really? So were mine! We had a lot to talk about. Well, I talked, she couldn't. So, she answered me with text messages. Did I miss much on Monday? I asked Susan if we had any homework. She said no, but everyone handed in an assignment at the end of class. Well, everyone but me.

🅼 Did you do the assigned reading from Friday? They just wrote reactions to that story from before and after we discussed it.

🆆 Yeah, I read it on the train. And I wrote my reaction upon reading it. Since I missed the class discussion, how can I write the post-discussion reaction?

🅼 Hmm, could you tell me about your initial reaction?

🆆 Well, I read all of the stories in our anthology by Eudora Welty as assigned. But, I was kind of confused by them. I mean, not much really happened in them. Like in the story *A Memory*…

it's just about a woman sitting on a beach, watching other people, and thinking about something that happened to her in the past.

M Yes, in a nutshell. Nothing significant happens.

W Exactly, I mean… nothing truly exciting, romantic, or tragic happens. There are no larger issues at play, no conflict, no twist ending.

M All accurate observations, but tell me, did you enjoy reading it?

W Actually, yeah, I did. It's kind of funny, really. In the story, she's watching other people at the beach and remembering something that happened to her. And when I was reading it, it was kind of like I was watching her watch them, and I started remembering similar things that had happened to me. When I realized that, it made me think about our writing assignment. Can I write about my own experiences for my story?

M Yes, of course you can. I think you actually understood her point quite well. It's as the old adage says, "Write what you know." That is exactly what Eudora Welty did for almost everything she wrote. She didn't always write about her own firsthand experiences, though. When she was young she worked for the Works Progress Administration during the Great Depression. She interviewed people, wrote down their stories, and photographed them. That was a huge influence on her work. Her story *Why I Live at the PO* is like that. She did incorporate myths and legends into some of her work, but those were thematic and plot elements. The stories were still set in her home, the American Southeast, and the people were like the ones she grew up around or worked with for the WPA.

W I see what you mean. So, I could write about my weekend experience, but maybe from my sister's perspective instead of mine.

M That sounds like an excellent idea. I look forward to reading it.

어휘

hometown n 고향 | **tonsil** n 편도선 | **recovery** n 회복 | **assignment** n 과제 | **reaction** n 반응 | **initial** adj 처음의 | **anthology** n 작품집 | **tragic** adj 비극적인 | **twist** n 반전 | **accurate** adj 정확한 | **observation** n 관찰 | **adage** n 속담 | **firsthand** adj 직접 체험한 | **incorporate** v 포함하다 | **myth** n 신화 | **legend** n 전설 | **thematic** adj 주제의, 주제와 관련된 | **perspective** n 관점

1. **Main Idea**

What are the speakers mainly discussing?

Ⓐ The importance of students being familiar with what they write

Ⓑ The story that the class discussed when the student was absent

Ⓒ The student's opinions about a story assigned for class discussion

Ⓓ The student's childhood memory and the theme of her paper

2. **Detail**

Why did the student miss the class?

Ⓐ She had to visit her sister who just had surgery.

Ⓑ She was ill and had to stay in the hospital for a few days.

Ⓒ She was enjoying Eudora Welty's stories too much.

Ⓓ She had to turn in a paper she had been working on.

3. **Function & Attitude**

Listen again to part of the conversation. Then answer the question.

> W I asked Susan if we had any homework. She said no, but everyone handed in an assignment at the end of class. Well, everyone but me.
>
> M Did you do the assigned reading from Friday? They just wrote reactions to that story from before and after we discussed it.

Why does the professor say this:

> M They just wrote reactions to that story from before and after we discussed it.

Ⓐ To persuade the student that the homework is simple

Ⓑ To tell the student that there was no homework

Ⓒ To ask the student to finish the homework right now

Ⓓ To show his surprise that the student did not read the book

4. **Connecting Contents**

Why does the student mention Welty's story *A Memory*?

Ⓐ To express the type of story she would rather read

Ⓑ To recommend a story for the professor to read later

Ⓒ To give an example from the assigned reading material

Ⓓ To compare it with interesting stories the class read earlier

1.

화자들은 주로 무엇에 대해서 논의하고 있는가?

Ⓐ 학생들이 쓰는 글에 대해 친숙해지는 것의 중요성

Ⓑ 학생이 결석했을 때 수업시간에 토론했던 소설

Ⓒ 수업 토론을 위해 과제로 내준 소설에 대한 학생의 의견

Ⓓ 학생의 유년기 추억과 글쓰기 과제의 주제

2.

학생은 왜 수업을 빠졌는가?

Ⓐ 막 수술을 마친 여동생을 방문해야 했다.

Ⓑ 아파서 며칠 동안 입원해야 했다.

Ⓒ 유도라 웰티의 소설들을 매우 즐기고 있었다.

Ⓓ 작업 중이던 글쓰기 과제를 제출해야 했다.

3.

대화의 일부를 다시 듣고 질문에 답하시오.

> 여 제가 수잔에게 숙제가 있었냐고 물어봤는데요. 숙제가 없다고 했지만 수업 마지막에 모두가 과제를 제출했어요. 음, 저를 뺀 모두가요.
>
> 남 금요일에 내준 읽기 과제를 했나요? 학생들은 그 이야기에 대해 토론하기 전과 후의 감상을 써낸 거예요.

교수는 왜 이렇게 말하는가:

> 남 금요일에 내준 읽기 과제를 했나요? 학생들은 그 이야기에 대해 토론하기 전과 후의 감상을 써낸 거예요.

Ⓐ 그 숙제가 간단하다고 학생을 설득하기 위해

Ⓑ 학생에게 숙제가 없었다고 말하기 위해

Ⓒ 학생에게 그 숙제를 지금 당장 끝마치라고 요구하기 위해

Ⓓ 학생이 그 책을 읽지 않아서 놀랐다는 것을 보이기 위해

4.

학생이 웰티의 소설 〈A Memory〉를 언급하는 이유는 무엇인가?

Ⓐ 차라리 읽기 더 낫다고 생각하는 소설 유형을 나타내기 위해

Ⓑ 교수가 나중에 읽어볼 만한 소설을 추천하기 위해

Ⓒ 과제로 내준 읽기 자료의 예를 들기 위해

Ⓓ 전 수업에서 읽었던 흥미로운 소설들과 비교하기 위해

5. Detail

According to the professor, what is true about Eudora Welty? Choose 2 answers.

Ⓐ **She usually wrote about the things she had experienced.**
Ⓑ She liked giving advice about how to become a writer.
Ⓒ She encouraged others to write about what they are familiar with.
Ⓓ **She used myths and legends in her stories for themes and plots.**

5.

교수에 의하면, 유도라 웰티에 대해 옳은 것은 무엇인가? 두 개를 고르시오.

Ⓐ 주로 자신이 경험했던 것에 대해서 글을 썼다.
Ⓑ 작가가 되는 방법에 대해 조언해 주는 것을 좋아했다.
Ⓒ 사람들에게 자신에게 친숙한 것에 대해서 글을 쓰라고 장려했다.
Ⓓ 주제와 줄거리를 위해 자신의 소설에 신화와 전설들을 활용했다.

Lecture 2

 AT02_4

[1-6] Listen to part of a lecture in a biology class.

Man: Professor | Woman: Student

Ⓜ As I promised you last time we met, I have information packets regarding the research trip I will be going on this summer. You may pick one up after class if you are interested in joining the expedition as an intern. To give you an idea of what we will be doing, I'll describe to you why we went last year and what we learned. In the Caribbean, the coral population has been dwindling. Can anyone tell me why this is important?

Ⓦ Of course, coral reefs are the most diverse biome on the planet. They support a wide variety of ocean species, and they benefit people as well. We eat many fish that need coral reefs to survive, but the reefs actually protect our coastlines from storms and waves.

Ⓜ That was a very thorough answer, Sally. Be sure you pick up one of these packets. The decline of these vital habitats is not a new trend; rather, it has been occurring for decades. However, only recently has it reached such a rapid pace, and we wanted to figure out why. In some parts of the world, the culprits behind coral disappearance are easily identified. Take the Great Barrier Reef off of the coast of Australia for example. There, a plague of crown of thorns starfish are literally eating up the coral polyps. Polyps are the small animals that actually create the coral structure by secreting the minerals that build it. But, those starfish aren't a big problem here, so we had a difficult task ahead of us.

생물학 강의의 일부를 들으시오.

남자: 교수 | 여자: 학생

🅼 저번 강의 때 약속했듯이, 올 여름에 제가 가게 될 연구 여행과 관련된 정보를 담은 패킷을 가져왔어요. 인턴으로 탐험에 참여하는 것에 흥미가 있다면 수업이 끝난 뒤 하나씩 가져가면 됩니다. 우리가 무엇을 하게 될지에 대해 알려주기 위해 왜 작년에 우리가 여행을 갔고, 무엇을 배웠는지 설명할게요. 카리브해에서 산호의 개체 수는 계속 줄어들고 있습니다. 이것이 왜 중요한지 누가 말해줄 수 있나요?

🅦 물론 산호초들이 지구상에서 가장 다양한 생물군계이기 때문입니다. 산호초들은 광범위한 해양 생물군을 부양하고, 인간에게도 이롭죠. 생존을 위해 우리는 산호초를 필요로 하는 어류를 많이 섭취하지만, 사실 산호초들은 우리의 해안 지대를 폭풍과 파도로부터 지켜주기도 합니다.

🅼 매우 자세한 대답이었어요, 샐리. 그 패킷들 중 하나를 꼭 가져가도록 하세요. 이 필수적인 서식지의 감소는 새삼스러운 현상은 아니고 오히려 수십 년에 걸쳐 발생하고 있습니다. 그러나 최근 들어 급격히 감소하면서 그 이유가 무엇인지를 알아보고 싶었던 거죠. 세계 몇몇 곳에서는 산호초의 소멸 뒤에 숨은 범인이 쉽게 밝혀지기도 합니다. 호주의 해안에 있는 그레이트배리어리프를 예로 들어 봅시다. 그곳에는 악마 불가사리 떼들이 말 그대로 산호충을 잡아먹고 있어요. 폴립은 산호를 형성하는 미네랄을 분비함으로써 실제로 산호의 구조를 만드는 작은 동물들입니다. 그러나 이 불가사리들은 여기서 중요한 문제가 아니기 때문에 우리에게는 어려운 과업이 기다리고 있었던 겁니다.

We found coral structures where about half of the corals were dead and covered in fleshy algae, while the algae free areas were healthy. So, at first glance the algae appeared to be responsible. However, we soon learned that the algae were just one factor in a larger process. The algae do not affect the coral directly. In between these areas of healthy and dead corals, we found a band of algae-free but sick and dying corals. Therefore, we speculated that some kind of disease was killing the corals. As it turned out, this also was not entirely true. We found many species of bacteria present in the area, but they were not feeding on the coral or releasing toxins that poisoned it. The bacteria present in the algae and the border area were killing the corals by using up all of the available oxygen! They were effectively suffocating the corals. But, this raised another question. What is supporting such a profusion of bacteria? Well, that is where the algae come in. They produce sugars that they release into the water, and these sugars feed the bacteria. This was confirmed by using antibiotics in the laboratory. The antibiotics killed off the bacteria in the diseased area and in the algae covered zone. The algae remained healthy, and many corals that were already covered in algae began to recover.

W That's a great discovery. We can use antibiotics to save the coral.

M Well, yes and no. It is very useful information, that much is true. However, there are many problems with such a simple solution. Firstly, antibiotics often do more harm than good. Remember, these experiments were conducted in a laboratory, i.e. in a controlled environment. We have no idea what effect it would have if we released those same compounds into the open ocean. They could kill off many strains of bacteria that actually benefit the corals as well as other species, which could be catastrophic. Not only that, but it would only be treating a symptom of the problem. You see, nature is all about balance, and the balance has been upset in the coral reefs by human activity. Warmer seawater due to global warming and agricultural runoff of fertilizer has caused the algae population to explode. On top of that, overfishing has reduced the number of fish that would normally feed on the algae. That is why we are returning to the reefs this summer. We need to find a comprehensive way to resolve the situation and save the coral reefs.

어휘

packet n 꾸러미 | expedition n 탐사 | describe v 묘사하다 | coral n 산호 | dwindle v 줄어들다 | diverse adj 다양한 | biome n 생물군계 | coastline n 해안 지대 | habitat n 서식지 | rapid adj 빠른 | culprit n 범인 | disappearance n 사라짐, 소실 | identify v 밝히다 | plague n 떼 | polyp n 폴립 | secrete v 분비하다 | fleshy adj 살집이 있는, 살찐 | algae n 해조, 해조류 | affect v 영향을 주다 | speculate v 추측하다 | effectively adv 효율적으로 | suffocate v 질식하게 하다 | profusion n 다량, 풍성함 | confirm v 확인하다 | laboratory n 실험실 | antibiotics n 항생제 | experiment n 실험 | conduct v 실행하다 | compound n 물질 | strain n 종류, 유형 | catastrophic adj 큰 재앙의 | symptom n 증상 | agricultural adj 농업의 | runoff n 유출 액체 | fertilizer n 비료 | explode v 폭발하다 | overfish v 남획하다 | comprehensive adj 포괄적인 | resolve v 해결하다

---

1. Main Idea
What is the lecture mainly about?
Ⓐ The history of preserving different coral species
Ⓑ **Reasons for and solutions to decreasing coral populations**
Ⓒ The lasting influence of antibiotics in the open ocean
Ⓓ The characteristics of coral reefs and their habitats

2. Detail
According to the lecture, which of the following are benefits that coral reefs provide? Choose 2 answers.
Ⓐ Purifying polluted ocean water
Ⓑ **Supporting diverse ocean species**
Ⓒ **Protecting coastlines from storms**
Ⓓ Indirectly helping fish to grow

3. Connecting Contents
Why does the professor mention crown of thorns starfish?
Ⓐ **To give the students an example of a coral reef predator**
Ⓑ To compare the lives of starfish and coral reefs in general
Ⓒ To explain how they help coral reefs to fight algae
Ⓓ To emphasize that they are near extinction these days

1.
강의는 주로 무엇에 대한 것인가?
Ⓐ 다양한 산호 종 보존의 역사
Ⓑ 감소하는 산호 개체 수의 이유와 해결책
Ⓒ 열린 바다에서 항생제가 미치는 지속적인 영향
Ⓓ 산호초들의 특징과 서식지

2.
강의에 의하면, 다음 중 산호초가 주는 이점들은 무엇인가? 두 개를 고르시오.
Ⓐ 오염된 바닷물 정화
Ⓑ 다양한 해양 생물 부양
Ⓒ 폭풍으로부터 해안선 보호
Ⓓ 물고기의 성장에 대한 간접 도움

3.
교수는 왜 악마 불가사리를 언급하는가?
Ⓐ 산호초 포식자의 한 예를 제시하려고
Ⓑ 불가사리와 산호초의 삶을 전반적으로 비교하려고
Ⓒ 산호초가 해조에 대항하는 것을 어떻게 그들이 도와주는지 설명하려고
Ⓓ 최근 그들이 멸종 위기에 처했다는 것을 강조하려고

4. **Function & Attitude**

Why does the professor say this:

> M But, those starfish aren't a big problem here, so we had a difficult task ahead of us.

Ⓐ To indicate that finding the real cause is almost impossible
Ⓑ To say that there are many different dangerous species
Ⓒ To tell the students that getting rid of starfish was hard
Ⓓ To emphasize that the main problem was elusive

5. **Detail**

According to the lecture, which of the following is true?

Ⓐ Algae were releasing harmful toxins into the ocean.
Ⓑ Bacteria were taking all the oxygen away from corals.
Ⓒ Bacteria helped algae to release a large amount of sugar.
Ⓓ Algae kept corals from getting enough nutrients for survival.

6. **Detail**

Why does the professor say using antibiotics to save the coral is problematic?

Ⓐ Corals will spread at an unnecessarily rapid rate.
Ⓑ Experiments using antibiotics often failed.
Ⓒ The ocean is far different from a controlled environment.
Ⓓ Antibiotics usually cause severe side effects.

Lecture 3

 AT02_5

[1-6] Listen to part of a lecture in an astronomy class.

Woman: Professor

W Uranus is the seventh planet from the Sun, and it orbits between Saturn and Neptune. It is the third largest planet in our solar system. Uranus shares a similar internal structure with Neptune that consists of a rocky core coated in a thick mantle of ice and a heavy atmosphere. The thick icy mantle differentiates them from the other giants, which have little surface outside of their inner core and are composed almost entirely of gas. For this reason, Jupiter and Saturn are called gas giants, and Uranus and Neptune are called ice giants. This name is further supported by the fact that Uranus has the coldest atmosphere of the eight planets, which can reach below -224 degrees Centigrade. That is even colder than Neptune, which is farther away from the Sun.

Uranus' atmosphere is composed mostly of hydrogen and helium — like those of Jupiter and Saturn — but it also contains much more water, methane, and ammonia. Methane is actually the third most abundant chemical in its atmosphere. Methane absorbs red wavelengths from sunlight, and it reflects the blue ones, so the high methane content is what gives Uranus its uniform blue color. Like the other giants, Uranus also possesses a ring system, many moons, and a magnetosphere.

The characteristic that makes Uranus unique among the planets in our solar system is its axial tilt. All eight planets orbit the Sun on a flat plane. Each of the planets also rotates on its own axis at the same time. The axis of a planet is an imaginary line drawn between its north and south poles. For most of the planets, their orbital axes are more or less vertical. For example, the Earth's poles roughly point up and down from the solar plane; the angle is not truly vertical, and the degree of tilt varies, but it is fairly perpendicular to the plane.

This is not true of Uranus. At some point in its history, a large object or objects struck the planet, and knocked it onto its side. Uranus' axis does not point up and down from the plane. Rather, it points toward and away from the Sun. As Uranus orbits the Sun, its poles trade places. One year on Uranus is 84 years on Earth. That means that for 42 years, its south pole is pointed toward the Sun, and for the next 42 years its north pole is aimed at the Sun. This has a dramatic effect on its seasons, as each pole experiences summer, or day, for half of the year and winter, or night, for the other half.

For most of its year, the atmosphere appears to be a bland, motionless blue. This is deceptive, as the planet's rotation actually causes powerful winds to constantly swirl around it. That is what gives the atmosphere such a smooth appearance. At the equator, the winds go in the opposite direction from the planet's rotation and they blow at 50 to 100 meters per second. From 20 degrees away from the equator to the poles, the winds travel in the same direction as the planet's rotation, and

를 가지고 있고 그것이 섭씨 -224도까지 도달할 수 있다는 사실에 의해 더 의의를 가집니다. 그것은 해왕성의 대기보다 낮은데, 이는 태양으로부터 더 멀리 떨어져 있죠.

천왕성의 대기는 목성이나 토성처럼 대부분 수소와 헬륨으로 이루어져 있지만 더 많은 양의 물, 메탄, 그리고 암모니아도 포함하고 있어요. 메탄은 사실 천왕성의 대기에서 세 번째로 풍부한 화학 물질입니다. 메탄은 햇빛으로부터 적색 파장을 흡수하고 파란 파장을 반사하는데, 그래서 높은 양의 메탄이 천왕성으로 하여금 균일한 푸른 빛을 내도록 만드는 것이죠. 다른 자이언트들과 마찬가지로 천왕성도 고리 시스템과 많은 달, 그리고 자기권을 가지고 있습니다.

천왕성을 우리 태양계 내의 다른 행성들 가운데서 독특하게 만드는 특징은 바로 자전축 기울기입니다. 모든 여덟 개의 행성들은 평면에서 태양 주위를 돌죠. 각 행성은 또한 동시에 자기만의 축에서 회전하고 있습니다. 행성의 축은 그 행성의 북극과 남극 사이에 그어진 가상의 선이에요. 대부분의 행성들에게 궤도의 축은 거의 수직에 가깝습니다. 예를 들어, 지구의 양극은 태양계의 수평면에서 대략적으로 위와 아래를 가리키죠. 각도가 진짜로 수직은 아니고 기울기가 다르지만 평면에 꽤나 직각으로 축이 이루어져 있어요.

천왕성의 경우는 그렇지 않습니다. 천왕성의 역사 가운데 한 시점에서 한 커다란 물체나 물체들이 천왕성에 충돌했고 천왕성을 옆으로 기울게 만들었어요. 천왕성의 축은 평면에서 위와 아래를 가리키고 있지 않습니다. 오히려 태양을 향하거나 태양에서 멀어지는 축을 가지고 있죠. 천왕성이 태양 주변을 돌 때 양극의 위치가 바뀌게 됩니다. 천왕성에서의 1년은 지구의 84년이에요. 그 말은, 42년간 천왕성의 남극은 태양을 향해 있고 다음 42년간은 북극이 태양을 향해 있다는 의미입니다. 각 극이 1년의 절반은 여름, 즉 낮이나 나머지 절반은 겨울, 즉 밤을 겪다 보니 이는 천왕성의 계절에 극적인 영향을 미쳤어요.

1년 중 대부분 천왕성의 대기는 단조롭고 움직임이 없는 푸른빛으로 나타납니다. 천왕성의 회전이 사실 강한 바람으로 하여금 계속해서 주변을 돌면서 불도록 만들기 때문에 이는 눈속임에 가까워요. 이것이 천왕성의 대기가 그토록 매끄러운 모습을 하도록 만드는 겁니다. 적도에서 바람은 천왕성의 회전과는 반대의 방향으로 부는데 초속 50에서 100미터로 불죠. 적도에서 20도 떨어져서부터 각 극까지 바람은 행성의 궤도와 같은 방향으로 불고 세기가 더 셉니다. 이러한 바람은 초속 150에서 200미터까지 달하지만 양 극에서는

they are stronger. These winds reach 150 to 200 meters per second, but at the poles, wind strength falls to nothing. The air at the poles is calm.

During the transition periods, when the equatorial region has both day and night, the planet has a short period of observable weather. During its short spring and summer, fierce storms tear through the atmosphere creating bands of different shades of blue and dark spots. During the transition of March to May of 2004, the atmosphere looked more like Neptune's, with large clouds and wind speeds of up to 230 meters per second. This may make it sound like scientists know a lot about Uranus, but we really do not. Much of what happens below the atmosphere can only be speculated upon, and even our knowledge of the atmosphere is incomplete. We have not been able to observe the atmosphere for a full 84-year orbit. So much research remains to be done, and future probes will provide us with more accurate data from which to draw conclusions.

바람의 세기가 아예 사라집니다. 극에서의 대기는 조용하죠.

과도기 동안, 즉 적도 지역이 낮과 밤 둘 다를 경험하는 시기에 천왕성은 관찰 가능한 날씨가 있는 시기를 잠시 갖습니다. 짧은 봄과 여름 동안 격렬한 폭풍이 대기를 흐트러뜨려서 여러 다양한 빛깔의 푸른빛과 어두운 자국들을 만들어냅니다. 2004년의 3월에서 5월의 과도기 시기 동안 대기는 해왕성에 가까워 보였는데 커다란 구름들이 있었고 풍속은 초속 230미터까지 올라가기도 했습니다.

이 때문에 과학자들이 천왕성에 대해 많이 아는 것처럼 들릴 수 있지만, 우리가 아는 건 많지 않아요. 대기 아래에서 일어나는 일의 대부분은 그저 추측만 할 수 있을 뿐이고, 대기에 대한 우리의 지식 역시 불완전합니다. 우리는 84년 전체 주기 동안 천왕성을 관찰하지 못했어요. 그래서 앞으로 행해져야 할 많은 연구들이 남아있고, 미래의 탐사선들이 그것으로부터 결론을 내릴 수 있는 더욱 정확한 자료들을 우리에게 제공해줄 겁니다.

어휘

orbit v 궤도를 돌다 | solar system 태양계 | internal structure 내부 구조 | rocky adj 바위로 된 | coated adj 뒤덮인, 겉을 입힌 | mantle n 맨틀 | atmosphere n 대기 | differentiate v 구별하다 | giant n 거대 혹성 | surface n 표면 | inner core 내핵 | methane n 메탄 | ammonia n 암모니아 | abundant adj 풍부한 | absorb v 흡수하다 | wavelength n 파장 | reflect v 반사하다 | uniform adj 균일한, 한결같은 | possess v 소유하다 | ring system 고리 시스템 | magnetosphere n 자기권 | axial tilt 자전축 기울기 | flat plane 평면 | rotate v 회전하다 | imaginary adj 가상의 | vertical adj 수직의, 세로의 | vary v 서로 각기 다르다, 달라지다 | perpendicular adj 직각의 | strike v 때리다, 부딪치다 | trade v 교환하다, 바꾸다 | dramatic adj 극적인 | bland adj 단조로운 | motionless adj 움직임 없는 | deceptive adj 기만적인, 현혹하는 | rotation n 회전, 자전 | swirl v 빙빙 돌다 | smooth adj 매끄러운 | equator n 적도 | transition period 과도기 | observable adj 관찰 가능한 | fierce adj 격렬한, 맹렬한 | band n 무리 | speculate v 추측하다, 짐작하다 | incomplete adj 불완전한, 미완성의 | probe n 탐사선 | accurate adj 정확한 | conclusion n 결론

---

1. **Main Idea**

What is the lecture mainly about?

Ⓐ Characteristics of Uranus that make it an ice giant
Ⓑ Features that distinguish Uranus from other planets
Ⓒ The relationship between Uranus and Neptune
Ⓓ The difference between Uranus and other planets' axial tilts

1.

강의는 주로 무엇에 대한 것인가?

Ⓐ 천왕성을 아이스 자이언트로 만드는 특징들
Ⓑ 천왕성을 다른 행성들과 다르게 만드는 특색들
Ⓒ 천왕성과 해왕성의 관계
Ⓓ 천왕성과 다른 행성들의 자전축 기울기 차이

2. Detail

What are the characteristics of Uranus? Choose 2 answers.

Ⓐ It contains more gas than Jupiter and Saturn do.
Ⓑ Its core and mantle composition are similar to those of Neptune.
Ⓒ It has a larger core and thicker mantle than Neptune.
Ⓓ Its temperature is the lowest out of the eight planets.
Ⓔ Its internal structure is composed of a thin mantle.

3. Detail

Why does Uranus have a uniform blue color?

Ⓐ It is mostly composed of hydrogen and helium.
Ⓑ It has a high content of methane in its atmosphere.
Ⓒ It has a ring system that reflects certain wavelengths.
Ⓓ It possesses a very thin atmosphere that absorbs sunlight.

4. Inference

What can be inferred about Uranus' axial tilt?

Ⓐ It is closer to horizontal than it is to vertical.
Ⓑ Its angle varies widely throughout its orbit.
Ⓒ It does not possess geographic poles.
Ⓓ It becomes nearly perpendicular every 42 years.

5. Detail

What is true about the atmosphere of Uranus?

Ⓐ It is motionless as the planet orbits the Sun very slowly.
Ⓑ Its wind blows most strongly at the center of its axis of rotation.
Ⓒ It is the most placid around the South and North poles.
Ⓓ Its winds move in the same direction as the planet's rotation at the equator.

6. Connecting Contents

Why does the professor mention future probes?

Ⓐ To explain that there are already many probes studying Uranus
Ⓑ To imply that Uranus has the potential to provide valuable resources
Ⓒ To emphasize that further research should be done regarding Uranus' weather
Ⓓ To tell the students that what we know about Uranus is very limited

---

2.

천왕성의 특징은 무엇인가? 두 개를 고르시오.

Ⓐ 목성과 토성보다 더 많은 기체를 갖고 있다.
Ⓑ 내핵과 맨틀 구성이 해왕성과 흡사하다.
Ⓒ 해왕성보다 더 큰 내핵과 더 두꺼운 맨틀을 가지고 있다.
Ⓓ 여덟 개의 행성들 중 가장 낮은 기온을 가지고 있다.
Ⓔ 내부 구조는 얇은 맨틀로 이루어져 있다.

3.

천왕성은 왜 균일한 푸른빛을 띠는가?

Ⓐ 대부분이 수소와 헬륨으로 구성되어 있다.
Ⓑ 대기에 높은 양의 메탄을 함유하고 있다.
Ⓒ 특정 파장을 반사하는 고리 시스템을 갖고 있다.
Ⓓ 햇빛을 흡수하는 매우 얇은 대기층을 갖고 있다.

4.

천왕성의 자전축 기울기에 대해 무엇을 추론할 수 있는가?

Ⓐ 수직이기보다는 오히려 수평에 더 가깝다.
Ⓑ 궤도 전반적으로 자전축의 기울기가 다양하게 변화한다.
Ⓒ 지리적인 극을 갖고 있지 않다.
Ⓓ 42년마다 기울기가 거의 직각에 가까워진다.

5.

천왕성의 대기에 대해 옳은 것은 무엇인가?

Ⓐ 천왕성이 태양 주변을 아주 천천히 돌아서 움직임이 없다.
Ⓑ 자전축의 중간에서 대기의 바람이 가장 강하다.
Ⓒ 남극과 북극 주변에서 가장 잔잔하다.
Ⓓ 바람은 적도에서의 천왕성 회전 방향과 같은 방향으로 이동한다.

6.

교수는 왜 미래의 탐사선들을 언급하는가?

Ⓐ 이미 많은 탐사선들이 천왕성을 연구하고 있다는 사실을 설명하기 위해
Ⓑ 천왕성이 귀중한 자원을 제공할 가능성이 있다고 시사하기 위해
Ⓒ 천왕성의 날씨에 대해 더 많은 연구가 계속되어야 한다고 강조하기 위해
Ⓓ 우리가 천왕성에 대해 아는 것은 매우 제한적이라고 학생들에게 말하기 위해

Actual Test 03

본서 | P. 76

Conversation 1	1. Ⓒ	2. Ⓐ	3. Ⓑ	4. Ⓐ	5. Ⓒ	
Lecture 1	1. Ⓒ	2. Ⓐ	3. Ⓑ	4. Ⓓ	5. Ⓑ, Ⓓ	6. Ⓐ
Conversation 2	1. Ⓑ	2. Ⓓ	3. Ⓒ	4. Ⓒ	5. Ⓐ	
Lecture 2	1. Ⓐ	2. Ⓑ	3. Ⓐ	4. Ⓑ	5. Ⓒ	6. Ⓑ
Lecture 3	1. Ⓒ	2. Ⓑ	3. Ⓒ, Ⓓ	4. Ⓐ	5. Ⓒ	6. Ⓓ

● 내가 맞은 문제 유형의 개수를 적어 보고 어느 유형에 취약한지 확인해 봅시다.

문제 유형	맞은 개수
Main Idea	5
Detail	11
Connecting Contents	2
Function & Attitude	6
Inference	4
Total	28

Conversation 1

 AT03_1

[1-5] Listen to part of a conversation between a student and a housing officer.

Man: Student | **Woman:** Housing officer

M Hello, who should I talk to about issues with my dorm room?

W That would be me, actually. What issue do you have with your current accommodations?

M I would like to move to a room with a fully functional kitchen in it. In regular dormitory rooms, we can only have the most basic of food preparation appliances. There is not only no room for large appliances, but there are also no outlets powerful enough to plug them into.

W Yes, well, there are many reasons for that. Firstly, it's school policy that the majority of dormitory rooms include only what is necessary to facilitate studying and sleep. As I am sure you are aware, many of our dormitories still use communal bathrooms.

M Yes, I know. And I am very thankful that my current room has its own bathroom. But, I would really like to be able to cook my own meals.

W May I ask why that is? Do you have specific dietary restrictions that our dorm cafeterias cannot meet? Do you have a food allergy?

M A food allergy? No, none that I am aware of. My dietary restrictions are due to the fact that I am a strict vegetarian. I'm a vegan actually. I do not consume any animal products, which makes it pretty much impossible for me to eat in any of the university cafeterias.

W The cafeterias are required to provide vegetarian options at every meal.

M Yes, and they do. Usually only one such meal is provided, which on its own gets pretty boring. But, they also usually do not conform to a vegan diet. A vegetarian pizza is a fine idea, but the crust usually contains milk and eggs, which come from animals. Even the salads usually contain cheese, eggs, or other animal products.

W I see your point. However, there are very few dorm rooms that have kitchens in them.

M I know. I had to pay extra for a room with its own restroom. I understand that premium accommodations must be paid for. Can't I just pay more for a room with a kitchen?

W: I'm afraid not. You see, such rooms are actually full-sized apartments, and they are reserved for students that have families.

M: Well, my sister, who is also a vegan, is currently a student here. Could we qualify for such an apartment together?

W: No… uh… Actually, I'm not sure. The apartments in Granger Hall are usually reserved for students with children, but I think that a few rooms are occupied by foreign exchange students. Some of whom are not actually related to their roommates.

M: But, that privilege is only given to foreign students? That's… I was about to say that that is unfair, but I guess it isn't really. It must be really difficult for foreign students to live in the regular dormitories.

W: Yes, it can be, depending on where they are from. May I ask why you don't just rent an apartment off of campus?

M: I've tried to, believe me. The only apartments that are within walking distance of the campus that are not currently occupied are ridiculously expensive. The closest ones that are within my price range are so far away that I would have to drive to class. And, I don't have a car.

W: There are many buses that come to campus from all over the city.

M: Yes, there are. I'm sorry if I wasted your time.

W: Don't be. You have raised many valid points. Our cafeterias may be inadequate for our students' needs, our housing regulations may be biased, and rental rates in the city are exorbitant. Although I think it is unlikely that you will be allowed to move to Granger Hall, I can present your case to my manager.

M: Thank you. That's all I can ask, really.

여: 안타깝지만 그건 안 돼요. 알겠지만, 그런 방들은 실제로 아파트 규모고, 가족이 있는 학생들을 위한 곳이거든요.

남: 음, 마찬가지로 비건인 제 여동생도 지금 이 학교에 다니고 있어요. 같이 그 아파트에 들어갈 자격이 될까요?

여: 아니요… 어… 사실, 잘 모르겠네요. 그레인저홀의 아파트들은 보통 자녀가 있는 학생들을 위한 곳이지만, 몇몇 방들은 외국인 교환 학생들이 쓰고 있는 것 같아요. 그들 중 몇몇은 사실 룸메이트와 가족 관계가 아니고요.

남: 하지만 그 특권이 외국 학생들에게만 주어진다고요? 그건… 불공평하다고 말하려고 했지만, 사실 아닌 것 같기도 하네요. 일반 기숙사에 사는 것이 외국 학생들에게는 분명 매우 힘들 거예요.

여: 네, 출신지에 따라 그럴 수 있어요. 그냥 교외에 있는 아파트를 임대하지 않는 이유를 물어봐도 되나요?

남: 시도해봤죠. 정말요. 걸어서 통학할 수 있는 지금 비어있는 유일한 아파트들은 터무니없이 가격이 비싸요. 제가 생각한 가격대 내의 가장 가까운 아파트들은 너무 멀어서 수업을 듣기 위해서는 차를 몰아야 하고요. 그리고 전 차가 없어요.

여: 도시 곳곳에서 우리 학교로 오는 버스들이 많이 있어요.

남: 네, 그렇죠. 제가 시간을 빼앗았다면 죄송합니다.

여: 그렇지 않아요. 학생은 중요한 문제점들을 제기했으니까요. 우리 학교의 구내식당이 학생들의 필요에 충분히 부응하지 못할 수 있고, 숙소 규정은 불공평할 수 있고, 그리고 도시의 임대 비용은 터무니없이 높아요. 학생이 그레인저홀에 들어올 가능성은 적겠지만, 상사에게 학생의 상황을 이야기할 수는 있어요.

남: 감사합니다. 제가 부탁 드리는 건 정말 그게 다예요.

어휘

accommodation n 숙소, 거처 | **functional** adj 기능 위주의, 실용적인 | **preparation** n 준비 | **appliance** n 기기 | **outlet** n 콘센트, 배출구 | **facilitate** v 가능하게 하다, 용이하게 하다 | **communal** adj 공용의, 공동의 | **specific** adj 구체적인, 분명한 | **dietary** adj 음식물의, 식이 요법의 | **restriction** n 제한 | **vegan** n 엄격한 채식주의자 (우유와 달걀 등의 유제품도 먹지 않음) | **consume** v 먹다, 소비하다 | **animal product** 동물성 식품 | **conform** v 따르다, 순응하다 | **premium** adj 고급의, 아주 높은 | **reserve** v 예약하다 | **qualify** v 자격을 얻다 | **privilege** n 특권, 특혜 | **ridiculously** adv 터무니없이 | **price range** 가격대, 가격폭 | **valid** adj 타당한, 유효한 | **inadequate** adj 불충분한, 부적당한 | **regulation** n 규정, 규제 | **biased** adj 편향된, 선입견이 있는 | **exorbitant** adj 과도한, 지나친

1. **Main Idea**

What is the conversation mainly about?

Ⓐ Filling out a complaint form about the student cafeteria's food
Ⓑ Receiving permission to use a fully functional kitchen
Ⓒ **Trying to get a dormitory room that fits the student's needs**
Ⓓ Explaining the hardships that one could face living as a vegan

2. **Function & Attitude**

Listen again to part of the conversation. Then answer the question.

> W: I see your point. However, there are very few dorm rooms that have kitchens in them.
> M: I know. I had to pay extra for a room with its own restroom. I understand that premium accommodations must be paid for. Can't I just pay more for a room with a kitchen?

Why does the student say this:

> M: Can't I just pay more for a room with a kitchen?

Ⓐ **To show his willingness to meet any requirements the university may have**
Ⓑ To indicate that he thinks the university policy is unfair
Ⓒ To emphasize the importance of his dietary restrictions
Ⓓ To show that he understands why he is not allowed to have premium accommodations

3. **Detail**

What is true about the policy regarding premium accommodations?

Ⓐ They have more gas heaters and outlets in the kitchen for the residents.
Ⓑ **Students have to pay more money to use premium accommodations.**
Ⓒ Students can enjoy various vegetarian and vegan meal options there.
Ⓓ They only accept students who are married or have children.

4. **Inference**

What can be inferred about the housing officer?

Ⓐ **She still has to follow dormitory regulations.**
Ⓑ She is unable to fix the broken kitchen appliances.
Ⓒ She always immediately reports problems to her manager.
Ⓓ She is usually able to solve problems right away.

1.
대화는 주로 무엇에 대한 것인가?

Ⓐ 학생 구내식당의 음식에 대한 불만 사항 작성하기
Ⓑ 완전히 기능을 갖춘 부엌 사용에 대한 허가 받기
Ⓒ 학생의 필요에 부합하는 기숙사 방 찾아보기
Ⓓ 비건으로 생활하며 직면할 수 있는 어려움을 설명하기

2.
대화의 일부를 다시 들으시오. 그리고 질문에 답하시오.

> 여: 무슨 말을 하는 건지 알겠어요. 하지만, 부엌이 딸린 기숙사는 매우 적어요.
> 남: 알아요. 개인 화장실이 딸린 방을 쓰기 위해 추가로 돈을 더 내야 했거든요. 고급 숙소는 돈을 지불해야 한다는 걸 이해해요. 돈을 더 내고 부엌이 딸린 방을 쓸 수는 없나요?

학생은 왜 이렇게 말하는가:

> 남: 돈을 더 내고 부엌이 딸린 방을 쓸 수는 없나요?

Ⓐ 대학에서 제시할 수도 있는 어떠한 요구 사항에도 맞추겠다는 의지를 보이려고
Ⓑ 대학의 규정이 불공평하다고 생각한다는 것을 알리려고
Ⓒ 자신의 식습관 제한에 관한 중요성을 강조하려고
Ⓓ 왜 고급 숙소에 들어갈 수 없는지 이해하고 있다는 것을 보이려고

3.
고급 숙소에 관한 규정에 대해 옳은 것은 무엇인가?

Ⓐ 입주자들을 위해 부엌에 더 많은 가스 히터와 콘센트를 보유하고 있다.
Ⓑ 학생들은 고급 숙소를 사용하기 위해서 돈을 더 내야만 한다.
Ⓒ 학생들은 그곳에서 다양한 채식주의자 및 비건 메뉴를 즐길 수 있다.
Ⓓ 결혼했거나 자녀가 있는 학생들만 받는다.

4.
기숙사 직원에 대해 무엇을 추론할 수 있는가?

Ⓐ 그래도 기숙사 규정에 따라야만 한다.
Ⓑ 고장 난 부엌 기기들을 고치지 못한다.
Ⓒ 언제나 상사에게 즉각 문제를 보고한다.
Ⓓ 보통은 문제를 즉시 해결할 수 있다.

5. Detail

What does the housing officer offer to do for the student?

Ⓐ Have maintenance check out the shared kitchen as soon as possible

Ⓑ Make an exception for him to live in the dormitory mentioned

Ⓒ Tell the student's situation to her manager to see if there is any chance

Ⓓ Assign a room in Granger Hall to the student and his sister

5.

기숙사 직원은 학생을 위해 무엇을 해주겠다고 하는가?

Ⓐ 유지보수팀이 가능한 한 빨리 공용 부엌을 점검할 수 있도록 한다.

Ⓑ 언급된 기숙사에서 남자가 살 수 있도록 예외로 해준다.

Ⓒ 가능성이 있는지 알아보기 위해 그녀의 상사에게 상황을 말한다.

Ⓓ 그레인저홀에 있는 방 하나를 학생과 그의 여동생에게 배정한다.

Lecture 1

[1-6] Listen to part of a lecture in a sociology class.

Man: Student | Woman: Professor

사회학 강의의 일부를 들으시오.

남자: 학생 | 여자: 교수

W Today we will be discussing a man whose life's work may have had a profound effect upon your life, whether you know it or not. Odds are good that many of you grew up in the suburb of a larger city, in a neighborhood full of homes that were more or less similar in size and shape. The practice of constructing homes in that way actually goes back to the 1940s, when William Levitt and his brother Alfred began building their affordable housing communities. They were quite successful, eventually amassing substantial wealth, and William is often referred to as the "Inventor of the Suburb."

The Levitt story actually began a little earlier, around the beginning of the Great Depression, when Abraham Levitt, the brothers' father, founded the real estate development company, Levitt & Sons. William soon became the president of the company and oversaw every aspect outside of the design of the homes, which was his brother's realm of expertise. Prior to World War II, the brothers built many homes and communities on Long Island for wealthy clients. However, after serving with the Seabees during the war, William... Yes, Matthew, you have a question?

M Yes, sorry to interrupt, but what is a Seabee?

W Actually, that's a pretty good question. It stands for Construction Battalion, CB, which came to be said as Seabee. They were a special unit within the United States Navy that built bases and airfields

여 오늘 우리는 여러분이 알든 모르든 자기 필생의 업적이 여러분의 삶에 깊은 영향을 끼쳤을지도 모르는 남자에 대해 논의할 겁니다. 여러분 중 다수가 큰 도시의 교외 지역에서 크기나 생김새가 거의 비슷한 집들로 가득한 동네에서 자랐을 가능성이 높죠. 그런 방식으로 집을 짓는 관행은 사실 1940년으로 거슬러 올라가는데, 그것은 윌리엄 레빗과 그의 형제인 알프레드가 저비용 주택 단지를 짓기 시작했던 때입니다. 그들은 꽤나 성공했고 결국 상당한 부를 축적했는데, 윌리엄은 "교외의 창시자"라고 종종 일컬어지기도 합니다.

레빗 형제의 이야기는 사실 좀 더 일찍인 대공황이 시작되던 무렵 시작되었는데, 그때는 형제의 아버지였던 아브라함 레빗이 Levitt & Sons라는 부동산 개발 회사를 설립했던 때였죠. 윌리엄은 곧 회사의 사장이 되었고 형제의 전문 분야였던 주택 디자인을 넘어서서 모든 분야를 감독했어요. 2차 세계대전 전에 레빗 형제는 부유한 고객들을 위해 롱아일랜드에 많은 집과 단지를 지었습니다. 그러나 전쟁 동안 Seabees와 함께 복무하게 되면서, 윌리엄은... 네, 매튜, 질문이 있나요?

남 네, 끼어들어서 죄송합니다만, Seabee가 무엇인가요?

여 사실, 꽤 좋은 질문이에요. 건설 부대(Construction Battalion)라는 뜻의 CB가 Seabee로 불리게 된 겁니다. 태평양의 섬들에 주로 매우 재빠르게 군 기지와

mostly on islands in the Pacific — usually very quickly.

Now where was I... Oh, yes. After William returned from the war, he felt sorry for many of his fellow veterans who had to return to high-rent, low-quality apartments. He decided that his company would redirect its efforts to providing affordable houses to veterans and other middle and lower class people. In order to do so, they employed an assembly line form of construction.

In Henry Ford's famous assembly line method of building cars, the vehicles traveled along the line and workers repeated the task they were trained to do on each one as it passed. Of course, this would not work for houses, so the workers moved from house to house, completed their assigned tasks and then moved on to the next one. For this method to work, all of the houses were exactly the same. They were built from the same materials, they had the same room layout, everything... and one popular style they used was called the "Cape Cod," which was based upon the traditional homes of New England.

They built their first such community near Hempstead, Long Island, which they named Levittown. They built this community at an astonishing pace, and families began moving into the neighborhood as early as 1947. The homes cost from 7 to 8 thousand dollars, and some mortgages only required monthly payments of $57. Even at the time, these were amazingly low prices. Over the next two decades, the company built a total of 140,000 homes throughout the United States, and even a development near Paris, France. They eventually sold the company to International Telephone and Telegraph in 1968 for 90 million dollars.

The legacy of their innovation is still with us today. Their intention was to build affordable homes to accommodate families. One way they managed to keep costs down was by placing the bathroom next to the kitchen, which put all of the plumbing on one side of the house. To accommodate the families, the kitchen and the living room window both faced toward the street, allowing the mother to work in the kitchen but still be able to observe her children at play in the street. This dynamic shifted in a later design called a "Ranch House."

비행장을 짓는 미 해군 안의 특별 부대였어요.

어디까지 얘기했었죠... 아, 맞아요. 윌리엄은 전쟁에서 돌아온 뒤 높은 월세의 질 낮은 아파트로 돌아가야 하는 참전 용사 동료들을 안타깝게 여겼습니다. 그의 회사가 참전 용사들과 다른 중산층과 노동자 계급에게 저비용 주택들을 제공하는 것에 노력을 전용해야 한다고 결심했죠. 그렇게 하기 위해 그들은 공사를 위한 조립 라인 형식을 이용했어요.

핸리 포드의 유명한 자동차 조립 라인 방식에서는 자동차들이 라인을 따라갔고, 노동자들은 그것들이 지나갈 때 각 자동차에 자신이 교육받은 작업을 반복했습니다. 물론, 이 방식은 집에는 적용할 수가 없었기에 노동자들이 한 집에서 다른 집으로 움직이며 맡은 일들을 한 뒤 다음 집으로 이동했어요. 이 방법이 제대로 실행되기 위해서는 모든 집들이 완전히 똑같아야 했죠. 모두 같은 재료로 지어졌으며, 같은 방 배치를 가졌고, 그 외 모든 것들도요... 그리고 그들이 사용했던 인기 있는 스타일은 "Cape Cod"라고 불렸는데, 이는 뉴잉글랜드 지역의 전통적인 집들에 기반한 것이었습니다.

그들은 그러한 첫 번째 주택 단지를 롱아일랜드의 햄프스테드 근처에 지었고 레빗타운이라는 이름을 붙였어요. 그들은 이 주택 단지를 놀라운 속도로 지었고, 가족들 이 이미 1947년부터 입주하기 시작했습니다. 집들의 가격은 7,000~8,000 달러였는데, 어떤 주택 융자금은 한 달에 57달러밖에 요구하지 않았죠. 이것은 그 당시에도 놀라울 정도로 낮은 가격이었습니다. 향후 20년 동안 이 회사는 미국 전역에 총 14만 채의 집을 지었고 심지어 프랑스 파리 근처의 단지도 지었습니다. 결국 1968년에 이 회사를 International Telephone and Telegraph에게 9천만 달러로 매각했어요.

이들의 혁신이 남긴 유산은 오늘날에도 여전합니다. 이들의 의도는 가족들을 수용하기 위한 저비용의 집들을 짓는 것이었죠. 비용을 절약하기 위해 이들이 행한 한 방식은 부엌 옆에 화장실을 배치하여 집의 한 쪽에 모든 배관 시설을 놓는 것이었어요. 가족들의 편의를 위해 부엌과 거실 둘 다 길가를 향해 있었고, 어머니가 부엌에서 일하면서 아이들이 길에서 노는 것을 지켜볼 수 있도록 했죠. 이 역동성은 "Ranch House"라고 불린 추후의 디자인으로 전환되었습니다.

These homes had the living room in the back of the structure with its large window facing into the backyard. This seemingly subtle change had a huge effect. Home life became more private, and people interacted less with their neighbors, whom they had to leave the house to see.

The Levitts have also received their share of criticism. Their suburbs ate up huge amounts of land that could have been used for farming or other purposes. They also tended to cater to the racist attitudes of the era, creating new white-only communities, which furthered racial divisions.

이 집들은 거실의 큰 창문이 뒤뜰을 향한 채로 집 구조의 뒤쪽으로 거실을 두었습니다. 이 미묘해 보이는 변화는 큰 효과를 가져왔습니다. 가정 생활이 더 개인적인 것이 되었고, 사람들은 집을 나가서야 볼 수 있는 이웃들과 덜 교류하게 되었죠.

레빗 형제는 그들 몫의 비판 또한 받았습니다. 이들의 교외 주택 단지들은 농사나 다른 목적에 쓰일 수도 있었던 엄청난 크기의 토지를 차지했어요. 이들은 또한 그 시대의 인종차별주의적 분위기에 영합하려는 경향이 있어 새로운 백인 거주 단지를 만들었고, 이는 인종차별을 심화시켰습니다.

어휘

profound adj 깊은 | **odds** n 공산, 가능성 | **suburb** n 교외 | **construct** v 건축하다 | **affordable** adj 입수 가능한, (가격이) 알맞은 | **amass** v 쌓다, 축적하다 | **substantial** adj 상당한 | **inventor** n 창시자, 발명가 | **real estate** 부동산 | **oversee** v 감독하다 | **aspect** n 측면, 양상 | **realm** n 영역 | **expertise** n 전문 지식 | **client** n 고객 | **interrupt** v 가로막다, 방해하다 | **airfield** n 비행장 | **veteran** n 참전 용사 | **redirect** v 다시 보내다 | **employ** v 쓰다, 고용하다 | **assembly line** 조립 라인 | **construction** n 건축, 건설 | **task** n 일, 과제 | **exactly** adv 완전히, 정확히 | **layout** n 배치 | **traditional** adj 전통적인 | **astonishing** adj 놀라운 | **pace** n 속도 | **mortgage** n 융자 | **legacy** n 유산 | **innovation** n 혁신 | **intention** n 의도 | **plumbing** n 배관 | **dynamic** n 역학 | **backyard** n 뒤뜰 | **subtle** adj 미묘한 | **private** adj 개인의, 사적인 | **interact** v 교류하다, 소통하다 | **cater to** ~에 영합하다 | **racial** adj 인종의 | **division** n 분열, 분배

1. Main Idea
What is the lecture mainly about?
- Ⓐ The impact that the Seabees had on the Levitt brothers
- Ⓑ The difference between two styles of house designs
- **Ⓒ The legacy and influence of the Levitt brothers**
- Ⓓ The popularity of affordable housing communities

1.
강의는 주로 무엇에 대한 것인가?
- Ⓐ Seabees가 레빗 형제에게 끼쳤던 영향
- Ⓑ 두 가지 주택 설계 양식의 차이점
- **Ⓒ 레빗 형제의 유산과 영향**
- Ⓓ 저비용 주택 단지의 인기

2. Connecting Contents
Why does the professor mention Henry Ford?
- **Ⓐ To compare the Levitt brothers' house building process to his car building method**
- Ⓑ To introduce a historical figure who had a heavy influence on the Levitt brothers
- Ⓒ To explain why Henry Ford was the main competitor of the Levitt brothers
- Ⓓ To emphasize the fact that building houses and cars are quite different

2.
교수는 왜 헨리 포드를 언급하는가?
- **Ⓐ 레빗 형제의 집 건축 과정을 그의 자동차 조립 방법과 비교하려고**
- Ⓑ 레빗 형제에게 큰 영향을 준 역사적 인물을 소개하려고
- Ⓒ 왜 헨리 포드가 레빗 형제의 주요 경쟁자였는지 설명하려고
- Ⓓ 집을 짓는 것과 자동차를 조립하는 것은 매우 다르다는 것을 강조하려고

3. Detail

According to the professor, what was the ultimate goal of the Levitt brothers?

- Ⓐ Influencing the house building trend in the United States
- **Ⓑ Helping American families to buy affordable houses**
- Ⓒ Launching new construction projects internationally
- Ⓓ Having a town named after their family

4. Detail

Which of the following is true about the Cape Cod style?

- Ⓐ Each house had its own unique appearance.
- Ⓑ Its room layout followed the Ranch House style.
- Ⓒ People often preferred it to apartments.
- **Ⓓ It was modeled after New England homes.**

5. Detail

Which of the following are characteristics of the Ranch House? Choose 2 answers.

- Ⓐ It was similar to traditional homes on Long Island.
- **Ⓑ It had a big window facing the backyard.**
- Ⓒ The kitchen and bathroom used separate plumbing.
- **Ⓓ The living room was located in the back of the house.**

6. Function & Attitude

Listen again to part of the lecture. Then answer the question.

> W The homes cost from about 7 to 8 thousand dollars, and some mortgages only required monthly payments of $57. Even at the time, these were amazingly low prices.

Why does the professor say this:

> W Even at the time, these were amazingly low prices.

- **Ⓐ To highlight the fact that the Levitt brothers succeeded in building affordable houses**
- Ⓑ To remind the students that today's mortgages are unbelievably high
- Ⓒ To emphasize the dedication and commitment of the Levitt brothers
- Ⓓ To indicate that it wasn't really possible to build houses at such a low price

3.

교수에 의하면, 레빗 형제의 궁극적인 목표는 무엇이었는가?

- Ⓐ 미국의 주택 건축 추세에 영향을 주는 것
- **Ⓑ 미국 가정들이 저비용 주택을 구입하는 데 도움을 주는 것**
- Ⓒ 국제적으로 새로운 건설 프로젝트에 착수하는 것
- Ⓓ 가족의 이름을 붙인 마을을 갖는 것

4.

Cape Cod 스타일에 대해 옳은 것은 무엇인가?

- Ⓐ 각 집은 나름대로의 독특한 외관을 지녔다.
- Ⓑ 방 배치는 Ranch House 스타일을 따랐다.
- Ⓒ 사람들은 아파트보다 이 스타일을 선호했다.
- Ⓓ 뉴잉글랜드 주택을 따라 지어졌다.

5.

다음 중 Ranch House의 특징은 무엇인가? 두 개를 고르시오.

- Ⓐ 롱아일랜드의 전통적인 집들과 비슷했다.
- Ⓑ 뒤뜰을 향하는 큰 창문이 있었다.
- Ⓒ 부엌과 거실은 분리된 배관을 사용했다.
- Ⓓ 거실은 집 뒤편에 위치했다.

6.

강의의 일부를 다시 듣고 질문에 답하시오.

> 예 집들의 가격은 7,000~8,000 달러였는데, 어떤 주택 융자금은 한 달에 57달러밖에 요구하지 않았죠. 이것은 그 당시에도 놀라울 정도로 낮은 가격이었습니다.

교수는 왜 이렇게 말하는가:

> 예 이것은 그 당시에도 놀라울 정도로 낮은 가격이었습니다.

- Ⓐ 레빗 형제가 저비용 주택을 짓는 데 성공했다는 사실을 강조하려고
- Ⓑ 오늘날의 주택 융자는 믿기 어려울 정도로 높다는 것을 학생들에게 상기시켜주려고
- Ⓒ 레빗 형제의 전념과 헌신을 강조하려고
- Ⓓ 그렇게 낮은 가격으로 주택을 짓는 것이 정말로 가능하지는 않았다고 말하려고

Conversation 2

[1-5] Listen to part of a conversation between a professor and a student.

Man: Student | Woman: Professor

M Good afternoon, Professor.

W Yes, Mr. Krieger, please have a seat.

M Mr. Krieger, you'd think I'd have gotten used to that by now. Mr… it still sounds strange to me for a teacher to call me mister.

W Would you prefer it if I called you Stefan? You are planning to get your Ph.D. after all, so soon enough everyone will call you doctor.

M That is true. No, Mr. Krieger is fine, I guess. Um, anyways, I have something I want to discuss with you.

W I noticed that you seemed rather upset when I reminded the class about your paper's page count. Is that what you wanted to talk about? Are you having trouble finding enough material?

M Um, no, actually, I have the opposite problem. There is so much that I want to include, but you gave us an upper limit as well.

W Yes, I did. Ten to twenty pages, as I recall. I want you to be concise in your analysis; however, that does not mean that you have to leave out material that you think is useful to the reader. You can always add an appendix.

M Now, why didn't I think of that…

W Have you ever included an appendix with a paper before? Just like any other part of a well-written research paper, there are certain rules to be followed.

M No, but I do have my style guide.

W Excellent, then we can move on to another matter.

M Another matter?

W As you are no doubt aware, the campus library recently received a donation from the estate of Gerhard Foch, the renowned historian. I and some other faculty have been given the task of cataloging the collection before we incorporate it into the library. We are each allowed to bring two student assistants who are working on their master's degrees. I was wondering if you would like to take part.

M Me? Of course I would! But, why me?

W: Well, as your desire to expand your paper further proves, you are an avid historian. So, I think that this would be a great experience for you.

M: Thank you very much, Professor. When do we start?

W: The collection will be delivered next month. But, due to final exams we cannot begin on our task until summer vacation. We expect it to take at least a month to properly catalog. Dr. Foch had an immense collection of books and artifacts that he amassed over the five decades of his career.

M: Um, just out of curiosity, would I be able to receive credit for doing this?

W: No, but there are side benefits. Of course, you will not be paid, but you will technically be an employee of the university. You can include this on your résumé later when you are looking for internships or other positions. The university will also provide you with housing if required. Do you live in campus housing right now?

M: Yes, I am staying in Henker Dormitory.

W: They will probably move you into the staff housing for the summer then. We can take care of the official paperwork next week. I will contact you. If you see Judith in the hallway, please send her in. She may also be working with us this summer.

어휘

remind v 상기시키다 | **material** n 자료, 재료 | **opposite** adj 반대의 | **concise** adj 간결한 | **analysis** n 분석 | **appendix** n 부록 | **donation** n 기부 | **estate** n 유산 | **renowned** adj 저명한 | **historian** n 역사가 | **catalog** v 분류하다 | **incorporate** v 포함하다 | **assistant** n 조교 | **expand** v 확장하다 | **avid** adj 열정적인 | **properly** adv 제대로 | **immense** adj 거대한, 엄청난 | **artifacts** n 인공물, 유물 | **amass** v 모으다, 수집하다 | **curiosity** n 궁금함 | **technically** adv 엄밀히 따지면 | **official** adj 공식의 | **hallway** n 복도

---

1. **Main Idea**

Why did the student want to talk to the professor?

Ⓐ He needed to ask the professor to allow him to participate in a field project.
Ⓑ **He wanted to discuss how he should include research material in his paper.**
Ⓒ He came to persuade the professor to give him more time for an assignment.
Ⓓ He felt worried that his paper would need to include some maps and charts.

2. **Detail**

What feature of his paper is the student concerned about?

Ⓐ The relevance of some of his sources
Ⓑ The data collected from his field project
Ⓒ The conciseness of his writing style
Ⓓ **The number of pages the paper will have**

3. **Function & Attitude**

What is the student's attitude toward the project the professor mentioned?

Ⓐ He is thrilled that he can research the topic he wanted to use for his paper.
Ⓑ He thinks it is rather boring compared to other types of historical projects.
Ⓒ **He finds it to be very interesting, and is amazed that he could be a part of it.**
Ⓓ He is uncertain if he would be the right candidate for such a big project.

4. **Detail**

According to the professor, what is true about the upcoming project that she mentioned?

Ⓐ It needs more donations from historians.
Ⓑ It requires 50 staff members to complete.
Ⓒ **It will provide the student with housing.**
Ⓓ It will begin during the winter vacation.

5. **Inference**

What is the student's next step for participating in the project?

Ⓐ **He is going to do the required paperwork sometime next week.**
Ⓑ He will start applying for housing to stay in during the winter vacation.
Ⓒ He is going to have a meeting with Judith regarding the project.
Ⓓ He will collect more information about Gerhard Foch and his work.

2.
학생은 과제의 어떤 점을 걱정하고 있는가?

Ⓐ 일부 자료의 타당성
Ⓑ 현장 연구에서 수집한 데이터
Ⓒ 글쓰기의 간결성
Ⓓ 과제의 페이지 수

3.
교수가 언급한 프로젝트에 대한 학생의 태도는 어떠한가?

Ⓐ 과제에 쓰고 싶었던 주제를 연구하게 되어 매우 기뻐한다.
Ⓑ 다른 종류의 역사 프로젝트들에 비해 좀 지루하다고 생각한다.
Ⓒ 매우 흥미롭게 여기며 자신이 참여할 수 있다는 것에 놀라워한다.
Ⓓ 그렇게 큰 프로젝트에 자신이 정말 적합한 후보자인지 확신이 없다.

4.
교수에 의하면, 그녀가 언급한 곧 있을 프로젝트에 대해 옳은 것은 무엇인가?

Ⓐ 역사학자들의 기부가 더 많이 필요하다.
Ⓑ 완료하는 데 50명의 인력이 필요하다.
Ⓒ 학생에게 기숙사를 제공할 것이다.
Ⓓ 겨울 방학 중에 시작할 것이다.

5.
프로젝트에 참가하기 위해 학생이 다음에 할 일은 무엇인가?

Ⓐ 다음 주 중 필요한 서류 작업을 할 것이다.
Ⓑ 겨울 방학 동안 머물기 위해 기숙사 신청을 시작할 것이다.
Ⓒ 프로젝트와 관련해 주디스와 회의를 할 것이다.
Ⓓ 게하드 포슈와 그의 연구에 대해 더 많은 정보를 수집할 것이다.

Lecture 2

[1-6] Listen to part of a lecture in a social science class.

Man: Student | Woman: Professor

W As I am sure you are all aware, the parking lot behind Voltaire Hall currently is being repaved, which actually ties in nicely with the topic we are going to discuss. Today parking lots and roads are paved with asphalt, but that is actually a fairly recent invention.

The first roads were basically just wide dirt paths where repeated foot traffic prevented vegetation from reclaiming the soil. These often became impassable due to rainfall reducing them to mud. One of the earliest examples of a paved road is what we call a corduroy road. These are made by placing logs across a path tightly together, and they are pretty durable. Many examples have been unearthed in archaeological digs relatively intact. They were widely used in northern Europe, where bogs and marshes are prevalent, so paths are rarely dry.

The most famous roads in Europe, however, were paved with stone. As the Roman Empire expanded, its roads did as well to allow better administration of its territories. Their most lasting roads were actually fairly complex. They consisted of a roadbed of gravel, sand and rubble that was tamped down to form a stable base and then paved with flat stones. This layering of materials allowed water to seep through into the soil without compromising the road surface, and many of them have survived to this day.

However, people in drier areas had a different problem to deal with. Their dirt roads would produce great clouds of dust when traffic was heavy. As early as the ninth century, the streets of Baghdad were routinely given a coating of tar to combat this problem. It was a pretty good method, but when it did rain, they were still pretty useless. Further innovation did not come for another thousand years or so. Early in the nineteenth century, a Scottish inventor named John Loudon McAdam developed a process for road building dubbed macadamisation.

M Wait, John McAdam, macadamisation... he named it after himself?

사회과학 강의의 일부를 들으시오.

남자: 학생 | 여자: 교수

여 여러분 모두 알고 있겠지만 볼테르홀 뒤편의 주차장이 재포장 중인데, 이것이 우리가 오늘 얘기해 볼 주제와 정말 잘 들어맞네요. 요즘 주차장과 도로들은 아스팔트로 포장이 되어 있는데, 그것은 사실상 꽤 최근에 발명된 것입니다.

최초의 도로는 기본적으로 사람들이 계속 지나다니면서 초목이 땅 위로 다시 자라날 수 없도록 한 넓은 흙길일 뿐이었습니다. 이 흙길은 비가 와서 그곳을 진흙으로 만들어버리기 때문에 종종 통과할 수 없는 곳이 됐었죠. 초기 포장 도로의 예제들 중 하나는 목재포도라고 불리는 것입니다. 이 도로는 길에 통나무를 단단히 함께 놓아서 만들어지고, 꽤나 견고하죠. 많은 예들이 고고학적 발굴지에서 비교적 손상되지 않은 상태로 발굴되었습니다. 그것들은 유럽 북부에서 널리 쓰여졌는데, 그곳은 늪지와 습지가 일반적이라 길이 말라있는 경우가 드뭅니다.

하지만 유럽에서 가장 유명한 도로는 돌로 포장되어 있었습니다. 로마 제국이 확장되었을 때, 영토를 더 잘 관리하기 위해서 도로 역시 확장되었습니다. 로마 제국에서 가장 오래 지속된 도로는 사실상 꽤나 복잡했습니다. 그 도로는 자갈, 모래, 돌을 꾹꾹 눌러서 안정된 바닥을 만들고 그런 다음 평평한 돌로 포장된 노반으로 이루어져 있었습니다. 이러한 겹쳐진 재료들은 물이 도로의 표면을 해치지 않으면서 토양으로 스며들 수 있게 해줬으며, 이러한 도로 중 대다수가 오늘날까지 남아 있습니다.

하지만 더 건조한 지역에 사는 사람들은 다른 문제에 대처해야 했습니다. 그들의 흙길은 통행량이 많으면 먼지 구름이 엄청나게 발생했습니다. 이미 9세기경에는 이러한 문제를 해결하기 위해 바그다드 도로들에 일상적으로 타르 코팅이 칠해졌습니다. 이것은 꽤 좋은 방법이었지만, 비가 오면 여전히 매우 소용이 없었습니다. 그 이후 약 천 년간 더 나은 발명이 등장하지 않았지요. 19세기 초반, 스코틀랜드의 존 루돈 맥애덤이라는 발명가가 머캐덤 포장법(매캐더마이제이션)이라고 불리는 도로 건설을 위한 과정을 개발해냈어요.

남 잠깐만요. 존 맥애덤과 머캐덤 포장법... 그가 자신의 이름을 따서 지은 것인가요?

W I'm not sure, but it was certainly named for him. I'll look into that later… He put a layer of larger stones, about 75 millimeters, overlaid with another layer of smaller stones, no more than 20 millimeters. His road was 30 feet wide and gradually sloped down from the center to allow proper drainage. He believed that no binding agent should be used as the stones would naturally settle and match up their surfaces. The stones in the top layer were smaller than the iron wagon wheels of the time, so it acted as a fairly solid surface. His method was quite effective at resisting rainwater, but it still produced dust in the summer.

Then in 1901, Edgar Purnell Hooley patented what he called tarmac, which is short for tar-penetration macadam. His patented technique involved mixing macadam gravel with tar before laying it on the roadbed. Then it was compacted with a steamroller. He founded a company called Tarmac Limited, which became quite profitable as he repaved roads throughout England. During the Second World War, tarmac started being used to pave airfields, which is why we still refer to airstrips as tarmac, whether or not they are actually made from it. Much like macadam before it, tarmac spread to the United States, but Americans preferred to use asphalt instead of tar. At first it was collected from lakes in Venezuela, but it was later produced as a byproduct of oil processing. Frederick Warren began using it in a process he called bitulithic, but is commonly referred to as hot-mix asphalt. HMA is unique in that it retains some of its liquid properties, particularly in hot weather. In fact, on particularly hot days, passing vehicles and even people's feet will leave marks in the pavement that gradually disappear in the next few moments. HMA is the most widely used road paving material today, but dirt roads, corduroy roads, and macadam are all still used, particularly in rural areas.

1. **Main Idea**
What is the lecture mainly about?
- (A) **The history of road paving**
- (B) The creation of tar and tarmac
- (C) The lasting influence of John McAdam
- (D) The characteristics of hot-mix asphalt

2. **Detail**
What does the professor say about corduroy roads?
- (A) They were not usable during the rainy season.
- (B) **Logs were used to strengthen the ground.**
- (C) They were among the first asphalt-paved roads.
- (D) They were commonly used in dry regions.

3. **Function & Attitude**
Why does the professor say this:

> W However, people in drier areas had a different problem to deal with.

- (A) **To compare roads in regions with varied climates**
- (B) To emphasize that dry areas had more difficulties
- (C) To show respect for people in drier areas for their road making efforts
- (D) To discuss the difficulties of living in dry regions

4. **Inference**
What can be inferred about John Loudon McAdam's road building process?
- (A) Large flat stones were put on the bottom for safety.
- (B) **Stones of different sizes were used without other binding material.**
- (C) Tar and gravel were combined together to resist rainwater.
- (D) Wood and tar needed to be used for the base.

5. **Connecting Contents**
Why does the professor mention the Second World War?
- (A) To give the students a historical example
- (B) To contrast asphalt with tar use in the United States
- (C) **To explain how the use of tarmac became popular**
- (D) To illustrate a point about macadamisation

6. **Detail**
According to the lecture, which of the following is true?
- (A) John McAdam invented tarmac and macadam.
- (B) **Hot-mix asphalt is not completely solid in hot weather.**
- (C) Asphalt gained wide popularity during World War II.
- (D) Most roadways in the U.S. are paved with tarmac.

1.
이 강의는 주로 무엇에 대한 것인가?
- (A) **도로 포장의 역사**
- (B) 타르와 타맥의 창조
- (C) 존 맥애덤의 지속적인 영향력
- (D) 아스팔트 혼합물의 특징

2.
교수가 목재포도에 대해 언급한 바는 무엇인가?
- (A) 비가 오는 계절에는 사용할 수 없었다.
- (B) **통나무들은 땅을 강화시키기 위해 사용되었다.**
- (C) 최초의 아스팔트 포장 도로 중 하나였다.
- (D) 건조한 지역에서 흔히 사용되었다.

3.
교수는 왜 이렇게 말하는가:

> 여 하지만 더 건조한 지역에 사는 사람들은 다른 문제에 대처해야 했습니다.

- (A) **다양한 기후를 가진 지역의 도로를 비교하려고**
- (B) 건조한 지역들에는 더 많은 어려움이 있었다는 것을 강조하려고
- (C) 더 건조한 지역의 사람들이 도로 건축에 기울였던 노력을 존중하려고
- (D) 건조한 지역에서 사는 것의 어려움에 대해 논의하려고

4.
존 루돈 맥애덤의 도로 건설 과정에 대해 무엇을 추론할 수 있는가?
- (A) 안전을 위해 크고 판판한 돌들을 바닥에 배치했다.
- (B) **다른 결합 물질 없이 서로 다른 크기의 돌들이 사용되었다.**
- (C) 빗물에 침식되지 않게 하기 위해 타르와 자갈이 함께 혼합되었다.
- (D) 목재와 타르가 기반에 사용되어야 했다.

5.
교수가 제2차 세계대전을 언급한 이유는 무엇인가?
- (A) 학생들에게 역사적인 예를 제시하기 위해
- (B) 미국에서의 아스팔트와 타르 사용을 비교하기 위해
- (C) **타맥의 사용이 어떻게 대중화되었는지 설명하기 위해**
- (D) 머캐덤 포장법에 대한 요점을 설명하기 위해

6.
강의에 의하면, 다음 중 옳은 것은 무엇인가?
- (A) 존 맥애덤은 타맥과 머캐덤을 발명했다.
- (B) **아스팔트 혼합물은 더운 날씨에서는 완전한 고체 상태가 아니다.**
- (C) 아스팔트는 제2차 세계대전 동안 폭넓은 인기를 얻었다.
- (D) 대부분의 미국 도로는 타맥으로 포장되어 있다.

Lecture 3

[1-6] Listen to part of a lecture in an ecology class.

Man: Professor | Woman: Student

M The Amazon River is not the longest river in the world, but its drainage basin is easily the largest. This vast supply of water feeds the largest rain forest in the world and the diversity of life it contains. The flora and fauna of the Amazon Rainforest are incredibly varied and numerous, but why is this so? Now, that may seem like a foolish question, but hear me out. If we look back through the fossil record, nearly every species will share a genetic ancestor somewhere in their history. For some, this was hundreds of millions of years ago, but other divergences happened much more recently. Once these groups have diverged far enough, they can no longer mate with each other, thereby creating a new species. This process is called speciation.

Normally, speciation occurs as a result of an animal population being divided by a major geographic barrier like a mountain range or an ocean. Such complete isolation allows the animals to evolve independently and frequently results in incompatibility if they are ever reintroduced. This process is called allopatric speciation, and it is responsible for a great majority of modern species. However, since the Amazon River basin is essentially one giant river valley, such complete division of an animal population seems unlikely. So, why is there such stunning variety present? Some scientists have argued that the rivers of the Amazon present a much greater barrier than previously thought. For smaller species, like ants for example, even a small river may present a significant obstacle, but more on that later.

Although it is a fairly homogenous ecosystem, the very nature of the Amazon Basin may explain why such diversity exists. The levels of the rivers usually fluctuate wildly during the course of a normal year, so some species may simply choose to remain in the areas they are periodically isolated to. These smaller groups allow genetic changes to manifest more quickly, creating new species in close proximity to the parent group. This is an example of a pattern called peripatric speciation. Conversely, even with the lack of significant barriers, sometimes distance alone can bring about change. In such a large habitat, species will often spread to cover immense ranges. Inevitably, some smaller groups will become isolated and the usual process of divergence occurs. This pattern is called parapatric speciation. Later, these species may encounter each other again, and may subsequently live in the same region, but remain distinct species. When this occurs, it is referred to as sympatry. However, sympatry can also occur as a result of a distinct process called sympatric speciation. There are many examples of this in nature, but the most complete is that of the Attini tribe.

W The Attini tribe? Professor, I thought you were talking about animal species, not native peoples.

M I am. As I am using the term, tribe refers to an animal classification between subfamily and genus. The Attini tribe is divided into two genera that include 47 species of ants. These ants are commonly referred to as leafcutter ants. They slice off sections of tree leaves with their jaws, which they transport back to their hives. Within their hives, they expose the leaves to a fungus that provides them with their food supply. The ants provide the fungus with food and safety, and the fungus provides them with a dependable food supply — a very nice example of mutually beneficial symbiosis. Now, all of the fungus these many species of ants use are in the same family, but they and the ants that use them are exclusive. There are structural differences between the two genera of ants, but the speciation they exhibit has occurred as a result of their farming techniques. You see, the ants are fiercely territorial, and they kill any intruders to their hives. So, one population of ants and the fungus they farm has evolved in isolation from the other ant groups and the fungi that they use. They occupy the same geographic area, but they have become distinct species that cannot interbreed: both ants and fungi. So, this is speciation that has occurred without barriers or any other form of geographic isolation. They have become different while living together, making it true sympatric speciation.

수 있습니다. 그렇게 거대한 서식지에서 종들은 종종 드넓은 범위를 뒤덮으면서 퍼져나갑니다. 불가피하게 몇몇 작은 그룹은 고립될 것이고, 흔히 있는 분기 과정이 일어나죠. 이 패턴은 근지역 종분화라고 불립니다. 나중에 이들 종들은 다시 서로 마주치게 되고 그 뒤에는 같은 지역에서 살 수도 있겠지만, 뚜렷하게 다른 종으로 남게 됩니다. 이런 것이 발생할 때 이것은 동지역성이라고 불립니다. 그러나 동지역성은 동소적 종분화라고 불리는 별개의 과정의 결과로 인해 일어날 수 있습니다. 자연에는 이 현상의 예가 많지만, 가장 완벽한 예는 아티니 족입니다.

여 아티니 족이요? 교수님, 저는 교수님께서 부족이 아니라 동물의 종에 대해 말씀하시는 거라고 생각했는데요.

남 동물의 종에 대해 말하고 있는 겁니다. 제가 이 용어를 쓰듯이, '족'이라는 단어는 아과와 속 사이의 동물 분류를 의미해요. 아티니 족은 47종의 개미를 포함한 두 개의 속으로 나뉩니다. 이 개미들은 흔히 가위개미라고 불리죠. 턱으로 나뭇잎의 일부를 잘라내어 집으로 가져오거든요. 이들은 집 안에서 그들에게 먹이를 제공해주는 균류에 이 나뭇잎들을 노출시킵니다. 개미들은 균류에 음식과 안전을 제공하고, 균류는 개미들에게 의지할 수 있는 음식 공급처가 되죠. 서로에게 이로운 공생 관계의 아주 좋은 예입니다. 자, 많은 종들의 개미들이 이용하는 모든 균류는 같은 과에 속해 있지만, 이 균류와 이들을 이용하는 개미들은 독점적입니다. 두 속의 개미들 사이에는 구조적 차이가 있지만, 이들이 보이는 종분화는 그들의 영농 기술의 결과로 인해 발생한 것입니다. 알다시피, 개미들은 지독히도 텃세가 심해서 집에 침입하는 누구든지 죽이죠. 그래서 한 개체의 개미들과 그들이 재배하는 균류가 다른 개미 그룹과 그들이 재배하는 균류와 고립되어 진화했습니다. 같은 지리적 지역을 점령하고 있으나 이종 교배가 불가능한 아예 다른 종이 되어버린 것이죠. 개미와 균류 둘 다요. 그래서 이는 장애물이나 다른 지리적 고립의 형태 없이 발생한 종분화입니다. 함께 살아가는 동안 달라지게 되었고, 진정한 동소적 종분화를 만든 거죠.

어휘

drainage basin 유역 | **vast** adj 어마어마한, 방대한 | **diversity** n 다양성, 포괄성 | **flora** n 식물군 | **fauna** n 동물군 | **incredibly** adv 엄청나게 | **numerous** adj 수없이 많은 | **foolish** adj 바보스러운 | **fossil record** 화석 기록 | **genetic** adj 유전적인 | **ancestor** n 조상 | **divergence** n 분기, 차이 | **mate** v 짝짓기하다 | **speciation** n 종분화 | **population** n 인구 | **geographic** adj 지리적인 | **barrier** n 장애물 | **isolation** n 고립 | **evolve** v 진화하다 | **independently** adv 독립적으로 | **incompatibility** n 양립할 수 없음 | **allopatric speciation** 이지역종 형성 | **division** n 분할 | **stunning** adj 놀라운 | **significant** adj 큰, 중요한 | **homogenous** adj 동일한 | **ecosystem** n 생태계 | **fluctuate** v 변동하다 | **periodically** adv 주기적으로 | **manifest** v 나타나다 | **proximity** n 가까움, 근접 | **peripatric speciation** 근소적 종분화 | **conversely** adv 역으로 | **habitat** n 서식지 | **inevitably** adv 불가피하게 | **parapatric speciation** 근지역 종분화 | **encounter** v 맞닥뜨리다 | **subsequently** adv 그 뒤에, 나중에 | **sympatry** n 동지역성 | **tribe** n 족 (아과와 속 사이의 분류) | **subfamily** n 아과 | **genus** n 속 | **hive** n 둥지, 집 | **expose** v 노출하다 | **fungus** n 균류, 곰팡이 | **dependable** adj 믿을 수 있는 | **mutually** adv 서로, 상호간에 | **exclusive** adj 독점적인 | **structural** adj 구조적인 | **fiercely** adv 지독하게, 격렬하게 | **territorial** adj 세력권을 주장하는 | **intruder** n 침입자 | **interbreed** v 이종 교배하다 | **sympatric speciation** 동소적 종분화

---

1. Main Idea
What is the lecture mainly about?
Ⓐ The characteristics of various flora and fauna in the Amazon
Ⓑ The comparison of the Amazon River ecosystem and those of other rivers
Ⓒ **The different types of speciation and their examples**
Ⓓ The process by which organisms develop symbiotic relationships

2. Detail
According to the lecture, how should speciation be defined?
Ⓐ A way of discovering a new species in the forest
Ⓑ **A process that changes a species to a new one**
Ⓒ A method that a species uses for seasonal migration
Ⓓ A method that animals use to survive environmental change

3. Detail
What does the professor mention as causes of speciation?
Choose 2 answers.
Ⓐ Large population
Ⓑ Food chain
Ⓒ **Geographic obstacles**
Ⓓ **Distance**

1.
강의는 주로 무엇에 대한 것인가?
Ⓐ 아마존의 다양한 식물군과 동물군의 특징
Ⓑ 아마존강의 생태계와 다른 강들의 생태계 비교
Ⓒ 여러 종류의 종분화와 그 예시
Ⓓ 생물들이 공생 관계를 발전시키는 과정

2.
강의에 의하면, 종분화는 어떻게 정의될 수 있는가?
Ⓐ 숲에서 새로운 종을 발견하는 방법
Ⓑ 한 종을 새로운 종으로 바꾸는 과정
Ⓒ 계절 이동을 위해 한 종이 사용하는 방법
Ⓓ 환경적 변화에서 생존하기 위해 동물들이 사용하는 방법

3.
교수는 종분화의 원인으로 무엇을 언급하는가?
두 개를 고르시오.
Ⓐ 많은 개체
Ⓑ 먹이 사슬
Ⓒ 지리적 장애물
Ⓓ 거리

4. Function & Attitude

Listen again to part of the lecture. Then answer the question.

> M However, sympatry can also occur as a result of a distinct process called sympatric speciation. There are many examples of this in nature, but the most complete is that of the Attini tribe.
>
> W The Attini tribe? Professor, I thought you were talking about animal species, not native peoples.

Why does the student say this:

> W The Attini tribe? Professor, I thought you were talking about animal species, not native peoples.

- Ⓐ **To express her confusion about the new topic the professor introduced**
- Ⓑ To tell the professor that he has made a mistake about the lecture topic
- Ⓒ To show the professor that she studied the Amazon ecosystem thoroughly
- Ⓓ To point out that she has never heard of a tribe called the Attini before

5. Inference

According to the lecture, what can be inferred about sympatric speciation?

- Ⓐ It occurs when two different species compete for survival.
- Ⓑ It is a rare process which only happens to ant species.
- Ⓒ **It does not require geographic barriers or distance.**
- Ⓓ It shows that the environment is in danger because of human activities.

6. Function & Attitude

What is the professor's opinion about the symbiosis of leafcutter ants?

- Ⓐ He is certain that it ultimately is a doomed type of relationship.
- Ⓑ He believes that it can help the ants to find good leaves more easily.
- Ⓒ He doubts if it really is a necessary relationship for the ants.
- Ⓓ **He thinks that it is a good strategy for both the ants and the fungus.**

4.

강의의 일부를 다시 듣고 질문에 답하시오.

> 남 그러나 동지역성은 동소적 종분화라고 불리는 별개의 과정의 결과로 인해 일어날 수 있습니다. 자연에는 이 현상의 예가 많지만, 가장 완벽한 예는 아티니 족입니다.
>
> 여 아티니 족이요? 교수님, 저는 교수님께서 부족이 아니라 동물의 종에 대해 말하시는 거라고 생각했는데요.

학생은 왜 이렇게 말하는가:

> 여 아티니 족이요? 교수님, 저는 교수님께서 부족이 아니라 동물의 종에 대해 말씀하시는 거라고 생각했는데요.

- Ⓐ 교수가 소개한 새로운 주제에 대한 혼란을 표현하기 위해
- Ⓑ 강의 주제에 대해 교수가 실수를 했다고 말하기 위해
- Ⓒ 아마존 생태계를 깊게 공부했다는 것을 보여주기 위해
- Ⓓ 아티니라는 부족을 한 번도 들어보지 못했다고 지적하기 위해

5.

강의에 의하면, 동소적 종분화에 대해 무엇을 추론할 수 있는가?

- Ⓐ 두 개의 다른 종이 생존을 위해 경쟁할 때 일어난다.
- Ⓑ 개미 종에게만 일어나는 희귀한 과정이다.
- Ⓒ 지리적 장애물이나 거리는 필요하지 않다.
- Ⓓ 인간 활동으로 인해 환경이 위험에 처한다는 것을 보여 준다.

6.

가위개미의 공생에 대한 교수의 의견은 무엇인가?

- Ⓐ 결국에는 불운한 종류의 관계라고 확신한다.
- Ⓑ 개미들이 좋은 나뭇잎을 더 쉽게 찾을 수 있도록 도와줄 수 있다고 믿는다.
- Ⓒ 개미들에게 꼭 필요한 관계인지 의심한다.
- Ⓓ 개미와 균류 모두에게 좋은 전략이라고 생각한다.

Actual Test 04

본서 | P. 88

Conversation 1	1. C	2. A	3. A, C	4. B	5. D	
Lecture 1	1. B	2. D	3. A, C	4. B	5. B	6. D
Conversation 2	1. C	2. B	3. A	4. C	5. B	
Lecture 2	1. B	2. C	3. A	4. A, D	5. A	6. C
Lecture 3	1. C	2. B	3. B	4. C	5. B	6. A

● 내가 맞은 문제 유형의 개수를 적어 보고 어느 유형에 취약한지 확인해 봅시다.

문제 유형	맞은 개수
Main Idea	5
Detail	11
Connecting Contents	2
Function & Attitude	5
Inference	5
Total	28

Conversation 1

[1-5] Listen to part of a conversation between a student and an employee at the campus bookstore.

Man: Student | Woman: Bookstore employee

W Greetings, can I help you?

M Uh, I'm not sure. I asked for directions at the reception desk, and the young lady sent me here. She said to walk down the hall and take the first right turn.

W That is how you get here. Are you looking for books? If you are, this is the right place.

M Yes, it would be, but I would like to order some T-shirts.

W Is this for a campus organization?

M Yes, it is. I would like to order some shirts for the astronomy club.

W Well, then you are still in the correct place! We sell standard university clothing here, but clubs can also order custom designed shirts, hats, etc. here. Do you have a design ready? We just need to fill out some paperwork. Then we can send it to the company that produces all of our university affiliated clothing.

M Alright, that sounds good. Here is the design.

W The planets of the solar system. This seems appropriate for the astronomy club… except there are only eight planets on this shirt. Where's Pluto?

M That's because Pluto is no longer considered to be a planet. In 2006, a council of astronomers met and decided that since Pluto is smaller than other non-planetary objects, and its orbit crosses Neptune's, it cannot be counted as a true planet. It was reclassified as a dwarf planet.

W A dwarf planet? I imagine that there was some uproar about that.

M Yes, there was. But, that plays right into our design. You see on the front here, at the top above the planets, where it says Major? Well, on the back side, we included the dwarf planets along with Pluto and labeled it Minor. We chose that design to emphasize that astronomy can be taken as either a major or a minor, and we hope that this will interest more students in studying the subject.

W Are these all of the dwarf planets in the Solar System?

M: The main five, yes. At the bottom you can see six others that are still disputed. So, we titled them Electives. That shows that you can take astronomy classes even if it isn't your major or minor.

W: That is actually pretty clever. Did you come up with the idea?

M: No, I didn't. I was unable to attend that meeting. That is why I am here today. They gave me the task of ordering the T-shirts because I wasn't there.

W: Alright. Then we need to know how many you want to order, what sizes you need them in, and what color scheme you would like to use.

M: Well, we want 40 shirts. We need 5 small shirts, 10 medium shirts, 15 large shirts, and 10 extra large shirts.

W: Colors?

M: Uh, actually, I don't know. What colors are there to choose from?

W: Hmm… Most clubs use the university's colors, so purple, black, and white for shirt colors, and gold is also available for writing.

M: Do you have some sample patterns? I'd like to take them to the next meeting and ask the other club members for their opinions.

W: Sure, there are some standard patterns, or you can create your own. Just let me open up the file on this computer. Then I can print a copy out for you.

어휘

direction n 길 찾기, 방향 | **reception desk** 안내 데스크 | **organization** n 단체, 조직 | **astronomy** n 천문학 | **standard** adj 일반적인, 보통의 | **custom designed** 맞춤 디자인한 | **paperwork** n 서류 작업 | **affiliated** adj 제휴된, 연계된 | **solar system** 태양계 | **appropriate** adj 적절한 | **council** n 협의회, 의회 | **astronomer** n 천문학자 | **planetary** adj 행성의 | **orbit** n 궤도 | **reclassify** v 재분류하다 | **dwarf planet** 왜소행성 | **uproar** n 소란, 논란 | **label** v 라벨[이름]을 붙이다 | **emphasize** v 강조하다 | **dispute** v 분쟁[논란]을 벌이다 | **title** v 제목을 붙이다 | **task** n 일, 과제 | **color scheme** 색채 조합

---

1. Main Idea

What is the conversation mainly about?

Ⓐ Organizing a student club meeting at the university bookstore
Ⓑ Debating the controversy of Pluto being a dwarf planet
Ⓒ Having t-shirts ordered for a student organization
Ⓓ Designing the patterns of the astronomy club shirts

1.

대화는 주로 무엇에 대한 것인가?

Ⓐ 대학교 서점에서 학생 동아리 모임 조직하기
Ⓑ 왜소행성이 된 명왕성에 대한 논쟁을 두고 토론하기
Ⓒ 학생 동아리를 위한 티셔츠 주문하기
Ⓓ 천문학 동아리 셔츠의 패턴 디자인하기

2. **Function & Attitude**

What is the employee's opinion about the astronomy club shirt?

Ⓐ **She thinks it is brilliantly designed.**
Ⓑ She is worried that it might be too complex.
Ⓒ She believes it is worth the price.
Ⓓ She thinks purple and black are necessary.

3. **Detail**

What does the student say about the planets in the solar system? Choose 2 answers.

Ⓐ **Pluto is excluded from the list of planets.**
Ⓑ Neptune is still considered a dwarf planet.
Ⓒ **Pluto is too small to be considered a planet.**
Ⓓ There are six main dwarf planets.

4. **Detail**

What is true about the club's shirt?

Ⓐ It implies that astronomy majors should participate.
Ⓑ **It suggests that non-majors can join the club as well.**
Ⓒ It will be sold during the first astronomy club meeting.
Ⓓ It helped to bring many non-major students to the club.

5. **Inference**

What will the student do next?

Ⓐ Choose the colors to be included in the shirt pattern
Ⓑ Call the club members to hear their opinions about the colors
Ⓒ Follow the woman to design some sample patterns for the shirt
Ⓓ **Receive a copy of sample patterns to show to club members**

2.
천문학 동아리 셔츠에 대한 직원의 의견은 무엇인가?

Ⓐ 멋지게 디자인되었다고 생각한다.
Ⓑ 너무 복잡하지 않을까 걱정된다.
Ⓒ 그 가격의 가치가 있다고 생각한다.
Ⓓ 보라색과 검은색이 필요하다고 생각한다.

3.
학생은 태양계의 행성에 대해 무엇이라고 말하는가?
두 개를 고르시오.

Ⓐ 명왕성은 행성 목록에서 제외되었다.
Ⓑ 해왕성은 여전히 왜소행성으로 여겨진다.
Ⓒ 명왕성은 행성으로 여겨지기에는 너무 작다.
Ⓓ 여섯 개의 주요 왜소행성이 있다.

4.
동아리 셔츠에 대해 옳은 것은 무엇인가?

Ⓐ 천문학 전공자들이 참여해야 한다는 것을 암시한다.
Ⓑ 비전공자들도 동아리에 가입할 수 있다고 제안한다.
Ⓒ 첫 번째 천문학 동아리 모임 때 판매될 것이다.
Ⓓ 많은 비전공자 학생들을 동아리로 데려오는 데 도움을 주었다.

5.
학생은 다음에 무엇을 할 것인가?

Ⓐ 셔츠 패턴에 포함될 색상들을 선택한다.
Ⓑ 색상과 관련된 의견을 얻기 위해 동아리 회원들에게 전화한다.
Ⓒ 셔츠의 샘플 패턴을 디자인하기 위해 여자를 따라간다.
Ⓓ 동아리 회원들에게 보여줄 샘플 패턴의 복사본을 받는다.

Lecture 1

 AT04_2

[1-6] Listen to part of a lecture in a biology class.

Man: Professor | Woman: Student

Ⓜ Not every flowering plant species relies upon other organisms for pollination; in fact, many practice what is called abiotic pollination, often by relying on the wind to disperse their pollen. However, the majority require some kind of pollinator organism to carry pollen from one flower to another. These

생물학 강의의 일부를 들으시오.

남자: 교수 | 여자: 학생

🅟 모든 개화 식물 종이 수분을 위해 다른 생물에 의존하는 것은 아닙니다. 사실, 많은 개화 식물 종은 꽃가루를 퍼뜨리기 위해 흔히 바람에 의존함으로써 비생물적 수분이라는 것을 실행합니다. 하지만 대다수의 경우에는 한 꽃에서 다른 꽃으로 꽃가루를 옮겨줄 일종의 꽃가루 매개자를 필요로 합니다. 이러한 꽃가루 매개자

pollinators are often invertebrates like butterflies and moths, beetles, flies, and of course bees. But, vertebrates like birds and bats often get involved as well. The relationship between a particular plant species and its pollinators is called pollination ecology. Simply put, the plant wants to attract a pollinator that is hungry and impatient, whereas the pollinator wants to eat as effortlessly as possible. However, the means by which a flower attracts the best possible pollinator is actually a complex relationship that depends upon many factors.

For the flower, what time of year it blooms as well as what time of day are important, as are how often it blooms, how many flowers bloom together, and the length of the blooming period. For example, many pollinators are migratory species, so a plant that attracts such species reaches its peak blooming cycle when that species is in the area. The physical characteristics of the flower specifically are also very important. The color, shape, and scent of a flower attract specific pollinators, and the nectar the flower produces to feed its visitor is also vital. For example, plants that attract nocturnal pollinators such as bats tend to have light colored petals — white, light yellow… Yes, Grace?

W Sir, you said bats. I thought that they have poor eyesight. Wouldn't scent be a better way to attract them?

M Their sense of smell does play an important role, but most bat species see quite well. Even the ones that use echolocation to find flying insects have decent vision. There's a species of water lily in the Amazon rainforest called Victoria amazonica, more commonly known as the giant Amazon water lily, which grows to immense proportions. Its chief pollinator is a type of scarab beetle that it attracts by using scent, color, and temperature. The first evening the flower blooms, it is female and has white petals and emits a strong pineapple-like scent. The flower also undergoes a chemical reaction that heats it up to 12 degrees Centigrade warmer than the surrounding air. This enables the scent to travel farther and offers the beetle a warm place to feed. After a beetle lands to eat, the flower closes around it, thereby ensuring that the beetle will be covered in pollen. Then the flower becomes male, turns red, and stops emitting the scent. When the beetle is released the next evening, it departs the now unattractive male flower to find another white female flower, which will fertilize with the pollen covering it. That's a pretty complicated process, right?

These relationships are also very delicate, and they can easily be disrupted. New plant species may distract pollinators when they are introduced, just as new organisms can compete with the original pollinators. One of the key ways this occurs is through agriculture. By creating fields of our crop plants, we can distract the majority of pollinators from other species in the area, and those plants will begin to disappear. Farmers in the rainforest have also introduced pollinators like bees to fertilize their crops, and this has disturbed the natural pollination relationships of the surrounding forest. Which raises another point... many of our crops depend on pollinator organisms to be fertilized, and without such fertilization, they will not produce the fruit or vegetables that we desire. When we use pesticides to prevent insects from consuming our plants, we may also be killing off the pollinators of those plants. If we eliminate pollinators, we are effectively ruining our crop yield, so pesticides should be very carefully applied.

변하고, 빨간색으로 바뀌며 향기를 더 이상 내뿜지 않습니다. 그 다음날 저녁에 풍뎅이가 풀려날 때, 풍뎅이는 다른 흰 암꽃을 찾기 위해 이제는 매력적이지 않은 그 수꽃을 떠나고, 그 흰 암꽃은 풍뎅이를 덮고 있는 꽃가루와 수정할 것입니다. 상당히 복잡한 과정이죠?

이런 관계들은 또한 매우 섬세하며 쉽게 방해를 받습니다. 새로운 생물들이 기존의 꽃가루 매개자들과 경쟁하는 것처럼, 새로운 식물 종이 도입되면 그것들이 꽃가루 매개자들을 분산시킬 수도 있습니다. 이것이 발생하는 주된 방식 중 하나가 농업을 통해서입니다. 농작물 밭을 만듦으로써 우리는 대다수 꽃가루 매개자들을 그 지역에 있는 다른 종들로부터 분산시킬 수 있으며, 그 식물들은 사라지기 시작할 것입니다. 우림에 있는 농부들은 그들의 농작물을 수정시킬 벌 같은 꽃가루 매개자를 도입했고, 이것은 주변 숲의 자연적인 수분 관계들을 어지럽혀 놓았습니다. 그것이 또 다른 문제점을 야기하는데... 우리가 키우는 농작물들은 꽃가루 매개자의 수분에 의존하고, 이러한 수분 없이는 우리가 원하는 과일과 채소를 생산하지 않을 것입니다. 곤충들이 우리가 키우는 식물들을 먹지 못하게 농약을 사용한다면, 이 식물들의 꽃가루 매개자들을 죽일 수도 있습니다. 우리가 꽃가루 매개자들을 제거한다면 곡물 수확을 실질적으로 망치는 것이기 때문에 농약은 매우 신중하게 사용되어야 합니다.

어휘

rely v 의지하다, 신뢰하다 | **organism** n 생물 | **pollination** n 수분 | **practice** v 실천하다, 연습하다 | **abiotic** adj 무생체의, 생물이 아닌 | **disperse** v 흩어지다, 해산하다 | **pollen** n 꽃가루 | **invertebrate** n 무척추동물 | **vertebrate** n 척추동물 | **particular** adj 특정한 | **ecology** n 생태학 | **impatient** adj 서두르는 | **effortlessly** adv 노력하지 않고 | **complex** adj 복잡한, 복합적인 | **migratory** adj 이동성의 | **peak** adj 최상의, 한창인 | **specifically** adv 특별히, 따로 | **nectar** n 꿀 | **nocturnal** adj 야행성의 | **petal** n 꽃잎 | **eyesight** n 시력 | **scent** n 향기 | **echolocation** n 반향 위치 측정 | **decent** adj 괜찮은, 제대로 된 | **rainforest** n 우림 | **immense** adj 거대한 | **proportion** n 크기, 규모 | **scarab** n 풍뎅이 | **emit** v 내뿜다, 발산하다 | **undergo** v 겪다 | **chemical reaction** 화학 반응 | **disrupt** v 방해하다, 지장을 주다 | **agriculture** n 농업 | **distract** v 집중이 안 되게 하다, 산만하게 하다 | **pesticide** n 농약, 살충제 | **eliminate** v 제거하다 | **yield** n (농작물 등의) 산출량

1. **Main Idea**

What is the lecture mainly about?

- Ⓐ The characteristics of various plant pollinators
- Ⓑ **The relationships between plants and their pollinators**
- Ⓒ The effects of agriculture on pollination ecology
- Ⓓ The destructive effects of some insects on pollination

2. **Detail**

What does the professor say is the ideal pollinator for a plant?

- Ⓐ An animal that is able to fly from one flower to another
- Ⓑ An animal that eats the pollen but not the nectar from the flower
- Ⓒ An animal that can transfer a lot of pollen to another flower
- Ⓓ **An animal that is hungry and quick to leave after feeding**

3. **Detail**

According to the professor, what are some features of a flowering plant that can affect how attractive it is to pollinators? Choose 2 answers.

- Ⓐ **Nectar**
- Ⓑ Size
- Ⓒ **Color**
- Ⓓ Location

4. **Inference**

According to the lecture, what can be inferred about the giant Amazon Water Lilies when they are red?

- Ⓐ They are ready to attract beetles for pollination.
- Ⓑ **They have recently opened after releasing a beetle.**
- Ⓒ They are heating up and emitting odor to attract pollinators.
- Ⓓ They are signaling that the plant has been fed upon.

5. **Connecting Contents**

Why does the professor mention agriculture?

- Ⓐ To tell the students that he believes it is the most destructive type of disturbance
- Ⓑ **To give an example of one factor that can disrupt natural pollination ecology**
- Ⓒ To illustrate how pollination ecology is affected by agriculture in a positive way
- Ⓓ To explain that it can provide new pollinators that could benefit the plants

---

1.

강의는 주로 무엇에 관한 것인가?

- Ⓐ 다양한 식물 꽃가루 매개자의 특징
- Ⓑ 식물과 꽃가루 매개자 간의 관계
- Ⓒ 농업이 수분 생태학에 끼치는 영향
- Ⓓ 몇몇 곤충들이 수분에 끼치는 파괴적 영향

2.

교수는 식물의 이상적인 꽃가루 매개자가 무엇이라고 말하는가?

- Ⓐ 한 꽃에서 다른 꽃으로 날아갈 수 있는 동물
- Ⓑ 꽃가루는 먹지만 꽃에서 나오는 꿀은 먹지 않는 동물
- Ⓒ 다른 꽃으로 많은 양의 꽃가루를 이동시키는 동물
- Ⓓ 굶주린 상태이며 먹은 뒤 빨리 떠나는 동물

3.

교수에 의하면, 꽃가루 매개자들에게 매력적으로 보일 수 있게 해주는 개화 식물의 특징은 무엇인가? 두 개를 고르시오.

- Ⓐ 꿀
- Ⓑ 크기
- Ⓒ 색깔
- Ⓓ 위치

4.

강의에 의하면, 거대한 아마존 수련이 빨간색일 때 그들에 대해 무엇을 추론할 수 있는가?

- Ⓐ 수분을 위해 풍뎅이를 끌어들일 준비가 되어 있다.
- Ⓑ 풍뎅이를 풀어준 지 얼마 안 됐다.
- Ⓒ 꽃가루 매개자를 끌어들이기 위해 온도를 높이고 향을 내뿜고 있다.
- Ⓓ 수련이 먹잇감이 됐다는 것을 표시하고 있다.

5.

교수는 왜 농업을 언급하는가?

- Ⓐ 가장 파괴적 유형의 방해물로 생각한다는 것을 학생들에게 말하기 위해
- Ⓑ 자연적인 수분 생태학을 방해할 수 있는 하나의 예시를 들기 위해
- Ⓒ 수분 생태학이 어떻게 농업에 의해 긍정적인 방향으로 영향을 받는지 보여주기 위해
- Ⓓ 식물에게 이로울 수 있는 새로운 매개자를 제공할 수 있다고 설명하기 위해

6. Function & Attitude

Listen again to part of the lecture. Then answer the question.

> W Sir, you said bats. I thought that they have poor eyesight. Wouldn't scent be a better way to attract them?
> M Their sense of smell does play an important role, but most bat species see quite well. Even the ones that use echolocation to find flying insects have decent vision.

Why does the professor say this:

> M Their sense of smell does play an important role, but most bat species see quite well.

Ⓐ To show the student that bats usually prefer scent over colors
Ⓑ To explain a pollinator mostly attracted to the scent of a flower
Ⓒ To illustrate that the majority of plants attract pollinators in daytime
Ⓓ To tell the student that she has stated a common misconception

---

Conversation 2

[1-5] Listen to part of a conversation between a student and a professor.

Man: Professor | Woman: Student

W Thank you for seeing me without an appointment, Professor Collins.
M No problem, Janice, my schedule is open this morning. What can I do for you?
W I was hoping to get some advice from you. I was thinking about transferring to another university.
M Really? May I ask why?
W Well, I'm not really satisfied with the teacher certification program here, so I was thinking of transferring to Central University. I heard that they have a very good program, and it is much closer to my parent's house, so I wouldn't have to stay in the dorms there.
M That is true, they do have a good program there, but it is actually quite similar to ours.
W Is it? Oh, I didn't realize that.

M: Yes, and I have a question for you. I can see that you clearly enjoy studying science. You always participate actively in lectures, and the laboratory assistants have said that they have to force you to leave so they can lock up for the night.

W: They told you that? It only happened… Ok, it happened a few times…

M: No need to be embarrassed. That kind of dedication is admirable. But, this is my question. Have you considered that maybe teaching just isn't right for you? Perhaps your true calling is being a scientist and not a high school science teacher.

W: Um, honestly, yes, I have. But, I figured that teaching would be an easier industry to get into. There is a lot of competition for research positions at universities and companies. Teaching would mean a steadier paycheck, you know?

M: Yes, I know. However, it seems clear to me that you may not really be cut out for teaching. Which is fine, not everyone can handle that profession. And if you are not happy preparing to do that kind of work, then doing it professionally will not make you any happier.

W: So, what do you think I should do?

M: I think you should change the focus of your major. Instead of science for secondary education, you should major in just science. Well, not just science. You will need to choose a type of science if you want to be a scientist. Which branch of science do you like the most?

W: Chemistry!

M: I figured as much.

W: Do you think I could become a chemical engineer? I would really like that.

M: Of course! First, you need to fill out the form to change your major, and then rearrange your schedule with your advisor. You cannot add any courses to your schedule for this semester, though.

W: That's fine. I can use the time to study in preparation for next semester.

M: Perfect, go see your advisor and she will prepare the form for you.

어휘

appointment n 약속 | transfer v 옮기다, 편입하다 | certification n 증명, 증명서 | participate v 참여하다 | actively adv 적극적으로 | laboratory n 실험실 | assistant n 조교 | dedication n 전념, 헌신 | calling n 소명 | industry n 산업 | competition n 경쟁 | steady adj 꾸준한, 변함 없는 | paycheck n 급료 | rearrange v 바꾸다, 재배열하다 | preparation n 준비

---

1. Main Idea
Why is the student talking to the professor?

A To determine which subject would be the best to major in
B To ask about the professor's experiences as a college student
C To get advice about transferring to a different university
D To decide which classes she needs to take the next semester

2. Detail
Which of these statements about the student is true?

A She is a senior at Central University.
B She is majoring in secondary education.
C She wants to live on campus for a while.
D She already took a few biology courses.

3. Function & Attitude
Why does the professor say this:

> M However, it seems clear to me that you may not really be cut out for teaching.

A To suggest that the student should consider a different kind of change
B To criticize the student for not looking for better options
C To tell the student how brave she is for deciding to be a teacher
D To give an example of his own poor decision-making in the past

4. Detail
What does the professor suggest the student do?

A Transfer to Central University
B Take more education courses
C Change her major to chemistry
D Visit her advisor for advice

1.
학생이 교수와 대화를 하는 이유는 무엇인가?

A 어떤 과목을 전공으로 택하면 가장 좋을지 결정하기 위해
B 교수가 대학생이었을 때의 경험에 대해 묻기 위해
C 다른 학교로 편입하는 것에 대한 조언을 얻기 위해
D 다음 학기에 어떤 과목들을 들어야 하는지 결정하기 위해

2.
다음 중 학생에 대해 옳은 것은?

A 센트럴 대학의 4학년생이다.
B 중등 교육을 전공하고 있다.
C 한동안 교내에서 살기를 원한다.
D 이미 몇 가지 생물학 과목들을 수강했다.

3.
교수는 왜 이렇게 말하는가:

> 하지만 학생이 교직에 안 맞을지도 모른다는 확신이 드네요.

A 학생이 다른 종류의 변화를 고려해봐야 한다고 제안하기 위해
B 그 학생이 더 좋은 선택지를 찾지 않는 것을 비난하기 위해
C 그 학생에게 그녀가 교사가 되기로 결정한 것이 얼마나 용기 있는 선택이었는지 말해주기 위해
D 과거에 자신이 잘못된 결정을 내렸던 예를 들기 위해

4.
교수는 학생에게 무엇을 할 것을 제안하는가?

A 센트럴 대학으로 편입하기
B 더 많은 교육학 과목을 수강하기
C 전공을 화학으로 바꾸기
D 조언을 얻기 위해 지도 교수를 만나보기

5. Inference

What will most likely happen next?

Ⓐ The professor will sign the form that the student has filled out.
Ⓑ **The student will go see her advisor to do some paperwork.**
Ⓒ The student will move back to her hometown and change her major.
Ⓓ The advisor will come to give the student the form she needs.

5.

다음에 무슨 일이 일어날 것 같은가?

Ⓐ 교수는 학생이 기입한 서류에 서명을 할 것이다.
Ⓑ 학생은 서류 작업을 하기 위해 지도 교수를 찾아갈 것이다.
Ⓒ 학생은 고향으로 돌아가 전공을 바꿀 것이다.
Ⓓ 지도 교수가 학생에게 필요한 서식을 주기 위해 올 것이다.

Lecture 2

[1-6] Listen to part of a lecture in an ancient history class.

Man: Professor | Woman: Student

M In ancient times, the maximum sustainable size of a city was often determined by the availability of fresh water. For this reason, many began as settlements on the banks of rivers or the shores of lakes. As the population grew, these initial water sources would become insufficient, and sometimes too heavily polluted to support the community. In order to compensate, people would locate nearby springs, dig wells, and collect rainwater in cisterns. Ultimately, these too would reach their limits, and the population would become fairly stable or decline. Eventually, engineers came up with a way to bring water into a city from many kilometers away: aqueducts.

Aqueducts were developed independently in many societies, but it was through ancient Rome that they reached their highest state of development. Roman aqueducts were not only very efficient, but they also developed into beautiful marvels of engineering. Considering how bad the city's water situation was, it is easy to see why they became so talented at constructing aqueducts. There were several springs within the city walls, but the water that came from them was infamous for its horrible taste. In addition, the water from the Tiber River was heavily polluted and rife with disease. So by around 300 BCE, the population's demand had long exceeded its supply. In 312 BCE, censor Appius Claudius Caecus commissioned the city's

고대 역사 강의의 일부를 들으시오.

남자: 교수 | 여자: 학생

고대에 유지 가능한 도시의 최대 크기는 이용 가능한 수원에 의해 종종 결정되었습니다. 이러한 이유 때문에 많은 도시들이 강둑이나 호수 주변의 정착지로 출발했죠. 인구가 늘어남에 따라 이런 초기의 수원은 부족하게 되고, 때때로 도시를 부양할 수 없을 만큼 너무 많이 오염되기도 합니다. 보충을 위해 사람들은 부근의 샘을 찾거나 우물을 파거나 물탱크에 빗물을 모았죠. 결국에는 이러한 것들도 한계에 달하고, 인구는 꽤 안정이 되거나 줄어들거나 합니다. 마침내 기술자들은 수 킬로미터가 떨어진 곳으로부터 도시로 물을 끌어오는 방법을 떠올리게 되었습니다. 바로 송수관이죠.

송수관은 많은 사회에서 독자적으로 발달되었지만, 가장 높은 발달 단계에 이르게 되었던 것은 바로 고대 로마를 통해서였습니다. 로마의 송수관은 매우 효율적이었을 뿐만 아니라 공학 기술의 아름다운 경이로움으로 발전하였습니다. 도시의 수도 상황이 얼마나 좋지 않았는지를 고려해 보면, 그들이 송수관 건설에 있어 어떻게 그러한 재능을 발휘하게 되었는지 쉽게 알 수 있습니다. 도시 성벽 안에는 여러 개의 샘이 있었지만 거기서 나오는 물은 지독한 맛으로 악명이 높았습니다. 게다가 티베르강 강물은 심하게 오염되어 질병이 들끓었습니다. 그래서 기원전 300년경, 사람들의 수요는 그 공급을 일찌감치 초과했죠. 기원 전 312년, 감찰관이던 아피우스 클라우디우스 스카이쿠스는 도시 최초

first aqueduct, the Aqua Appia. The spring that fed the aqueduct was located about 16 kilometers from Rome, and it ran through a buried conduit that dropped in elevation by just 10 meters by the time it reached the city. It supplied about 75,500 cubic meters of water per day into a fountain in the city's cattle market. This market was a public place at one of the lowest elevations in the city, making it ideal for this purpose… Yes, Helen, you have a question?

W Did you just say a buried conduit? I thought that the aqueducts were soaring bridges supported by complex arches, not buried pipes…

M Well, you're not wrong. Most of what we have left of them today is the arches and bridges that were used to span rivers and valleys. In fact, the second aqueduct built for Rome, the Old Anio, entered the city using an arch-supported conduit. Their construction rapidly spread throughout the empire, and hundreds were built. The arch supported bridges, sometimes called arcades, reached truly amazing heights and lengths, and they weren't just functional, they were beautiful. Many of them are popular tourist attractions even today. Surprisingly, a few of them are still used for their original purpose.

However, most of their length was underground conduits carved from stone, built with cement and brick, or made from clay or lead pipes. But these are no less of an engineering marvel. Remember what I said about the Aqua Appia? Over its entire 16 kilometer length, it only descended in elevation by 10 meters! That is a phenomenal achievement, and it was very necessary. They needed the water to descend gradually. If it flowed too quickly, it could cause serious problems. It would erode the conduit walls and reach the catchment pools at great speed, easily overflowing them. By 300 CE, a total of 11 aqueducts supplied Rome with a staggering amount of water from mountain springs as far as 90 kilometers away. Rome had a population of around 1,000,000 people at that time, but they had more water than what they knew what to do with. The water was used primarily for drinking and bathing — Rome had an extravagant bathing culture — and of course, some was diverted for irrigation and industry, but most of the rest was used to flush out waste from their extensive sewer system.

However, after the empire ended, most of the aqueducts were neglected. They still supplied water, but without regular care and maintenance, they began to fall apart. They would leak, bridges began to crumble, and many underground conduits became clogged with mineral deposits. Some were refurbished and upgraded during the Renaissance, but most of them have become ruins.

그러나 제국이 멸망한 이후, 대부분의 수도관은 방치되었죠. 그것들은 여전히 물을 공급했지만 유지 보수가 적절히 이루어지지 않아서 무너지기 시작했습니다. 수도관들은 새거나, 다리들은 무너지기 시작했고, 많은 지하 수로는 광물 침전물로 막히게 되었어요. 일부는 르네상스 시대에 개조되고 업그레이드 되었지만 대부분은 폐허가 되었습니다.

어휘

maximum adj 최대의 | **sustainable** adj 지속 가능한 | **availability** n 유효성, 유용성 | **settlement** n 정착 | **bank** n 둑, 제방 | **shore** n 기슭, 해안 | **population** n 인구 | **initial** adj 초기의, 처음의 | **insufficient** adj 부족한 | **polluted** adj 오염된 | **compensate** v 보상하다 | **cistern** n 물탱크, 수조 | **stable** adj 안정적인 | **decline** v 감소하다 | **aqueduct** n 송수관 | **independently** adv 독자적으로, 독립적으로 | **marvel** n 경이로운 것 | **construct** v 건설하다, 구성하다 | **infamous** adj 악명 높은 | **rife** adj 만연한 | **exceed** v 초과하다 | **commission** v 의뢰하다, 주문하다 | **conduit** n 도관 | **elevation** n 높이, 고도 | **fountain** n 분수 | **cattle** n 가축 | **ideal** adj 이상적인 | **soar** v 솟구치다, 치솟다 | **span** v 가로지르다 | **arcade** n 아케이드 (아치로 둘러싸인 통로) | **underground** adj 지하의 | **carve** v 조각하다, 깎아서 만들다 | **descend** v 내려가다 | **gradually** adv 서서히 | **erode** v 침식시키다, 풍화시키다 | **overflow** v 넘치다 | **staggering** adj 놀라운, 엄청난 | **primarily** adv 주로 | **extravagant** adj 사치스러운 | **divert** v 방향을 바꾸게 하다 | **irrigation** n 관개 | **flush** v 흘려 보내다 | **neglect** v 방치하다 | **crumble** v 무너지다, 부서지다 | **clog** v 막다, 막히다 | **deposit** n 침전물 | **refurbish** v 재단장하다

1. Main Idea
What is the lecture mainly about?

A The complex construction process of conduits
B The features of an ancient Roman technology
C The Roman Empire's need for water sources
D The difficulties of building and maintaining aqueducts

2. Function & Attitude
What is the professor's opinion about the Roman aqueducts?

A He doubts if it was necessary to build them with arches and bridges.
B He is amazed at how rapidly the water moved inside the conduits.
C He believes they contributed to the advancement of the empire.
D He thinks they put a limit on the population of the empire.

1.
강의는 주로 무엇에 관한 것인가?

A 도관의 복잡한 건설 과정
B 한 고대 로마 기술의 특징
C 로마 제국의 수원의 필요성
D 송수관의 건설과 유지의 어려움

2.
로마 송수관에 대한 교수의 의견은 무엇인가?

A 꼭 아치와 다리를 써서 지어야 했는지 의심한다.
B 물이 도관 내에서 빠르게 흘렀다는 데 놀라고 있다.
C 그것이 제국의 발전에 기여했다고 믿는다.
D 제국의 인구에 제한을 가했다고 생각한다.

3. Detail
What aspect of aqueducts was NOT mentioned in the lecture?

Ⓐ **The amount of time they took to build**
Ⓑ Their aesthetic value
Ⓒ How well constructed they were
Ⓓ The great distances they covered

4. Detail
According to the professor, what were requirements for building an effective aqueduct? Choose 2 answers.

Ⓐ **A gradual degree of descent**
Ⓑ A water source located far from the city
Ⓒ A water source near a mountain
Ⓓ **A downward route from the water source to the city**

5. Connecting Contents
Why does the professor mention the size of ancient Rome's population?

Ⓐ **To explain why the Romans needed to transport so much water**
Ⓑ To point out that the water source had to come from a higher elevation
Ⓒ To emphasize why water was so important for their survival
Ⓓ To describe the various methods of bringing water into the city

6. Inference
What can be inferred from the professor's explanations about the aqueducts after the end of the empire?

Ⓐ Their productivity is often praised by modern scientists.
Ⓑ Some of them are still used in some parts of Rome.
Ⓒ **Many of them no longer can function as aqueducts.**
Ⓓ They need special care to provide service to people.

3.
강의에서 언급되지 않은 송수관의 특징은 무엇인가?

Ⓐ 건설되는데 걸린 시간
Ⓑ 미적 가치
Ⓒ 얼마나 잘 건설되었는지
Ⓓ 걸쳐있던 엄청난 거리

4.
교수에 의하면, 효율적인 송수관을 건설하는 데 필요한 요건은 무엇인가? 두 개를 고르시오.

Ⓐ 점진적인 하강 각도
Ⓑ 도시에서 먼 곳에 위치한 수원
Ⓒ 산 근처의 수원
Ⓓ 수원에서 도시로 하향하는 루트

5.
교수는 왜 고대 로마 제국의 인구 규모를 언급하는가?

Ⓐ 로마인들이 왜 그렇게 많은 물을 수송해야 했는지 설명하기 위해
Ⓑ 수원이 높은 지대에 있어야 했다는 것을 지적하기 위해
Ⓒ 왜 물이 그들의 생존에 그렇게 중요했는지 강조하기 위해
Ⓓ 물을 도시로 가져오는 다양한 방법을 묘사하기 위해

6.
로마 제국이 멸망한 뒤의 송수관에 대한 교수의 설명에서 무엇을 추론할 수 있는가?

Ⓐ 그들의 생산성은 현대 과학자들에게 자주 칭송 받는다.
Ⓑ 몇 개는 여전히 로마 시대의 몇 곳에서 사용되고 있다.
Ⓒ 대다수가 더 이상 송수관의 기능을 할 수 없다.
Ⓓ 사람들에게 물을 제공하기 위해서 특별한 관리를 필요로 한다.

Lecture 3

[1-6] Listen to part of a lecture in an archaeology class.

Man: Student | Woman: Professor

W When Bill Saturno and his team began surveying the San Bartolo site, they were hoping to find something — anything really — connected to the Mayan civilization. The Maya lived in and around the Yucatan Peninsula from around 2000 BCE until the arrival of the Spanish in the early 1600s. Their culture reached its peak between 250 and 900 CE... This was the period during which they reached their highest levels of construction and artistic expression and is referred to as the Classic Period. During this period they built monumental pyramids, painted extensive murals, and developed their detailed hieroglyphic writing system. Their population also expanded to its greatest size, numbering several million people. The civilization consisted of a conglomeration of city states and the center of power changed periodically, with some cities ruled by others. After 900 CE, their society almost entirely disappeared due to a combination of factors. Some of them survived and tried to rebuild, but they never regained their former glory. Eventually, their cities were reclaimed by the jungle, and they vanished from history.

Saturno and crew were in an uninhabited stretch of the Guatemalan jungle in 2001 looking for traces of their civilization when they made a startling discovery. After a long day of surveying, Saturno ducked into a cave-like hollow to escape from the oppressive jungle heat. When he turned on his flashlight and aimed it at the walls around him, he learned that he was in no cave, but rather a room decorated with murals that would later prove to be contained in the base of a pyramid 85 feet tall... Yes, Nathan?

M Why didn't they know about the pyramid? I mean, 85 feet tall? That's more than half the height of the Great Pyramid at Giza. How could they miss that?

W: **Well, as I mentioned earlier, the jungle reclaimed their cities.** The city had been abandoned around 100 CE. After almost two millennia, it looked like a tall, fairly steep hill. They were on the jungle floor with layers of foliage blocking out the sky and obscuring the landscape. This is why their task was so difficult, and had produced so little results. After locating that room, however, Saturno knew that they had found something significant. The murals were carbon-dated to around 100 BCE, which was incredible! That pushed back the date for the earliest known Mayan paintings by 700 years! Not only that, but they were in remarkably good condition and extended for several meters along the wall. Saturno was certain that there had to be more buildings nearby, but without knowing exactly where to look, the search would be painstaking and arduous. Then Saturno received help from an unexpected source: NASA.

M: NASA? The National Aeronautics and Space Administration helped him out?

W: They are one and the same. NASA's satellites regularly scan the surface of the Earth using a variety of electromagnetic frequencies, and they offered him a map of the region taken with an infrared imaging system. If you'll direct your attention to this screen, I'll show you an image they gave him.

The blue and red areas are normal jungle vegetation, but the yellow spots you see are places where the jungle has grown over buildings and stone roads and plazas. Using this imagery, Saturno and his team went directly to the areas indicated and confirmed that there were indeed structures there. Today, the complex is known to contain 140 structures including two pyramids, a temple, a royal tomb, and a large residential area.

It is not entirely clear why the vegetation shows up as different colors on the scan, but there are theories. It may have to do with differences in water retention caused by the stone underlying the soil. There is also the possibility that the calcium carbonate from the limestone is leaching into the plants, changing them chemically. Either way, the method has proven to be very reliable.

어휘

survey v 조사하다 | peak n 정점 | construction n 건축 | artistic adj 예술의 | expression n 표현 | monumental adj 기념비적인 | extensive adj 대규모의 | mural n 벽화 | detailed adj 섬세한 | hieroglyphic adj 상형 문자의 | population n 인구 | expand v 확장하다 | civilization n 문명 | conglomeration n 집합체 | periodically adv 주기적으로 | combination n 결합 | former adj 이전의 | glory n 영광 | reclaim v 되찾다 | vanish v 사라지다 | uninhabited adj 사람이 살지 않는 | stretch n (길게 뻗은) 지역, 구간 | trace n 흔적 | startling adj 놀라운 | discovery n 발견 | duck v 숙이다, 수그리다 | hollow n 빈 공간 | escape v 탈출하다 | oppressive adj 억압하는 | flashlight n 손전등 | abandon v 버리다 | steep adj 가파른 | foliage n 나뭇잎 | obscure v 보기 어렵게 하다 | landscape n 풍경 | significant adj 중요한 | remarkably adv 굉장히 | painstaking adj 고통스러운, 공을 들이는 | arduous adj 고된 | unexpected adj 예상치 못한 | aeronautics n 항공학 | regularly adv 정기적으로 | surface n 지면 | electromagnetic adj 전자기의 | frequency n 주파 | infrared adj 적외선의 | vegetation n 초목 | confirm v 확인하다 | complex n 복합 건물, 단지 | temple n 사원 | tomb n 무덤 | residential adj 주거의 | retention n 보유, 잔류 | possibility n 가능성 | limestone n 석회암 | chemically adv 화학적으로 | reliable adj 믿을 만한

1. Main Idea
What is the lecture mainly about?
- Ⓐ Different methods used for discovering Mayan relics
- Ⓑ Reasons behind the disappearance of an ancient culture
- **Ⓒ Bill Saturno's discovery of an ancient settlement**
- Ⓓ Murals found in the ruins of the Mayan civilization

2. Detail
How did Bill Saturno discover the cave with ancient murals?
- Ⓐ He had a map that was provided by NASA.
- **Ⓑ He accidentally entered it while taking a rest.**
- Ⓒ He was equipped with electromagnetic imaging technology.
- Ⓓ He used a satellite to scan the surrounding area.

3. Detail
What significant role did NASA play in the discovery of Mayan ruins?
- Ⓐ NASA granted Saturno access to its space satellites.
- **Ⓑ NASA provided Saturno with infrared images.**
- Ⓒ NASA allowed Saturno to use their facilities for research.
- Ⓓ NASA gave Saturno a map from the ancient Mayans.

4. Detail
What do the shades of yellow in the infrared image represent?
- Ⓐ Rainforest
- Ⓑ Mountains
- **Ⓒ Ruins**
- Ⓓ Desert

1.
강의는 주로 무엇에 대한 것인가?
- Ⓐ 마야 유적 발견에 사용된 다양한 방법들
- Ⓑ 한 고대 문명이 소멸한 이유들
- **Ⓒ 빌 새터노의 고대 정착지 발견**
- Ⓓ 마야 문명의 폐허에서 발견된 벽화들

2.
빌 새터노는 고대 벽화가 있는 동굴을 어떻게 발견했는가?
- Ⓐ NASA에서 제공해 준 지도를 가지고 있었다.
- **Ⓑ 잠시 쉬는 동안 우연히 들어가게 되었다.**
- Ⓒ 전자기의 이미지 기술을 보유하고 있었다.
- Ⓓ 근처의 지역을 스캔하기 위해 위성을 사용했다.

3.
마야 유적의 발견에서 NASA는 어떤 중요한 역할을 했는가?
- Ⓐ NASA는 새터노에게 자신들의 우주 위성 이용을 승인했다.
- **Ⓑ NASA는 적외선 이미지를 새터노에게 제공했다.**
- Ⓒ NASA는 새터노가 연구에 자신들의 시설을 이용할 수 있도록 허락했다.
- Ⓓ NASA는 새터노에게 고대 마야인들의 지도를 주었다.

4.
적외선 이미지에 나타난 노란색은 무엇을 나타내는가?
- Ⓐ 열대 우림
- Ⓑ 산
- **Ⓒ 유적**
- Ⓓ 사막

5. **Inference**

What can be inferred about the discovery at San Bartolo?

Ⓐ The local people were aware of the location of the ancient ruins.
Ⓑ There are many ancient sites and ruins yet to be discovered.
Ⓒ The discovery could not have been made without NASA's help.
Ⓓ Saturno has found all of the Mayan ruins in Guatemala.

6. **Function & Attitude**

Listen again to part of the lecture. Then answer the question.

> Ⓜ Why didn't they know about the pyramid? I mean, 85 feet tall? That's more than half the height of the Great Pyramid at Giza. How could they miss that?
> Ⓦ Well, as I mentioned earlier, the jungle reclaimed their cities.

Why does the professor say this:

> Ⓦ Well, as I mentioned earlier, the jungle reclaimed their cities.

Ⓐ To remind the student of what the scientists were dealing with
Ⓑ To indicate that the student misunderstood what she said
Ⓒ To illustrate what happened to the cities after the Maya abandoned them
Ⓓ To explain the differences between the two environments the pyramids are found in

---

5.

산 바트롤로 발견에 대해 무엇을 추론할 수 있는가?

Ⓐ 지역 주민들은 고대 유적의 위치를 알고 있었다.
Ⓑ 아직 발견되지 않은 고대 현장과 유적이 많다.
Ⓒ NASA의 도움 없이 이 발견은 있을 수 없었을 것이다.
Ⓓ 새터노는 과테말라에 있는 모든 마야 유적들을 발견했다.

6.

강의의 일부를 다시 듣고 질문에 답하시오.

> 남 왜 그들은 피라미드에 대해 몰랐나요? 제 말은, 85피트나 되는데요? 기자의 대피라미드 높이의 반절보다 더 높잖아요. 어떻게 그걸 놓칠 수 있었죠?
> 여 음, 앞서 말했지만 도시는 다시 정글이 되었어요.

교수는 왜 이렇게 말하는가:

> 여 음, 앞서 말했지만 도시는 다시 정글이 되었어요.

Ⓐ 과학자들이 어떤 문제에 대처하고 있었는지를 학생에게 상기시키려고
Ⓑ 자신이 한 말을 학생이 오해했다고 말하려고
Ⓒ 마야인들이 도시들을 버린 이후 그 도시들에 무슨 일이 일어났는지 설명하려고
Ⓓ 피라미드들이 발견된 두 환경들 사이의 차이점들을 설명하려고

Actual Test 05

본서 | P. 100

Conversation 1	1. Ⓓ	2. Ⓐ	3. Ⓒ	4. Ⓐ	5. Ⓑ, Ⓒ	
Lecture 1	1. Ⓑ	2. Ⓓ	3. Ⓓ	4. Ⓐ, Ⓔ	5. Ⓐ	6. Ⓒ
Lecture 2	1. Ⓑ	2. Ⓓ	3. Ⓐ	4. Ⓒ	5. Ⓑ	6. Ⓒ
Conversation 2	1. Ⓒ	2. Ⓐ	3. Ⓒ	4. Ⓒ	5. Ⓑ	
Lecture 3	1. Ⓐ	2. Ⓑ	3. Ⓒ	4. Ⓓ	5. Ⓑ, Ⓒ	6. Ⓐ

● 내가 맞은 문제 유형의 개수를 적어 보고 어느 유형에 취약한지 확인해 봅시다.

문제 유형	맞은 개수
Main Idea	5
Detail	13
Connecting Contents	3
Function & Attitude	2
Inference	5
Total	28

Conversation 1

[1-5] Listen to part of a conversation between a student and a professor.

Man: Professor | Woman: Student

W: Professor Greene, do you have a minute?
M: Hi, Traci, I certainly do. Do you have a question?
W: Yes, but I'm not really sure how to ask it.
M: I'm always open to criticism. Fire away.
W: Oh, I'm not here to criticize; I just didn't understand something you said. You said that it is just as important to do public relations for yourself as it is for a company or other organization.
M: Yes, that is true.
W: But, how can you do that? How do you do PR for yourself? How do you create a positive image of yourself for other people?
M: It's quite simple really. You know how important it is to make a good first impression, right? It's the same thing. How you dress and act when you meet a prospective employer or customer is extremely important. Even the way that you answer the telephone is important. You may seem uninterested or rude, or you could sound warm and friendly. Which way do you think would be better?
W: Ok, I think I see what you mean. The way that we act affects the way that others think about us. So, it is important to make conscious decisions about our own behavior all of the time.
M: Exactly!
W: Well, I must have made some good decisions at the job fair last month.
M: Really?
W: Yes, two of the companies have offered me internship positions.
M: That's great! Have you decided which offer to accept?
W: That's the main reason I came here to see you today.
M: Okay, can you tell me about the positions?
W: One is at a talent agency called Face Forward. They specialize in helping aspiring entertainers get established. The other is at an online news service.
M: Those are two very different options.
W: I know, that is why it is so hard for me to choose. If they offered a salary, that could give me a deciding factor, but neither does.

M: Yes, that is true of most internship positions. They only offer practical experience. It all depends on what industry you want to get into. If you are interested in the entertainment industry, then working at a talent agency is a great idea. However, getting experience in journalism can open many doors for you.

W: Is that so? How?

M: Well, that's because it gives you the opportunity to do many different tasks: investigative journalism, writing, proofreading, editing, data entry, computer programming… the list goes on. And, you could still work with the entertainment industry. Most news sites have an entertainment section.

W: That's true. I hadn't thought about it that way. So, that position would definitely provide me with the most opportunity for experience.

M: Yes, that is how I see it.

W: Alright, then I think I know which one to choose. Thank you for your help, Professor Greene!

어휘

criticism n 비평, 비판 | **fire away** 말하세요, 질문하세요 | **public relations** 홍보 | **organization** n 조직, 단체 | **prospective** adj 유망한, 장래의 | **employer** n 고용주 | **customer** n 고객 | **conscious** adj 의식하는 | **specialize** v 전문적으로 다루다 | **aspiring** adj 장차 ~가 되려는 | **entertainer** n 연예인, 엔터테이너 | **establish** v 자리잡게 하다 | **salary** n 봉급 | **factor** n 요인 | **practical** adj 실질적인 | **industry** n 산업 | **journalism** n 저널리즘, 언론계 | **investigative** adj 조사의, 수사의 | **proofread** v 교정을 보다

---

1. Main Idea

Why did the woman go to see her professor?

Ⓐ To ask a question about the topic that was discussed in class

Ⓑ To question the connection between public relations and first impressions

Ⓒ To request the professor's opinion about personal public relations

Ⓓ To get guidance on a decision regarding the two internships she was offered

1.
여자는 왜 교수를 만나러 갔는가?

Ⓐ 수업 중에 논의된 주제에 관한 질문을 하기 위해

Ⓑ 홍보와 첫 인상과의 관계에 대해 질문하기 위해

Ⓒ 개인적 홍보에 대한 교수의 의견을 구하기 위해

Ⓓ 제안받은 두 인턴직에 관한 결정에 대해 교수의 지도를 받기 위해

2. **Function & Attitude**

Why does the professor say this:

> M I'm always open to criticism. Fire away.

Ⓐ **To encourage the student to ask anything she wants to**
Ⓑ To suggest the student work harder to understand the topic
Ⓒ To emphasize that criticizing someone can be hard at times
Ⓓ To tell the student that he likes it when students criticize him

3. **Detail**

What point does the professor make when he discusses answering the telephone?

Ⓐ People try to use personal public relations unconsciously in their daily lives.
Ⓑ Public relations can only be applied by businesses and corporations.
Ⓒ **Personal public relations is a good way to improve a person's reputation.**
Ⓓ Public relations should be practiced every day to be developed further.

4. **Inference**

What does the professor imply about the internship position at Face Forward?

Ⓐ **It might not be able to provide the range of work experience the student wants.**
Ⓑ He already knows some students that have applied at the talent agency.
Ⓒ It would be a better choice than interning at the online news service since it suits her.
Ⓓ Even though it is a talent agency, it rarely deals with the entertainment industry.

5. **Detail**

What does the professor say about the online news service internship? Choose 2 answers.

Ⓐ It is sponsored by the entertainment industry.
Ⓑ **It can provide experience in journalism.**
Ⓒ **It has diverse sections including entertainment.**
Ⓓ It organizes various events related to journalism.

Lecture 1

[1-6] Listen to part of a lecture in an art history class.

Man: Professor | Woman: Student

M The ceiling of the Sistine Chapel is considered to be one of the most significant artworks of the Renaissance. The frescoes that adorn the ceiling, commissioned by Pope Julius II, were painted by Michelangelo between 1508 and 1512. Pope Julius II was the nephew of the pope who had the original building constructed between 1477 and 1480, Pope Sixtus IV. That is where the name of the chapel comes from — the Latin name Sixtus in Italian is Sisto. The chapel serves as the Pope's private chapel, and the selection of a new pope also takes place there.

W Professor, I read an article that said Michelangelo was quite reluctant to accept this commission. Is it true?

M Yes, and he had many reasons. First and foremost, he considered himself a sculptor rather than a painter. The huge workload also meant that he would be unable to take on other projects as he worked on it. In fact, the other commission he had at the time was to make sculptures for the Pope's tomb, so it meant he would be wholly dependent upon the money that the Pope paid him. Despite his objections, the Pope insisted that he do the paintings. However, Michelangelo did win one major concession from Julius II. The Pope requested that Michelangelo replace the current ceiling, which depicted a starry, night sky, with a geometric design with the 12 Apostles painted as large figures along the walls. Michelangelo disliked the design, and called it a "poor thing." He had much grander ideas, and the Pope gave him pretty much a free hand in choosing the images to paint. His final composition includes 343 figures in various scenes from the Old Testament and portraits of prophets believed to have predicted the coming of Jesus.

When Michelangelo actually began to paint the frescoes, he was faced with a variety of challenges. Firstly, the fresco technique is very demanding. The paint is added to plaster that must be wet to hold the colors. This means that fresh plaster had to be applied every day for him to paint on. The plaster also dries fairly quickly, and that locks in the color. So he had to plan the images in advance and couldn't make many corrections. If you look at the ceiling today, you can still see where the divisions between some days of painting were, because of the plaster. For this reason, Michelangelo began with images that showed stories from later in the Bible. He wanted to paint the pictures of God and Creation after he had refined his skill.

W Didn't he take a break from work for a while?

M He did. He took a break from the project in 1510, and when he returned to it, his style had indeed changed. He used fewer figures and the images were much more expressive and dynamic. The scenes he painted in the final years of the project, like The Creation of Adam and Eve, are regarded as some of his best.

The second great challenge was where he had to paint. The ceiling of the chapel is huge, and it is about 20 meters above the floor! Since the chapel was actively being used, he could not use a simple platform that was built up from the floor. It was suggested that he use a scaffold hanging from ropes, but he discarded that idea since it would leave holes in the ceiling. Instead, he devised a platform that was supported by beams that went through the walls near the tops of the windows. After he had painted half of the fresco, the platform was moved and he painted the other side.

The third challenge he faced was the physical demands of the project. He could not see the painting from the floor, so he could not see whole images. He had to paint large pictures only inches away from his face. Since it was on the ceiling, he had to spend four years painting above his head, so his body suffered. His entire body hurt, especially his arms, legs, and back, and his eyesight was permanently damaged. He even wrote a poem describing his terrible working conditions. Upon completion of his monumental task, he received immediate and unanimous praise. Whether that acclaim eased his physical pain or not, it certainly secured his fame for centuries to come.

라서 색이 고정되어 버려요. 그래서 미켈란젤로는 그림을 그리기 전 미리 이미지를 계획해야 했고 수정을 많이 할 수가 없었습니다. 오늘날 천장을 보면 석회 때문에 그림이 그려진 날들 사이의 경계선들이 어디 있는지를 여전히 볼 수 있어요. 이 이유로 인해 미켈란젤로는 성경의 후반에 나오는 이야기들을 나타내는 그림을 먼저 시작했습니다. 그는 하나님과 천지창조에 대한 그림을 자신의 기술을 더 다듬은 뒤에 그리고 싶어 했어요.

여 일을 잠시 쉬지는 않았나요?

남 그랬습니다. 1510년에 일을 잠시 내려놓았고, 다시 돌아왔을 때는 실제로 기법이 달라져 있었어요. 더 적은 수의 인물들을 그렸고, 그림은 훨씬 더 표현력이 뛰어났고 역동적이었습니다. 그가 이 작업의 말년에 그린 장면들, 즉 아담과 이브의 창조와 같은 장면들이 미켈란젤로 최고의 작품들 중 하나로 여겨집니다.

두 번째의 힘겨운 도전은 그가 그림을 그려야 하는 곳이었습니다. 성당의 천장은 엄청나게 크고, 바닥으로부터 20미터나 됩니다! 당시에 성당이 실제로 활발하게 사용되고 있었기 때문에 바닥에 간단한 연단을 세워서 사용할 수가 없었습니다. 밧줄로 매단 비계를 사용하자는 제안도 있었지만 이 방법은 천장에 구멍을 남기게 되므로 그는 이 방법을 포기했어요. 그 대신 창문 위 근처의 벽들을 통과했던 기둥들로 지탱되는 단을 제작했습니다. 프레스코화의 절반을 그린 뒤 이 단을 옮겼고 그는 다른 쪽에 그림을 그렸어요.

그가 맞닥뜨린 세 번째의 어려움은 이 벽화가 가져온 신체적 부담이었습니다. 그는 바닥에서 그림을 볼 수 없었기 때문에 그림을 전체적으로 볼 수가 없었어요. 얼굴에서 몇 인치밖에 떨어지지 않은 곳에 거대한 그림들을 그려야 했습니다. 천장에 그리는 것이었기에 머리보다 높이 위치한 곳에 그림을 그리는 일에 4년을 보내야 했고 그로 인해 몸이 고통을 받았어요. 전신이 아팠으며, 특히 팔, 다리, 등에 통증이 있었고 시력은 영구적으로 손상을 입었습니다. 그는 끔찍한 작업 환경을 묘사하는 시를 쓰기까지 했어요. 이 기념비적인 벽화가 완성된 뒤 그는 즉각적이고 만장 일치의 찬사를 받았습니다. 이 칭송이 그의 신체적 고통을 덜어 주었든 아니든, 다음 수 세기 동안 그의 명성을 확실히 보장해주었죠.

어휘

ceiling n 천장 | Sistine Chapel 시스티나 성당 | fresco n 프레스코화 | commission v 의뢰하다, 주문하다 | construct v 건설하다 | private adj 개인 소유의 | selection n 선발, 선택 | reluctant adj 꺼리는, 주저하는 | accept v 받아들이다 | sculptor n 조각가 | workload n 작업량 | sculpture n 조각 | tomb n 무덤 | dependent adj 의지하는 | objection n 이의, 반대 | insist v 고집하다 | concession n 양보 | replace v 대신하다, 대체하다 | depict v 그리다, 묘사하다 | geometric adj 기하학의 | apostle n 사도 | grand adj 웅장한 | composition n 구성 요소 | Old Testament 구약 성서 | portrait n 초상화 | prophet n 선지자 | predict v 예측하다 | demanding adj 부담이 큰, 요구가 많은 | plaster n 석회 | correction n 수정 | division n 경계선 | refine v 개선하다 | expressive adj 표현력이 있는 | dynamic adj 역동적인 | platform n 단 | scaffold n 비계 | discard v 버리다, 폐기하다 | devise v 고안하다 | eyesight n 시력 | permanently adv 영구적으로 | completion n 완료, 완성 | monumental adj 기념비적인 | task n 과업, 업무 | immediate adj 즉각적인 | unanimous adj 만장일치의 | praise v 찬사, 칭찬 | acclaim n 칭송, 환호 | ease v 편하게 해주다 | secure v 보장하다 | fame n 명성

1. Main Idea
What is the lecture mainly about?

Ⓐ Some trivia regarding one of the most famous paintings of the Renaissance
Ⓑ A famous Renaissance artwork and the challenges it posed for its creator
Ⓒ Important characteristics of the Sistine Chapel and Michelangelo's painting
Ⓓ The difficulties that discouraged Michelangelo from painting frescoes

2. Detail
What is the main reason that made Michelangelo hesitate when taking the commission?

Ⓐ He usually preferred taking on stable projects from the government.
Ⓑ He didn't consider himself a better painter than his contemporaries.
Ⓒ He wanted to be able to work on other projects at the same time.
Ⓓ He viewed himself as more of a sculptor than a painter.

3. Connecting Contents
Why does the professor mention a geometric design?

Ⓐ To describe a popular style of art in churches during the Renaissance period in Italy
Ⓑ To explain how Michelangelo's style changed over the course of his work
Ⓒ To tell the students about the original design that was on the ceiling of the chapel
Ⓓ To show the power Michelangelo had over the subject matter for the commission

1.
강의는 주로 무엇에 대한 것인가?

Ⓐ 르네상스 시대의 가장 유명한 그림들 중 하나에 관련한 사소한 일들
Ⓑ 유명한 르네상스 작품과 그 작품이 창작자에게 제기한 도전들
Ⓒ 시스티나 성당의 중요한 특징들과 미켈란젤로의 그림
Ⓓ 미켈란젤로가 프레스코를 그리는 것을 단념시킨 어려운 점들

2.
그림 의뢰를 받아들였을 때 미켈란젤로를 망설이게 한 가장 주된 이유는 무엇인가?

Ⓐ 그는 보통 정부로부터 안정적인 일거리를 맡는 것을 선호했다.
Ⓑ 그는 자신이 동시대의 화가들보다 더 나은 화가라고 생각하지 않았다.
Ⓒ 그는 다른 프로젝트들도 동시에 맡고 싶어했다.
Ⓓ 그는 자신을 화가라기보다는 조각가라고 생각했다.

3.
교수는 왜 기하학적 디자인을 언급하는가?

Ⓐ 이탈리아의 르네상스 시대 동안 교회에서 인기를 끌던 예술 양식을 묘사하려고
Ⓑ 미켈란젤로의 작품이 진행됨에 따라 그의 화풍이 어떻게 바뀌었는지 설명하려고
Ⓒ 성당의 천장에 원래 있던 디자인에 대해 학생들에게 이야기하려고
Ⓓ 의뢰 받은 작품의 주제에 미켈란젤로가 가졌던 힘을 보여주려고

4. **Detail**

What were the problems with painting frescoes?

Choose 2 answers.

Ⓐ **The artist was not able to fix errors since the plaster dries quickly.**
Ⓑ The plaster dried quickly and started to break apart after painting.
Ⓒ It required too much water, which tended to obscure the painting.
Ⓓ Painters needed an assistant who could wet the plaster.
Ⓔ **Laying out a new plaster every day required a lot of work.**

5. **Detail**

Which method did Michelangelo use to paint on the 20-meter-high ceiling?

Ⓐ **He designed a floor that was supported by several beams.**
Ⓑ He constructed a temporary platform that stood on the ground.
Ⓒ He devised a large scaffold that was held up by thick ropes.
Ⓓ He sat on a little wooden board that hung from the ceiling.

6. **Inference**

What can be inferred about the influence of the commission on Michelangelo?

Ⓐ It brought him many more opportunities to paint frescoes.
Ⓑ It did not bring him the fame and praise he expected.
Ⓒ **It ended up having a lasting effect on Michelangelo's health.**
Ⓓ It eventually opened up the path to Michelangelo becoming a poet.

4.

프레스코화를 그리는 것의 문제점은 무엇이었는가?

두 개를 고르시오.

Ⓐ 석회가 빨리 마르기 때문에 화가는 잘못된 점을 고칠 수가 없었다.
Ⓑ 석회는 너무 빨리 말랐고 그림이 그려진 뒤에 부서지기 시작했다.
Ⓒ 너무 많은 물을 필요로 했고 그림을 흐려지게 만드는 경향이 있었다.
Ⓓ 화가들은 석회에 물을 적셔줄 조수를 필요로 했다.
Ⓔ 매일같이 새로운 석회를 바르는 것은 많은 노동을 필요로 했다.

5.

미켈란젤로는 20미터 높이의 천장에 그림을 그리기 위해 어떠한 방법을 사용했는가?

Ⓐ 몇 개의 기둥으로 지탱되는 층을 제작했다.
Ⓑ 바닥에 세운 임시 단을 만들었다.
Ⓒ 두꺼운 밧줄들에 매달린 커다란 비계를 고안했다.
Ⓓ 천장에 매달린 작은 나무 판자에 앉았다.

6.

이 작품의 의뢰가 미켈란젤로에게 끼친 영향에 대해 무엇을 추론할 수 있는가?

Ⓐ 프레스코화를 그릴 더 많은 기회들을 가져다 주었다.
Ⓑ 미켈란젤로가 기대했던 명성과 칭송을 가져다 주지 못했다.
Ⓒ 결국 미켈란젤로의 건강에 오래도록 지속되는 영향을 미쳤다.
Ⓓ 시인이 되는 길을 미켈란젤로에게 결과적으로 열어주었다.

Lecture 2

[1-6] Listen to part of a lecture in a botany class.

Man: professor

M Alright, take your seats. I want to continue our discussion on useful plant fibers. Last class, we talked about cotton and the many surprising ways it's used in various industries. I want to move on from that topic and discuss another useful fiber: hemp. First things first, let's talk about the plant itself. Hemp comes from the cannabis sativa plant, as does marijuana. But they come from different varieties of the plant, and unlike marijuana, consuming hemp won't cause intoxication of any sort. It's been cultivated for centuries for various purposes, including for its fibers.

Now, the list of things that make hemp fiber so cool is super long. Hemp fiber is tough and sturdy, even more so than cotton. Many cultures historically used the fibers to make shoes. Because it is so dense, processing it will result in a texture that many argue is even smoother and more luxurious than cotton. Plus, hemp fibers are naturally resistant to mold, mildew, and UV rays, making them perfect for outdoor or rugged applications. Can you imagine clothes that never get moldy? That seems like a big advantage! Hemp is also naturally antimicrobial, which reduces the need for chemical treatments in order to enhance hygiene in textiles and other applications. So in many ways, hemp is better for both our health and even for our environment when compared to other similar fibrous plants.

But where can you find hemp fiber in everyday life? Well, it's not as easy to spot as some of its competitors, but it is used in a variety of products. You might spot it in clothing, like shirts, pants, or shoes. Hemp fiber is also found in textiles for home goods, such as towels, bedding, and curtains. It is sturdy, so you'll also find hemp fiber in things like rope and canvas, and because it's so fibrous, it's used to produce bags, backpacks, and even concrete. Hempcrete, as it is called, is a building material made from the inner woody core of the hemp plant. This part of the plant is known as the hurd, and this is mixed with a lime-based binder. If you ask me, hemp really is one of the most underappreciated materials out there.

Now, let's address the obvious question: why isn't hemp fiber more widely used? Well, there's a bit of history behind that. Back in the day, hemp was a major player in various industries, including textiles and paper. However, with the rise of the timber industry in the 19th and 20th centuries, and the development of cotton processing techniques, hemp fell out of favor. The timber industry in particular wielded a good deal of political influence, and promotional campaigns were very successful in marketing timber as the material for construction and paper. Plus, many industries, including the cotton industry, spread propaganda equating hemp with marijuana. Marijuana is an illegal drug, and I am not advocating for its use, but you must admit, there was a lot of fear-mongering going on, especially given what I said about hemp being non-toxic at the beginning of the class.

However, times are changing. As we become more aware of the environmental impact of our choices, there's renewed interest in hemp and its sustainable properties. Regulations are evolving, and attitudes are shifting. With advancements in processing technology, hemp fiber is making a comeback in a big way.

Alright, you've taken in a lot of information, so let's break into smaller groups and share a few ideas about its significance.

이제 당연한 질문에 대해 이야기해 보죠. 왜 삼 섬유가 더 널리 사용되지 않을까요? 여기에 약간의 역사가 있습니다. 예전에는 삼이 섬유와 종이를 포함한 여러 산업에서 주요 역할을 했습니다. 하지만 19세기와 20세기에는 목재 산업이 부상했고, 면 처리 기술이 발전하면서 삼의 인기가 떨어졌습니다. 특히 목재 산업은 정치적인 영향력이 컸고, 목재를 건축과 종이를 위한 재료로 홍보하는 캠페인이 매우 성공적이었습니다. 게다가 면 산업을 포함한 여러 산업에서 삼을 마리화나와 동일시하는 선전을 퍼뜨리기도 했습니다. 마리화나는 불법 약물이고, 저는 마리화나의 사용을 옹호하는 건 아니지만, 특히 제가 수업 초반에 삼이 독성이 없다는 걸 말했다는 점을 고려하면, 두려움을 조장하는 부분이 많았다는 건 인정해야 합니다.

하지만 시대가 변하고 있습니다. 우리의 선택이 환경에 미치는 영향을 더 인식하게 되면서 삼과 그 지속 가능한 특성에 대한 관심이 다시 높아지고 있습니다. 규제도 변화하고 있고, 인식도 바뀌고 있습니다. 처리 기술의 발전과 함께 삼 섬유는 다시 큰 인기를 끌고 있습니다.

자, 이제 많은 정보를 접하셨으니 소규모 그룹으로 나누어 그 중요성에 대해 몇 가지 아이디어를 공유해 보겠습니다.

어휘

fiber n 섬유 | **industry** n 산업 | **variety** n 품종 | **intoxication** n 중독 | **cultivate** v 재배하다 | **sturdy** adj 견고한 | **luxurious** adj 고급스러운 | **mold** n 곰팡이 | **mildew** n 흰곰팡이 | **antimicrobial** adj 항균의 | **hygiene** n 위생 | **textile** n 직물 | **environment** n 환경 | **canvas** n 캔버스 | **concrete** n 콘크리트 | **construction** n 건설 | **propaganda** n 선전 | **fear-mongering** n 공포 조장 | **sustainable** adj 지속 가능한 | **regulation** n 규제

---

1. Main Idea

What is the main topic of the lecture?
Ⓐ The downfall of the hemp industry
Ⓑ The versatility of hemp
Ⓒ The best uses for hemp fibers
Ⓓ The resurgence of the hemp industry

1.

강의의 주요 주제는 무엇인가?
Ⓐ 삼 산업의 몰락
Ⓑ 삼의 다용성
Ⓒ 삼 섬유의 가장 좋은 용도
Ⓓ 삼 산업의 부활

2. Detail
According to the lecture, hemp fiber is superior to cotton because of its
- A Low density
- B Moisture absorption
- C Water repellent qualities
- **D Hygienic properties**

3. Detail
According to the lecture, hemp can be found in all of the following EXCEPT
- **A Hardware**
- B Bedsheets
- C Clothing and apparel
- D Backpacks

4. Function & Attitude
What is the professor's attitude toward hemp?
- A He is against marijuana use.
- B He believes the timber industry did a big disservice to America's consumers.
- **C He is a proponent of hemp's usefulness.**
- D He believes hemp is intriguing but has no place in today's society.

5. Detail
According to the lecture, why did hemp fall out of use?
- A The cotton industry wielded significant political lobbying power.
- **B Propaganda was aimed at associating hemp with marijuana.**
- C Consumers preferred the use of timber as a construction material for homes.
- D Children feared the effects of wearing clothes made from hemp.

6. Inference
What will the class most likely do next?
- A The class will learn about newer applications of hemp in the context of sustainability.
- B The class will learn about other sustainable plant fibers.
- **C The class will enter a discussion on the materials taught.**
- D The professor will answer any questions.

Conversation 2

[1-5] Listen to part of a conversation between a student and a radio station manager.

Man: Student | Woman: Radio station manager

M: Excuse me, is Marie Finch here?

W: Yes, please wait a moment… I am Marie. How can I help you?

M: First off, I would like to say that I really enjoy your radio show. I'm a big fan of 80s music.

W: Thank you. It's always good to hear from your audience even if only students can receive our radio signal. You are?

M: Oh, I'm David Gore. I'm the vice president of the Foreign Film Club on campus.

W: Really? I wasn't aware that we had one.

M: Well, we don't, yet… at least not officially. I was hoping you could help us with that. You see, the university's board of directors just passed a rule that says only student organizations that have received approval from the university may put up fliers to advertise on campus. But, if we cannot advertise, it is very hard for us to gain approval.

W: Yes, I remember hearing about that. That's a strange rule… It seems to be designed to keep new clubs from forming.

M: I know, and in order to receive approval, we need to have at least fifty people who regularly attend our events.

W: You can host events without officially being a club? How does that work?

M: There's no rule against students reserving a room for an event. In order to receive approval we need to have the same fifty people sign their name on a petition on three different dates. The problem is that we have been having trouble getting fifty people to attend even one event. So far we have a core of twenty people who come to every showing. They sometimes bring friends, but not many return later. And that is where I was hoping you could help us.

W: Oh, I get it. You want me to advertise your club on my show, right?

M: Exactly. The rule doesn't mention anything about radio advertisements.

W Hmm… That sounds like a very good way to circumvent the new rule, but I would have to ask my supervisor about that. I don't know what the rules are about advertising things like that. Unfortunately, he is on vacation this week, and I have no way of contacting him. He is in Canada fishing in a remote area.

M Oh, that's too bad…

W But, I'll tell you what I can do without approval. I can have you on my show as a guest. I'll introduce you and your club. Then we can discuss it in the breaks between songs. That will give you some publicity without actually advertising or officially endorsing your club. How does that sound?

M That sounds great. When could we do that?

W Right now, take a seat and put on these headphones. The song is almost over.

어휘

receive ⓥ 받다 | **signal** ⓝ 신호 | **officially** adv 공식적으로 | **board of directors** 이사회 | **approval** ⓝ 승인 | **advertise** ⓥ 광고하다 | **form** ⓥ 형성하다 | **regularly** adv 정기적으로 | **attend** ⓥ 참석하다 | **reserve** ⓥ 예약하다 | **petition** ⓝ 진정서, 탄원서 | **core** adj 핵심의 | **circumvent** ⓥ 피해 가다 | **supervisor** ⓝ 관리자 | **remote** adj 외진, 외딴 | **publicity** ⓝ 널리 알려짐 | **endorse** ⓥ 홍보하다, 보증하다

1. Main Idea
Why does the student come to the radio station?

Ⓐ To complain about the quality of the music played by the radio station
Ⓑ To suggest some new content for the radio show's program
Ⓒ To check if his club could be promoted on the show
Ⓓ To look to become an engineering manager at the radio station

2. Connecting Contents
Why does the student mention 80s music?

Ⓐ It is the reason why he likes listening to the woman's radio show.
Ⓑ It gave him the reason and determination for joining the radio station.
Ⓒ It inspired him when he was trying to solve his club advertising matter.
Ⓓ It is what gave him the idea of establishing the Foreign Film Club.

3. Detail

According to the student, what is true about the club?

Ⓐ It was made to discuss foreign music with other students.
Ⓑ Its meeting location will be posted on the student bulletin board.
Ⓒ **It needs to have a certain number of people to receive approval.**
Ⓓ It is looking for a new managerial staff to advertise a movie.

4. Detail

What did the board of directors make a new university policy?

Ⓐ All student organizations have to recruit at least 50 new members.
Ⓑ New student organizations need to post their advertisements on the bulletin board.
Ⓒ **Only organizations with the university's permission could post their fliers.**
Ⓓ The university will require all organizations to advertise themselves.

5. Inference

What will the student most likely do next?

Ⓐ Approve the club's plans for advertising
Ⓑ **Become a guest on the woman's radio show**
Ⓒ Realize his hopes of creating an official club
Ⓓ Look for some people to attend an event

3.
학생에 의하면, 그 동아리에 대해 옳은 것은 무엇인가?

Ⓐ 다른 학생들과 외국 음악에 대해 토의하기 위해 만들어졌다.
Ⓑ 동아리 모임 장소는 학생 게시판에 공지될 것이다.
Ⓒ 승인을 받기 위해서는 특정한 수의 인원이 있어야만 한다.
Ⓓ 영화를 광고하기 위해 새 관리직 직원을 찾고 있다.

4.
학교 이사회는 무엇을 신규 규정으로 만들었는가?

Ⓐ 모든 학생 단체들은 적어도 50명의 새 회원을 모집해야 한다.
Ⓑ 새로운 학생 단체들은 게시판에 광고를 게시해야만 한다.
Ⓒ 대학교의 허가를 받은 단체만 광고지를 게시할 수 있다.
Ⓓ 대학에서는 모든 단체들이 자체 광고를 하도록 요구할 것이다.

5.
학생은 다음에 무엇을 할 것 같은가?

Ⓐ 광고에 대한 동아리의 계획을 승인한다
Ⓑ 여자의 라디오 방송의 초대 손님이 된다
Ⓒ 공식 동아리를 만드는 소망을 이룬다
Ⓓ 동아리 행사에 참여할 사람들을 찾는다

Lecture 3

 AT05_5

[1-6] Listen to part of a lecture in an engineering class.

Man: Student | Woman: Professor

W People have been trying to build very tall structures almost since the first permanent buildings were constructed. Initially, these served the need for defense. The taller a building is, the greater the distance from which you can see an enemy approaching. Later, tall buildings took on religious and cultural significance as temples to gods and monuments to kings. Since the late 19th century, however, tall buildings have been built for residential and business purposes due to a lack of space in densely populated urban areas.

공학 강의의 일부를 들으시오.

남자: 학생 | 여자: 교수

여 최초의 영구적인 건물이 지어진 이래로 사람들은 아주 높은 구조물을 지으려고 노력해 왔습니다. 처음에 이 높은 건물들은 방어를 목적으로 지어진 것이었어요. 건물이 높으면 높을수록 적이 다가오는 거리를 더 멀리서부터 볼 수 있죠. 시간이 흐른 뒤 고층 건물들은 신들에게 바쳐진 신전이나 왕들의 기념비와 같이 종교적, 문화적 중요성을 갖게 되었습니다. 그러나 19세기 후반 이래 고층 건물들은 인구가 빽빽하게 밀집된 도시 지역의 공간 부족으로 주거와 사업을 목적으로 지어져 왔어요.

These skyscrapers incorporated metal and concrete in their construction in innovative ways. The first ones used wrought iron beams for support, but steel later replaced wrought iron, being both lighter and stronger. These metal skeletons allowed builders to make their buildings much taller, with large, open interior spaces. These buildings were not very appealing to people, though, because it was so difficult to reach the upper floors. That meant that rich people lived on the lower floors and poorer people on the higher ones. Of course, that all changed after the invention of the elevator.

Later, reinforced concrete was developed, making the walls stronger and even thinner. Reinforced concrete has a mesh of thin steel rods woven throughout it, providing both strength and flexibility. However, these lightweight towers soon became susceptible to a force that their thick-walled ancestors largely ignored: the wind.

When the weather is windy, the air typically blows from one general direction. This means that one face of a building will be subjected to higher positive pressure than the others, and the opposite face of the building will experience negative pressure. This is called *lateral loading*, and it can literally bend a building over to one side, particularly if it is very tall and thin-walled. When the pressure on the building lessens as the wind strength drops, it will bounce back. If this motion reaches a certain frequency, the buildings' movements will tear it apart and make it collapse.

To make matters worse, wind force does not simply push on buildings from one direction. Depending on geographic location, elevation, weather conditions, the amount of surface exposed, and the building's spatial relationship with nearby structures, the direction and strength of lateral loading will vary. On top of that, the building's own features such as height, size, and architectural features also influence the way that the building will react.

Therefore, it is vitally important that architects try to determine how a design will react to lateral loading from the wind profile of its proposed location. This is often achieved by building a scale model and placing it in a wind tunnel that has been calibrated to recreate the conditions at the building

M: site. A newer method, called computational fluid dynamics, or CFD, uses computer models to predict how the designed building would react to any imaginable loading situation. When used together with computer blueprints, CFD allows architects to alter their designs as soon as flaws in the structure are identified.

M: Professor, is computational fluid dynamics really that new? I mean, they have been using it in airplane design for decades.

W: That's true. CFD has been used with buildings in the past. But CFD is extremely complex, so before modern computers, it was difficult to get reliable results. The first application of CFD to a building was the Empire State Building in 1938. The skyscraper was completed in 1931, and at 102 stories and 381 meters tall, it was the tallest building in the world for almost 40 years. It is an incredibly sturdy building, which was proven when a medium-sized bomber aircraft struck it in 1945. Despite its robust construction, people had noticed that the wind had a noticeable effect on it. The study of the Empire State Building provided valuable data, but no one successfully built anything taller until the World Trade Center was completed in 1970. CFD is not an answer to all of the difficulties in predicting wind patterns, but it is very useful. One recent project that utilized it heavily was the Burj Khalifa in Dubai. While constructing the current tallest building, designers were struck with a unique problem to overcome. Normally, lateral loading affects the top section of a building most, but due to its particular characteristics, the skyscraper's highest lateral loading area is located closer to the middle of the building.

최신의 기술은 설계된 건물이 상상 가능한 어떤 하중 상황에 어떻게 반응할지 예측하기 위해 컴퓨터 모델을 사용합니다. 컴퓨터 청사진과 함께 사용될 때 CFD는 건축 구조에서 결함이 발견되자마자 건축가들이 설계를 수정하도록 해줄 수 있죠.

교수님, 전산 유체 역학이 정말로 그렇게 새롭나요? 제 말은, 지난 수십 년간 그 기술이 비행기 설계에 쓰여 왔잖아요.

맞아요. CFD는 옛날부터 건물에 사용되어 왔어요. 하지만 CFD는 극히 복잡한 기술이기 때문에 오늘날의 컴퓨터가 나오기 전에는 신뢰할 만한 결과를 얻기가 어려웠죠. CFD가 건물에 최초로 적용된 것은 1938년의 엠파이어 스테이트 빌딩입니다. 이 고층 건물은 1931년에 완공되었고 102층에 381미터의 높이로, 약 40년간 세계에서 가장 높은 건물이었습니다. 매우 튼튼한 건물인데, 이는 1945년에 중형 크기의 폭격기가 이 건물에 충돌했을 때 증명되었죠. 튼튼한 건축에도 불구하고 사람들은 바람이 이 건물에 눈에 띌 만한 영향을 주었다는 것을 알아차렸습니다. 엠파이어 스테이트 빌딩의 연구는 귀중한 자료를 제공해 주었지만 1970년에 세계 무역 센터가 완공되기 전까지는 누구도 이 건물보다 더 높은 건물을 성공적으로 건축하지 못했어요. CFD는 바람의 패턴을 예측하는 데 생겨나는 모든 어려움에 대한 답은 아니지만 그래도 매우 유용합니다. CFD를 많이 이용한 최근의 프로젝트는 두바이에 있는 부르즈 할리파예요. 현재 가장 높은 이 건물을 짓는 동안 설계자들은 극복해야 할 독특한 문제점에 부딪혔습니다. 보통 측방하중은 건물의 상층부에 가장 많은 영향을 주지만, 그 건물의 특이점들로 인해 측방하중이 가장 센 곳은 건물의 가운데와 가까웠어요.

어휘

structure n 구조물 | permanent adj 영구적인 | construct v 건설하다 | initially adv 처음에 | defense n 방어 | approach v 접근하다 | religious adj 종교적인 | cultural adj 문화적인 | significance n 중요성 | temple n 사원, 절 | monument n 기념물, 역사적 건축물 | residential adj 주택지의 | densely adv 빽빽하게 | populated adj 인구가 밀집한 | urban adj 도시의 | skyscraper n 고층 건물 | incorporate v 포함하다, 설립하다 | metal n 철 | concrete n 콘크리트 | innovative adj 혁신적인 | wrought iron 연철, 단철 | beam n 기둥 | steel n 강철 | replace v 대체하다 | skeleton n 골격, 뼈대 | interior space 내부 공간 | appealing adj 매력적인 | invention n 발명 | reinforced concrete 철근 콘크리트 | mesh n 철망 | steel rod 철골 | weave v 짜다, 엮다 | strength n 내구성 | flexibility n 유연함 | lightweight adj 가벼운 | susceptible adj 취약한 | ancestor n 선조 | ignore v 무시하다 | typically adv 일반적으로 | direction n 방향 | positive pressure 정압 | negative pressure 부압 | lateral loading 측방하중 | literally adv 문자 그대로 | particularly adv 특히, 특별히 | motion n 움직임 | certain adj 특정한 | frequency n 빈도 | collapse v 붕괴하다 | geographic adj 지리적인 | elevation n 해발 높이 | surface n 표면 | expose

ⓥ 노출하다 | **spatial** ⓐⓓⓙ 공간적인 | **vary** ⓥ 달라지다 | **react** ⓥ 반응하다 | **vitally** ⓐⓓⓥ 극도로, 지극히 | **wind profile** 바람 단면 | **proposed** ⓐⓓⓙ 제안된 | **achieve** ⓥ 달성하다 | **scale model** 축적 모형 | **wind tunnel** 풍동 | **calibrated** ⓐⓓⓙ 사용 전에 교정된 | **recreate** ⓥ 되살리다, 재현하다 | **computational fluid dynamics** 전산 유체 역학 | **predict** ⓥ 예측하다 | **imaginable** ⓐⓓⓙ 상상할 수 있는 | **computer blueprint** 컴퓨터 청사진 | **alter** ⓥ 변경하다 | **flaw** ⓝ 결함, 결점 | **identify** ⓥ 확인하다, 알아보다 | **decade** ⓝ 10년 | **extremely** ⓐⓓⓥ 극히 | **complex** ⓐⓓⓙ 복잡한 | **modern** ⓐⓓⓙ 현대의 | **reliable** ⓐⓓⓙ 신뢰할 만한 | **result** ⓝ 결과 | **application** ⓝ 적용 | **complete** ⓥ 완공하다 | **incredibly** ⓐⓓⓥ 믿을 수 없을 정도로 | **sturdy** ⓐⓓⓙ 튼튼한, 견고한 | **bomber aircraft** 폭격기 | **strike** ⓥ 치다, 부딪치다, 때리다 | **robust** ⓐⓓⓙ 튼튼한 | **notice** ⓥ 알아차리다 | **valuable** ⓐⓓⓙ 귀중한 | **unique** ⓐⓓⓙ 독특한 | **overcome** ⓥ 극복하다 | **normally** ⓐⓓⓥ 보통, 정상적으로

1. Main Idea
What is the main idea of the lecture?

Ⓐ **The effect of the wind on buildings and the application of CFD**
Ⓑ The history of famous tall buildings and the way they were constructed
Ⓒ The development of CFD and its application over time
Ⓓ The role that nearby structures play on the construction of buildings

2. Connecting Contents
Why does the professor mention the elevator?

Ⓐ To explain how it helped with building skyscrapers at the beginning of the 20th century
Ⓑ **To elaborate on how it changed the living environments of upper- and lower-class people**
Ⓒ To show its influence on the construction and exterior design of a building
Ⓓ To talk about the development of construction technology over time

3. Inference
What can be inferred about reinforced concrete?

Ⓐ It increased the chance of collapse since it made the walls thinner.
Ⓑ It allowed more space inside the building with its wrought iron beams.
Ⓒ **It caused buildings to be more vulnerable to the wind than before.**
Ⓓ It increased costs for the construction of skyscrapers.

4. Detail
What makes analyzing lateral loading difficult?

Ⓐ Modern buildings' tall and slender structures
Ⓑ Wind constantly blowing from the same direction
Ⓒ The negative pressure that buildings experience
Ⓓ **The many variables such as geography and weather**

1.
강의의 주제는 무엇인가?

Ⓐ 바람이 건물에 미치는 영향과 CFD의 적용
Ⓑ 유명한 고층 건물들의 역사와 그것들이 건설된 방법
Ⓒ CFD의 개발과 시간이 흐르며 이루어진 적용
Ⓓ 건물 건설에 있어 근처의 구조물들이 하는 역할

2.
교수는 왜 엘리베이터를 언급하는가?

Ⓐ 엘리베이터가 20세기 초반 고층 건물의 건설에 어떻게 도움을 줬는지 설명하기 위해
Ⓑ 엘리베이터가 상류층과 하층 계급의 주거 환경을 어떻게 바꿨는지 설명하기 위해
Ⓒ 건물의 건축과 외부 설계에 엘리베이터가 미친 영향을 보여주기 위해
Ⓓ 시간이 흐르며 이루어진 건축 기술의 발전에 대해 이야기하기 위해

3.
철근 콘크리트에 대해 무엇을 추론할 수 있는가?

Ⓐ 벽을 더 얇게 만들었기 때문에 붕괴의 위험을 더 증가시켰다.
Ⓑ 단철 기둥으로 건물 내부에 더 많은 공간을 가져다 주었다.
Ⓒ 건물들이 전보다 더 바람에 취약해지게 만들었다.
Ⓓ 고층 건물의 건설 비용을 더 증가시켰다.

4.
측방하중의 분석을 어렵게 만드는 것은 무엇인가?

Ⓐ 현대 건물들의 높고 가느다란 구조
Ⓑ 같은 방향에서 계속해서 불어오는 바람
Ⓒ 건물들이 겪는 부압
Ⓓ 지형과 날씨 같은 다양한 변수들

5. Detail

According to the lecture, which of the following are true about CFD? Choose 2 answers.

Ⓐ It is mostly used for airplanes and other types of vehicles nowadays.
Ⓑ It predicts a building's reactions to different burdening conditions.
Ⓒ It was first used on a building after the completion of the Empire State Building.
Ⓓ Its first full-scale use was for the World Trade Center, completed in 1970.
Ⓔ It is so complex that it is difficult to obtain trustworthy data from it.

6. Detail

What problem does the Burj Khalifa have that is different from other buildings?

Ⓐ The wind pattern most affects the middle part of the building.
Ⓑ The lateral loading of the building is much more severe than that of other buildings.
Ⓒ The difference between the lateral loading at the top and the bottom is huge.
Ⓓ The construction was more complicated due to the orientation of its surfaces.

5.

강의에 의하면, 다음 중 CFD에 대해 옳은 것은 무엇인가?
두 개를 고르시오.

Ⓐ 오늘날에는 비행기와 다른 종류의 탈것에 대부분 사용된다.
Ⓑ 다양한 압력 조건에 따른 건물의 반응 결과를 예측한다.
Ⓒ 엠파이어 스테이트 빌딩의 완공 이후 한 빌딩에 처음으로 사용되었다.
Ⓓ 최초로 완전히 사용된 경우는 1970년에 완공된 세계 무역 센터였다.
Ⓔ 너무 복잡해서 신뢰할 수 있는 자료를 얻기가 어렵다.

6.

다른 건물들과 다른 부르즈 할리파의 문제점은 무엇인가?

Ⓐ 바람의 패턴이 건물의 가운데에 가장 많은 영향을 준다.
Ⓑ 건물의 측방하중이 다른 건물들에 비해 더욱 심하다.
Ⓒ 건물의 상층부와 하층부의 측방하중 차이가 아주 크다.
Ⓓ 건물의 표층 방향 때문에 건축이 더 복잡했다.

Actual Test 06

본서 | P. 112

Conversation 1	1. Ⓒ 2. Ⓑ 3. Ⓐ 4. Ⓐ 5. Ⓒ
Lecture 1	1. Ⓐ 2. Ⓑ, Ⓒ 3. Ⓐ 4. Ⓓ 5. Ⓑ 6. Ⓑ
Lecture 2	1. Ⓒ 2. Ⓓ 3. Horns – Ⓒ / Antlers – Ⓐ, Ⓑ, Ⓓ, Ⓔ 4. Ⓐ 5. Ⓒ 6. Ⓓ
Conversation 2	1. Ⓑ 2. Ⓒ 3. Ⓒ 4. Ⓑ, Ⓒ 5. Ⓐ
Lecture 3	1. Ⓐ 2. Ⓓ 3. Ⓑ 4. Ⓒ 5. Ⓒ 6. Ⓓ

● 내가 맞은 문제 유형의 개수를 적어 보고 어느 유형에 취약한지 확인해 봅시다.

문제 유형	맞은 개수
Main Idea	5
Detail	9
Connecting Contents	6
Function & Attitude	5
Inference	3
Total	28

Conversation 1

[1-5] Listen to part of a conversation between two professors.

Man: Professor | Woman: Professor

M Marie! Hello! When did you get back? I thought that you were supposed to be gone for a few more weeks.

W Yes, well, that was the original plan.

M Did something happen? Is everyone alright?

W Yes, we're all fine. The weather didn't cooperate with us. We knew that we were leaving kind of late in the season, but the forecasters thought that this year's monsoon would be later and drier than last year.

M I take it that they were wrong?

W Yes, very much so! But, weather forecasting is not an exact science — definitely less so than archaeology.

M Yes, archaeology has become much more reliable with the technology available to us now. Speaking of which, how did your excavation go? Before the weather forced you to quit, I mean.

W Great, we made a lot of progress. Using satellite imagery really makes it easier to know where to look. The forests are so thick in Southeast Asia. If you go in without a destination in mind, you could search for weeks and never find anything — even if you were right next to a temple!

M Did you find any temples?

W Yes, we found a temple complex similar to that at Angkor Wat, but nowhere near as large. We aren't sure yet when it was constructed, but we took many samples that should help us figure that out when we analyze them in the laboratory.

M Excellent. Were you able to secure your dig site before you left?

W We certainly tried. It was on relatively high ground, kind of a low plateau that may have been an island in the past, so we hope it will survive this rainy season. We dug some channels to divert runoff from the dig site. Now we just have to wait.

M Yes, that is one of the hardest parts about working in the rainforest, you never know when a storm could wash away the ruins, or rebury them. By the way, how many students did you take along with you? I've been having trouble recruiting students for my desert research trip this winter.

W Do you think that might have something to do with the destination?

M That is possible, but the desert is quite pleasant in the late winter and spring. It isn't very hot, and there are flowers if it rains.

W I know, I know. I went on one of your excavations when I was a graduate student. It was a very useful experience. We had enough students this year, but some of them just barely signed up before the deadline. Students these days don't seem to like doing the real archaeology. It's strange, really. How are they going to get a true appreciation for the work if they never get their hands dirty? Analyzing samples and artifacts in the laboratory is important, but when you're on site you get so much more information from seeing the context firsthand.

M I couldn't agree with you more. It's a vital part of their training, and it really helps to have field work on your résumé. Of course, with the budget cuts, we can't take as many students with us as we used to anyway.

W Did I miss something when I was gone?

M No, I mean the cuts from last year, but you never know. The board of directors decides which departments get funding, and we aren't their top priority.

W Yes, I know. That is why we have to show results. I just hope we were able to retrieve enough data and artifacts to impress them on our shortened trip. So, I need to get to work.

여 목적지 때문일 수도 있다고 생각하시나요?

남 그럴 수도 있지만, 사막은 늦겨울과 봄에는 꽤 괜찮아요. 아주 덥지 않고, 비가 올 때는 꽃도 있죠.

여 알아요. 제가 대학원생이었을 때 교수님의 발굴지 중 한 곳에 참여했어요. 정말 유용한 경험이었죠. 올해엔 충분한 수의 학생들이 있었지만, 몇몇은 마감 바로 직전에 신청했어요. 요즘 학생들은 실제 고고학을 하는 것을 좋아하지 않는 것처럼 보여요. 정말 이상하죠. 한 번도 손을 더럽혀 보지 않고 어떻게 이 일의 진정한 가치를 알겠어요? 실험실에서 샘플과 인공 유물을 분석하는 것은 중요하지만, 현장에 있을 때 전후 사정을 직접 보는 것에서 훨씬 더 많은 정보를 얻을 수 있는데 말이죠.

남 전적으로 동의합니다. 그게 훈련의 가장 중요한 부분이고, 이력서에 현장 연구가 있는 것이 정말 도움이 되죠. 물론, 예산 삭감으로 예전처럼 많은 수의 학생들을 데려갈 수 없지만요.

여 제가 떠나 있었던 동안 무슨 일이 있었나요?

남 아니요, 작년의 예산 삭감을 말한 거지만, 모르죠. 이사회에서 어떤 부서가 지원을 받을지 정하고, 우리는 그들의 우선 순위가 아니니까요.

여 네, 알아요. 그래서 결과를 보여줘야 하는 거예요. 짧아진 이 여행에서 그들에게 깊은 인상을 줄 수 있을 만큼 저희가 충분한 자료와 인공 유물들을 회수할 수 있기를 바랄 뿐이에요. 그러니 이제 작업을 시작해야겠네요.

어휘

cooperate v 협조하다 | **forecaster** n 기상 요원 | **monsoon** n 우기, 장마 | **definitely** adv 분명히, 틀림없이 | **archaeology** n 고고학 | **reliable** adj 믿을 수 있는 | **excavation** n 발굴, 발굴지 | **satellite** n 위성 | **imagery** n 이미지, 화상 | **destination** n 목적지, 도착지 | **temple** n 사원 | **complex** n 복합 건물, 단지 | **construct** v 건설하다, 구성하다 | **analyze** v 분석하다 | **laboratory** n 실험실, 연구실 | **secure** v 안전하게 지키다, 보호하다 | **dig site** 발굴 현장 | **relatively** adv 상대적으로 | **plateau** n 고원 | **channel** n 도랑 | **runoff** n 땅 위를 흐르는 빗물 | **rainforest** n 우림 | **rebury** v 다시 매장하다 | **recruit** v 모집하다, 뽑다 | **deadline** n 마감일, 최종 기일 | **appreciation** n 감사, 가치의 평가 | **artifact** n 인공 유물 | **context** n 맥락, 전후 사정 | **firsthand** adv 직접 | **vital** adj 필수적인 | **budget cut** 예산 삭감 | **funding** n 자금 | **priority** n 우선 순위 | **retrieve** v 회수하다, 되찾다

1. **Main Idea**
What is the conversation mainly about?
- Ⓐ Receiving more funding from the school for upcoming excavations
- Ⓑ Persuading students to get more firsthand experience in the field
- **Ⓒ A recent research trip the woman went on with her students**
- Ⓓ Interesting samples the woman brought with her from an excavation site

2. **Detail**
What is true about the woman's recent excavation?
- Ⓐ They spent many days in the forest wondering where to excavate.
- **Ⓑ Bad weather conditions prevented her team from excavating further.**
- Ⓒ A storm eventually washed away the ruins that her team was studying.
- Ⓓ It took more time than she had expected since she was short of staff.

3. **Inference**
According to the lecture, what can be inferred about excavations in rainforests?
- **Ⓐ Weather conditions play an important role.**
- Ⓑ Excavation teams often get lost in the forest.
- Ⓒ Temples are usually found on high ground.
- Ⓓ Using satellite imagery is very difficult.

4. **Function & Attitude**
Why does the woman say this:

> W How are they going to get a true appreciation for the work if they never get their hands dirty?

- **Ⓐ To indicate that students need to participate directly in the field**
- Ⓑ To state that her students wouldn't enjoy actual field work that much
- Ⓒ To explain why she tries to encourage her students to travel as much as they can
- Ⓓ To express her disappointment that her students do not appreciate what they study

---

1.
대화는 주로 무엇에 대한 것인가?
- Ⓐ 다음 발굴을 위한 학교 지원 기금 받기
- Ⓑ 학생들이 현장에서 직접적인 경험을 더 하도록 설득하기
- **Ⓒ 여자가 학생들과 함께 갔던 최근의 리서치 여행**
- Ⓓ 발굴 현장에서 여자가 가져온 흥미로운 샘플들

2.
여자의 최근 발굴에 대해 옳은 것은 무엇인가?
- Ⓐ 어디를 발굴해야 할 지 고민하며 숲에서 며칠을 보냈다.
- **Ⓑ 악화된 날씨 상황으로 그녀의 팀은 더 이상의 발굴을 하지 못했다.**
- Ⓒ 여자의 팀이 연구하고 있던 유적을 폭우가 결국 휩쓸어가 버렸다.
- Ⓓ 인력이 모자랐기에 여자가 예상했던 것보다 시간이 더 걸렸다.

3.
강의에 의하면, 우림에서의 발굴에 대해 무엇을 추론할 수 있는가?
- **Ⓐ 기상 상태가 중요한 역할을 한다.**
- Ⓑ 발굴 팀은 종종 숲에서 길을 잃는다.
- Ⓒ 사원들은 보통 높은 지대에서 발견된다.
- Ⓓ 인공 위성 이미지 사용은 매우 어렵다.

4.
여자는 왜 이렇게 말하는가:

> 여 한 번도 손을 더럽혀 보지 않고 어떻게 이 일의 진정한 가치를 알겠어요?

- **Ⓐ 학생들이 현장에 직접 참여해야 한다는 것을 보여 주기 위해**
- Ⓑ 학생들이 실제 현장 연구를 그다지 즐기지 않을 것이라고 말하기 위해
- Ⓒ 학생들이 할 수 있는 한 많이 여행을 하도록 장려하려고 하는 이유를 설명하기 위해
- Ⓓ 학생들이 자신들이 공부하는 것의 가치를 모르기에 실망스럽다는 것을 표현하기 위해

5. Detail

What does the man say about budget cuts?

Ⓐ He expects there to be more budget cuts in the future.
Ⓑ The board of directors values the archaeology department.
Ⓒ **They limited the number of students excavation teams could take.**
Ⓓ Because of them, professors are trying to research abroad more.

Lecture 1

[1-6] Listen to part of a lecture in an earth science class.

Man: Student | Woman: Professor

W We have been keeping accurate records of weather and climate change for, well not for all that long really. Just a few centuries… The first thermometers were invented in the early to mid seventeenth century. In order to find out what happened with the world's weather before those records began, we can go by written eyewitness accounts, but those are very subjective. To gain an accurate picture of the climate before that time, we must look to nature. There are many ways to do this, but all of the ways rely on determining the amount of precipitation at a given time in the past. We can analyze tree rings or ice cores, but these methods have limitations. Thankfully, there is a third source for such data, and they are located all over the world: caves.

In caves, there are often fantastic sculptures created by dripping water called stalagmites. For paleoclimatologists, scientists who study the past of Earth's weather, these sculptures of nature are a valuable resource. Some even rank them among the most important records of the planet's past climate that we have.

M Professor, what about stalactites? They are made in the same way, aren't they?

W True, they are. Water filters down through the soil and bedrock and drips from the ceiling of the cave. This water contains minerals, mostly calcium carbonate, which is deposited on the floor, but some stays on the ceiling as well. Over time, these deposits grow into spikes on the floor called stalagmites and ones on the ceiling called stalactites. Given sufficient time, they can merge into a column of stone. So, yes, stalactites would be equally useful, except that they form from the ceiling, so it is hard to take samples from them.

Along with the calcium carbonate contained in the water, there are also trace amounts of the radioactive element uranium. Like other radioactive elements, uranium decays at a stable rate, and the byproduct is thorium. Thorium, however, is not soluble in water. So, any thorium found in a layer of calcite in a stalagmite formed from radioactive decay in that stalagmite, and it tells us precisely how old that layer is. The thickness of that layer of calcite tells us how much rain there was that year. Therefore, each layer of calcite in a stalagmite can tell us precisely when it was formed and how much precipitation there was at that time. One such stalagmite came from Wanxiang Cave in Gansu Province, China, and it has revealed some very interesting information.

By analyzing the layers of the stalagmite, scientists have created an incredibly accurate record of rainfall in China spanning nearly 2,000 years. This record showed three periods of severe drought that lasted for decades: from 860 to 930, 1340 to 1380, and 1589 to 1640 CE. During these periods the usual monsoon weather pattern from the Indian Ocean fell off, which drastically reduced rainfall in central and northern China. When these periods are compared to the historical record, a startling pattern is revealed. Each of these massive droughts corresponded with the fall of a Chinese dynasty: the Tang, Yuan, and Ming respectively.

Since around 1100 BCE, Chinese philosophers have discussed a concept called the "Mandate of Heaven." According to this idea, emperors rule only with the consent of the gods. If the emperor is just and wise, then he receives their blessings. But if he becomes tyrannical, their support is withdrawn, and the dynasty will collapse. Looking at the data revealed by analyzing the stalagmite, it seems that they may have been correct. During these periods of severe drought famine swept the land, leading to rebellion and intense warfare, which ultimately toppled the dynasties. So, the Mandate of Heaven actually did determine the fate of the empire, but it was through rainfall rather than the will of the gods.

으로 자랍니다. 충분한 시간이 주어지면 그것들은 돌기둥으로 합쳐집니다. 따라서, 맞아요, 종유석도 천장에서 형성되기 때문에 표본을 얻기가 힘들다는 것을 제외하면 마찬가지로 유용하죠.

물에 함유된 탄산석회와 더불어 방사능 물질인 소량의 우라늄도 들어 있어요. 다른 방사능 물질처럼 우라늄은 안정적인 비율로 부패하고, 그 부산물이 토륨입니다. 하지만 토륨은 물에 용해되지 않아요. 따라서, 석순의 방해석층에서 발견되는 모든 토륨은 그 석순의 방사능 부패물에서 형성되었으며, 그것은 이 층이 얼마나 오래되었는지 정확하게 알려줍니다. 그 방해석층의 두께는 그 해에 비가 얼마나 내렸는지 말해주죠. 따라서 석순의 각 방해석층은 그것이 언제 형성되었고 그때 비가 얼마나 내렸는지 정확하게 알려줍니다. 그러한 석순 중 하나는 중국 간쑤 지역의 완샹동굴에서 나온 것으로, 그것은 매우 흥미로운 정보를 보여주었습니다.

석순의 층들을 분석함으로써 과학자들은 거의 2000년에 걸친 놀랍도록 정확한 중국의 강수 기록을 만들어냈습니다. 이 기록은 수십 년간 지속된 심한 가뭄 기간이 세 번 있었다는 것을 보여주는데요, 바로 860~930년, 1340~1380년, 1589~1640년입니다. 이 기간 동안 인도양의 영향을 받는 일반적인 몬순 날씨 패턴이 줄어들었고, 이는 중국 중부와 북부의 강수량을 극적으로 감소시켰습니다. 이 기간들을 역사 기록과 비교하면 놀라운 패턴이 드러납니다. 각각의 가뭄 기간은 중국 왕조의 몰락, 즉, 당, 원, 명과 각각 일치합니다.

기원전 1100년경부터, 중국 철학자들은 "천명"이라는 개념에 대해 논의해왔습니다. 이 개념에 따르면, 황제는 신의 허락이 있어야만 다스릴 수 있습니다. 만약 황제가 공정하고 현명하다면, 그는 신들의 축복을 받습니다. 하지만 만약 그가 독재를 하면, 신들의 지지는 철회되고, 왕조는 몰락하게 됩니다. 석순 분석에 의해 드러난 자료를 보면, 그들이 옳았을지도 모릅니다. 이 극심한 가뭄 동안 기근이 나라를 휩쓸었는데 이는 반란과 전쟁으로 이어졌고, 결국 왕조들을 무너뜨렸습니다. 따라서 천명은 실제로 제국의 운명을 결정했지만, 그것은 신의 뜻이라기보다는 강수를 통해서였습니다.

어휘

accurate adj 정확한 | climate n 기후 | thermometer n 온도계 | eyewitness n 목격자, 증인 | subjective adj 주관적인 | precipitation n 강수 | tree ring 나이테 | limitation n 제한, 한계 | sculpture n 조각품 | stalagmite n 석순 | paleoclimatologist n 고기후학자 | stalactite n 종유석 | filter v 여과하다, 거르다 | bedrock n 기반, 기반암 | deposit v 침전시키다, 두다 | sufficient adj 충분한 | merge into ~에 합병하다 | column n 기둥 | trace n 극미량, 조금 | radioactive adj 방사능의 | decay v 부패하다 | stable adj 안정된, 견실한 | byproduct n 부산물 | thorium n 토륨 | soluble adj 녹는, 용해성의 | calcite n 방해석 | precisely adv 바로, 정확히 | thickness n 두께, 겹 | drought n 가뭄 | drastically adv 극단적으로 | startling adj 놀라운 | correspond v 일치하다, 부합하다 | mandate n 지시, 명령 | consent n 동의, 허락 | tyrannical adj 폭군의, 압제적인 | famine n 기근 | rebellion n 반란, 모반 | intense adj 극심한, 강렬한 | warfare n 전쟁, 전투 | ultimately adv 궁극적으로 | topple v 넘어지다

1. Main Idea
What is the lecture mainly about?
A **A method used for discovering Earth's climatic history**
B Stalagmites that are formed in different climates
C Types of cave structures found on different continents
D The impact of the Mandate of Heaven on Chinese society

2. Detail
Which of the following are characteristics of stalagmites?
Choose 2 answers.
A They are usually formed during a period of heavy rainfall.
B **They are useful for determining past amounts of rainfall.**
C **Minerals like calcium carbonate in the water make them grow.**
D They are dangerous because of their radioactive nature.

3. Detail
According to the professor, what information did the Wanxiang Cave in China reveal?
A **The climate of the region dating back for 2,000 years**
B Records written about four droughts in the last 2,000 years
C The size that stalagmites can reach inside of a cave
D The origin of the philosophy of the Mandate of Heaven

1.
강의는 주로 무엇에 관한 것인가?
A 지구 기후의 역사를 발견하기 위해 사용되는 방법
B 다른 기후에서 형성된 석순들
C 다른 대륙에서 발견된 동굴 구조의 형태들
D 중국 사회에 천명이 끼친 영향

2.
다음 중 석순의 특징은 무엇인가? *두 개를 고르시오.*
A 주로 비가 많이 오는 기간에 형성된다.
B 과거의 강수량을 결정하는 데 유용하다.
C 물에 함유된 탄산석회 같은 광물로 인해 자란다.
D 방사능 특성 때문에 위험하다.

3.
교수에 의하면, 중국의 완샹동굴이 밝혀낸 정보는 무엇인가?
A 2000년을 거슬러 올라간 그 지역의 기후
B 지난 2000년간 있었던 네 번의 가뭄에 대해 쓰여진 기록
C 동굴에서 석순이 도달할 수 있는 크기
D 천명 철학의 유래

4. **Detail**

Why is uranium important to the study described?

Ⓐ It leaves a residue when it decays, which forms stalagmites.
Ⓑ It helps in detecting stalagmites underground.
Ⓒ It is what keeps the stalagmites in caves intact.
Ⓓ It allows stalagmite layers to be accurately dated.

5. **Connecting Contents**

Why does the professor mention the Mandate of Heaven?

Ⓐ To explain how the climate of Gansu Province affected the whole of China
Ⓑ To show that climate changes in China coincided with its political situation
Ⓒ To compare different methods of determining the amount of rainfall
Ⓓ To point out that severe drought in the region was a common thing

6. **Inference**

What can be inferred about studying caves in order to determine the amount of rainfall?

Ⓐ It revealed that the Sun is the sole factor for the growth of stalagmites.
Ⓑ It provides more accurate results than analyzing tree rings and ice cores.
Ⓒ It showed that some countries would be unable to utilize this method.
Ⓓ It supports the evidence that the amount of rainfall depends on stalagmites.

Lecture 2

 AT06_3

[1-6] Listen to part of a lecture in a zoology class.

Man: Student | Woman: Professor

W During our last session, we discussed the differences between horns and antlers. What do you remember about that?

M Antlers are found on male cervids which are deer and their cousins. They are made wholly of bone, and usually are branched. Oh, and they are shed every year. So the males have to grow a new pair for each mating season, which is a huge investment of energy for them.

W Are antlers only found on male cervids?

M Ah… no… Female reindeer also have antlers. But they tend to be smaller; I forget why…

W That's fine. You said more than enough. Yes, they are smaller because they are not used for combat. They signify the female's health and thereby her access to food. And that shows her rank in the herd. Now, how about horns? How are they different?

M Horns are not shed, and they continue to grow throughout the animal's life. They are found on bovid animals like cows and antelope. They have a bone core covered in a sheath of keratin, they do not branch, and both males and females have them, although the female horns tend to be smaller as they are used for defense instead of offense.

W With that taken care of, let's move on to the function of horns in animals that are not mammals. Now, many animals have the word "horn" in their names, but they do not actually have true horns. Take the horned owl for example. It appears to have two horns on its head, but those are actually tufts of feathers.

This little fellow, however, has genuine horns. The Jackson's chameleon has three horns that protrude from its brow and snout, and they are much larger in the male chameleons. They have bone cores and keratin sheaths just like a bovid's horns. Like their bovine cousins, chameleons use their horns to attract mates and to fight over them. A male will open its mouth, lower its horns, and charge at its opponent. If it meets the other lizard horns-to-horns, they will twist and push, trying to knock each other off of the branch. But the animals will sometimes ram into softer areas like an eye or the opponent's flank, which can cause serious damage.

Chameleons also use their horns for interspecies communication. The habitats of different chameleon species often overlap. They are very territorial during mating season, but if a chameleon sees another one with different horns, it will be less likely to challenge it. That would be a waste of its time since the other chameleon would not compete with it for mating rites. It has also been observed that the horns can act as a defensive weapon. Hawks often pluck lizards out of trees, but they are less likely to eat chameleons with long horns.

Many beetles also have weapons on their bodies that look like horns and antlers. They are extensions of the insect's hard exoskeleton, so they are made of chitin instead of keratin, and they do not have bones. But they do have similar shapes and serve the same purposes. Dung beetles often have such armor, and they use it to fight for and protect the dung that they use to feed their young. Mating pairs of tunneling dung beetles will create balls of animal dung that they quickly roll away from the larger pile. They often have to fight off other beetles that try to steal their dung, and their horns are useful for this.

After they dig a deep tunnel, they put the dung balls in underground chambers and the female lays eggs in them. Then the male will place himself higher up in the tunnel to keep out other dung beetles and other parasite species that may try to lay their own eggs in the dung. The males have a variety of horns, tusks, antlers on their heads, and spikes on their forelegs that they use against invaders. They will lock up with intruder beetles and turn in circles as they push and shove. Eventually, the weaker male will break free and retreat, but these battles can last for over an hour. These chitin weapons take a similar toll on the beetles as antlers do on deer. They require energy to develop, but the larger they are the better the insect can fight. That can also help it to attract a mate.

많은 딱정벌레들 또한 뿔이나 가지뿔처럼 보이는 무기를 몸에 갖고 있습니다. 이것들은 딱정벌레의 딱딱한 외골격이 연장된 것이기에 케라틴이 아니라 키틴으로 만들어졌고, 뼈가 없습니다. 그러나 비슷한 모양을 갖고 있으며 같은 목적을 위해 이용되죠. 쇠똥구리들도 그러한 무기를 자주 갖추고 있으며, 새끼들에게 먹이는 똥을 서로 차지하려고 싸울 때나 지키기 위해 뿔을 이용합니다. 터널을 파는 쇠똥구리 한 쌍은 동물의 똥으로 큰 더미에서 빠르게 공을 만들어내어 굴립니다. 똥을 빼앗아가려는 다른 쇠똥구리와 자주 싸워야 하고, 뿔은 이럴 때 유용하죠.

깊은 터널을 판 뒤 그들은 똥으로 만든 공들을 지하 방에 놓고 암컷이 그 안에 알을 낳습니다. 그 뒤 수컷은 다른 쇠똥구리와 똥 안에 자기 알을 낳으려고 할 수도 있는 그 외의 기생충 종들을 막기 위해 터널의 더 위쪽에 자리를 잡죠. 수컷은 침입자들을 상대로 사용하는 다양한 종류의 뿔과 엄니, 가지뿔을 머리에 달고 있으며 앞다리에는 뾰족한 가시가 있습니다. 침입자 쇠똥구리와 달라붙어 서로를 밀치면서 빙빙 돌죠. 결국 더 약한 수컷이 몸을 떼고 물러나지만, 이 싸움은 한 시간 넘게 지속될 수도 있습니다. 이 키틴 무기는 사슴에게 가지뿔이 그러하듯 쇠똥구리에게 비슷한 부담을 줄 수 있어요. 발달시키는 데 에너지가 필요하지만, 더 클수록 벌레가 더 잘 싸울 수 있죠. 또한 짝짓기 상대를 끌어들이는 데도 도움이 됩니다.

어휘

discuss v 논의하다 | horn n 뿔 | antler n 가지진 뿔, 가지뿔 | cervid n 사슴과의 동물 | deer n 사슴 | wholly adv 완전히, 전적으로 | branch v 갈라지다, 나뉘다 | shed v 떨어뜨리다, 흘리다 | mating season 짝짓기 철 | investment n 투자 | reindeer n 순록 | impressed adj 깊은 인상을 받은 | combat n 싸움, 전투 | signify v 의미하다, 뜻하다 | thereby adv 그렇게 함으로써, 그것 때문에 | access n 접근, 이용 | herd n (짐승의) 떼 | bovid n 소과의 동물 | sheath n 싸개, 집 | keratin n 케라틴 | defense n 방어 | offense n 공격 | function n 기능 | mammal n 포유류 | owl n 올빼미, 부엉이 | appear to ~인 것처럼 보이다, 나타나다 | tuft n 다발, 술 | feather n 깃털 | genuine adj 진짜의 | chameleon n 카멜레온 | protrude v 돌출되다, 튀어나오다 | brow n 이마 | snout n 코, 주둥이 | bovine adj 소의 | attract v 끌어들이다 | charge v 돌격하다, 공격하다 | opponent n 적수, 상대 | lizard n 도마뱀 | knock off ~를 쳐서 치워버리다, 해치우다 | ram into ~을 들이받다 | flank n 측면, 옆구리 | damage n 피해, 손상 | interspecies n 종간 | communication n 소통, 커뮤니케이션 | habitat n 서식지 | overlap v 겹치다 | territorial adj 텃세권을 주장하는 | challenge v 싸움을 걸다, 도전하다 | compete v 경쟁하다 | mating rite 짝짓기 의식 | observe v 관찰하다 | weapon n 무기 | hawk n 매 | pluck v 뽑다, 뜯다 | beetle n 딱정벌레 | extension n 연장 | insect n 곤충 | exoskeleton n 외골격 | chitin n 키틴질 | serve v ~의 역할을 하다 | dung beetle 쇠똥구리 | armor n 갑옷 | tunneling dung beetle 터널을 파는 쇠똥구리 | pile n 더미, 무더기 | steal v 훔치다 | underground adj 지하의 | chamber n 방 | lay v 알을 낳다 | parasite n 기생충 | tusk n 엄니, 상아 | spike n 뾰족한 것, 스파이크 | foreleg n 앞다리 | invader n 침략자 | intruder n 불법 침입자 | shove v 밀치다, 떠밀다 | retreat v 물러나다 | toll n 피해, 타격

1. Main Idea
What is the main topic of the lecture?

Ⓐ The differences between horns and antlers
Ⓑ The reasons that animals grow horns and antlers
Ⓒ The various animals that have horns and antlers
Ⓓ The energy investment that horns and antlers require

2. Function & Attitude
Listen again to part of the lecture. Then answer the question.

> W Are antlers only found on male cervids?
> M Ah… no… Female reindeer also have antlers. But they tend to be smaller; I forget why…
> W That's fine. You said more than enough.

Why does the professor say this:

> W You said more than enough.

Ⓐ To indicate that she is disappointed with the student's answer
Ⓑ To point out that the student made an error in his answer
Ⓒ To show that the student failed to answer the question
Ⓓ To inform the student that he gave more detail than she expected

3. Connecting Contents
The speakers list the characteristics of horns and antlers. Indicate which characteristic belongs to which bodily structure.

	Horns	Antlers
Ⓐ Common on male animals		✓
Ⓑ Shed and regrown every year		✓
Ⓒ Have a keratin sheath over bone	✓	
Ⓓ Usually have a branched structure		✓
Ⓔ Signify the health of the animal		✓

4. Connecting Contents
Why does the professor mention the horned owl?

Ⓐ To provide an example of a misleadingly named organism
Ⓑ To illustrate that even birds sometimes grow horns
Ⓒ To indicate an animal that preys on chameleons
Ⓓ To emphasize how common horns are in nature

5. Detail

According to the professor, what is the characteristic of the horns of Jackson's chameleons?

Ⓐ They are used to defend against predators.
Ⓑ They are not able to inflict actual damage.
Ⓒ They are structurally the same as bovids'.
Ⓓ They grow from the top of their heads.

6. Inference

What can be inferred about dung beetles?

Ⓐ Their horns have bone cores like mammal horns.
Ⓑ Most species are very large for beetles.
Ⓒ Their horns are not used to compete for mates.
Ⓓ Female dung beetles do not typically protect their nests.

5.
교수에 의하면, 잭슨 카멜레온의 뿔이 가진 특징은 무엇인가?

Ⓐ 포식자를 상대로 방어하는 데 사용된다.
Ⓑ 실제로 손상을 입힐 수는 없다.
Ⓒ 소과 동물들과 구조적으로 같다.
Ⓓ 머리 맨 위에서 자란다.

6.
쇠똥구리에 대해 무엇을 추론할 수 있는가?

Ⓐ 포유류의 뿔과 같이 이들의 뿔도 중심 뼈를 갖추고 있다.
Ⓑ 대부분의 종들이 딱정벌레치고 매우 크다.
Ⓒ 이들의 뿔은 짝짓기 상대를 위해 경쟁하는 데 쓰이지 않는다.
Ⓓ 암컷 쇠똥구리는 대체로 자신의 둥지를 지키지 않는다.

Conversation 2

 AT06_4

[1-5] Listen to part of a conversation between two students.

Man: student | Woman: student

W Hey! Did you finish registration?
M Yes, but I must say I'm not really looking forward to next semester.
W Why? Is there some problem with your schedule?
M I'm taking a full 18 credits next semester. You remember how last semester I was able to take only 12 because I had to go back and forth between school and home?
W Oh yes, for your mother. I remember she's been sick.
M Right. So now, I'll have a really full load. All that's left is my core requirements, so I'm signed up for all upper-level English classes. I'm taking an advanced writing theory class, a medieval literature class, and to top it all off, I'm doing a teaching seminar. I heard it's really tough. I'll have to shadow one of the professors and basically become a TA.
W Hey! I'm signed up for that too! I'm sure we'll have different professors though.
M That's great! We can talk about it with each other. I know the seminar isn't a requirement, but it seems like everyone who wants to do a masters in English does it, especially if they want to go into teaching literature.

두 학생 간의 대화의 일부를 들으시오.

남자: 학생 | 여자: 학생

여 안녕하세요! 등록은 다 하셨어요?
남 네, 그런데 솔직히 다음 학기가 별로 기대되진 않네요.
여 왜요? 시간표에 무슨 문제가 있어요?
남 다음 학기에 18학점 꽉 채워 듣거든요. 지난 학기에는 학교와 집을 오가느라 12학점밖에 못 들었다는 거 기억하시죠?

여 아, 네. 어머니 때문에요. 어머니가 아프셨던 거 기억해요.
남 맞아요. 그래서 이번엔 정말 꽉 찬 일정이에요. 이제 남은 건 필수 과목들뿐이라서 전부 상급 영어 과목을 신청했어요. 고급 글쓰기 이론 수업, 중세 문학 수업, 그리고 설상가상으로 교육 세미나를 듣기로 했어요. 정말 힘들다고 들었어요. 교수님들 중 한 분을 따라다니며 기본적으로 조교가 되어야 해요.

여 아! 저도 그거 신청했어요! 교수님은 다르겠지만요.
남 그거 좋네요! 서로 얘기할 수 있겠어요. 세미나는 필수 과목은 아니지만, 영어 석사과정을 준비하는 사람들은 거의 다 듣는 것 같더라고요. 특히 문학 교육에 들어가고 싶으면요.

W That's certainly true. That's exciting that you're applying to grad school. I'm actually still undecided about it. I can't seem to get past the idea of my student loans piling up even higher. But I've still signed up for the seminar just in case. Are you taking the senior thesis class?

M Yes! With Dr. Harrison?

W That's it! That's great. I'm glad we're taking it together, because I heard she's really tough.

M Yeah, me too. I can't believe we're already going to be seniors! Whatever happened to your paper on minority cultures in modern literature? Did you get that published?

W My professor hasn't gotten back to me on it. Honestly, I feel like it's not going to work out.

M Do you know Dr. Davis, the professor who teaches modern literature? He's looking for a student to coauthor a paper. I think he wants to present something at the annual literature symposium. You should reach out to him! I don't know him that well, and I'm not sure what he's going to present on, but I do know that a lot of his research focuses on things like minority representation in literature. There might be a chance that your interests overlap!

W Interesting! Do you know when the symposium is?

M I think it's coming up in April. You should find out right away! You know what, I suddenly remembered reading in the student newspaper what he's presenting on. It's on something like slavery in late 19th-century literature. That could be a good match for your interests. I'm also realizing that if this happens, it will work in your favor for your senior thesis! I'm sure our professor will let you build on the research you've done, especially if it gets presented at a conference.

W Wow, thanks Mike. Maybe I'll talk to Dr. Davis right after this. I know his office is on this side of the campus. I'll let you know how it goes. Have you signed up for summer classes?

M I have. I'm taking just a one-credit class. I did the calculations, and I'll be short one credit by the time graduation comes around. I just need an elective, so I'll be taking a music class. It should be kind of fun, actually! What about you?

여 그건 맞아요. 대학원에 지원하신다니 정말 신나는 일이네요. 저는 사실 아직 결정 못 했어요. 학자금 대출이 계속 쌓여만 간다는 생각을 떨쳐낼 수가 없어요. 그래도 혹시 몰라서 세미나는 신청했어요. 혹시 졸업 논문 수업도 신청하셨어요?

남 네! 해리슨 교수님 수업이요?

여 맞아요! 좋네요. 같이 듣게 되어서 정말 다행이에요. 그녀가 엄격하다고 들었거든요.

남 네, 저도요. 벌써 우리가 4학년이 된다는 게 믿기지 않네요! 혹시 소수 문화에 관한 현대 문학 논문은 어떻게 됐어요? 출판됐나요?

여 교수님께서 아직 답을 안 주셨어요. 솔직히 잘 안 될 것 같아요.

남 현대 문학을 가르치시는 데이비스 교수님 아세요? 교수님이 논문을 공동 저술할 학생을 찾고 계세요. 연례 문학 심포지엄에서 발표하실 계획이신 것 같아요. 교수님께 연락해 보세요! 제가 그 교수님을 잘 알지는 못하고, 그가 무엇을 발표할지도 확실하지 않지만, 그가 문학에서 소수자 묘사 같은 주제로 연구를 많이 하신다고 알고 있어요. 아마 당신 관심사와 겹칠 수도 있을 것 같아요!

여 흥미롭네요! 혹시 심포지엄이 언제인지 아세요?

남 4월쯤인 것 같아요. 빨리 알아보는 게 좋을 것 같아요! 아, 갑자기 학생 신문에서 교수님이 발표하실 주제에 대해 읽었던 기억이 나네요. 19세기 후반 문학에서의 노예제에 관한 내용이었던 것 같아요. 당신의 관심사와 잘 맞을 수 있겠어요. 만약 그렇게 된다면, 졸업 논문에도 큰 도움이 될 거예요! 우리 교수님께서 당신이 이미 한 연구를 발전시킬 수 있도록 허락하실 거라고 확신해요. 특히 그것이 학회에서 발표된다면 말이에요.

여 와, 고마워요. 마이크. 이따가 바로 데이비스 교수님께 말씀드려봐야겠어요. 교수님 사무실이 캠퍼스의 이쪽에 있으니까요. 어떻게 됐는지 알려드릴게요. 여름 수업 신청하셨어요?

남 네. 1학점짜리 수업 하나 들을 거예요. 제가 계산해 보니까 졸업할 때 1학점이 부족하더라고요. 그냥 선택 과목이 하나 필요해서 음악 수업을 들으려고요. 사실 재밌을 것 같아요! 당신은요?

W I've signed up for summer classes, but not here. I've decided to take courses at a community college. I also just need six elective credits, so I've signed up for an art class and a lower-level psychology class. Like I said, these loans are seriously piling up, so I'm really hoping to keep costs down.
M That's a good idea! Why didn't I think of that?

저도 여름 수업 신청했는데, 여기서 듣지는 않아요. 커뮤니티 칼리지에서 들으려고 해요. 저도 선택 과목 6학점만 남아서, 미술 수업이랑 초급 심리학 수업을 신청했어요. 말씀드렸듯이, 학자금 대출이 정말 많이 쌓이고 있어서, 비용을 좀 줄이고 싶어요.

좋은 생각이네요! 왜 난 그런 생각을 못 했을까요?

어휘

registration n 등록 | schedule n 일정 | credit n 학점 | back and forth 왔다 갔다 | core requirement 필수 과목 | upper-level adj 고급의 | advanced adj 고급의 | medieval adj 중세의 | seminar n 세미나 | shadow v 따라다니다 | TA (teaching assistant) n 조교 | masters n 석사 | undecided adj 미정의 | student loan 학자금 대출 | senior thesis 졸업 논문 | minority n 소수 | coauthor v 공동 저술하다 | symposium n 심포지엄 | representation n 표현, 묘사 | overlap v 겹치다 | slavery n 노예제 | literature n 문학 | conference n 학회 | elective n 선택 과목

1. Main Idea
What is the conversation mainly about?
Ⓐ The students feeling overworked from their schedules
Ⓑ The students' plans for the next semester
Ⓒ Difficult classes they are both signed up for
Ⓓ How they are planning for graduate school

2. Detail
Why has the male student registered for 18 credits next semester?
Ⓐ He is preparing for graduate school.
Ⓑ His teaching seminar takes up six credits.
Ⓒ He couldn't take a full course load last semester.
Ⓓ He has to attend school from home.

3. Function & Attitude
What is the female student's attitude toward her education?
Ⓐ She feels she can get the same quality of education at a cheaper institution.
Ⓑ She wonders if the education at the university is worth the high tuition.
Ⓒ She finds her degree to be increasingly unaffordable.
Ⓓ She is frustrated with the unresponsiveness of some of her professors.

1.
이 대화는 주로 무엇에 관한 것인가?
Ⓐ 학생들이 일정 때문에 과로를 느끼는 것
Ⓑ 다음 학기에 대한 학생들의 계획
Ⓒ 두 학생 모두 신청한 어려운 수업들
Ⓓ 그들이 대학원 준비를 어떻게 하고 있는지

2.
남학생이 다음 학기에 18학점을 등록한 이유는 무엇인가?
Ⓐ 그는 대학원 준비를 하고 있다.
Ⓑ 그의 교육 세미나가 6학점을 차지한다.
Ⓒ 지난 학기에 학점을 다 채워 수업을 들을 수 없었다.
Ⓓ 그는 집에서 학교에 다녀야 한다.

3.
여학생은 그녀의 교육에 대해 어떤 태도를 가지고 있는가?
Ⓐ 그녀는 더 저렴한 기관에서 같은 수준의 교육을 받을 수 있다고 생각한다.
Ⓑ 그녀는 대학교에서의 교육이 높은 학비에 비해 가치가 있는지 궁금해한다.
Ⓒ 그녀는 자신의 학위가 점점 더 감당하기 어려워지고 있다고 생각한다.
Ⓓ 그녀는 일부 교수들의 무반응에 좌절하고 있다.

4. Detail

How will publishing the female student's work benefit her?

Choose 2 answers.

Ⓐ It will open many doors for her in her aspirations to join the teaching profession.
Ⓑ **Her work will be presented at a literature conference.**
Ⓒ **Her work can potentially be used toward her senior thesis.**
Ⓓ She can use the publication in her graduate school applications.
Ⓔ The publication can be counted for course credit.

5. Inference

What will the female student most likely do next?

Ⓐ **She will consult with Dr. Davis about a collaboration.**
Ⓑ She will go to the community college she is registered at.
Ⓒ She will prepare for her senior thesis.
Ⓓ She will persuade Mike to take classes at a different college.

4.

여학생의 연구를 출판하는 것이 그녀에게 어떻게 도움이 되는가? 두 개를 고르시오.

Ⓐ 그녀가 교직에 들어가려는 꿈에 많은 기회를 열어줄 것이다.
Ⓑ 그녀의 연구는 문학 학회에서 발표될 것이다.
Ⓒ 그녀의 연구는 졸업 논문에 사용될 가능성이 있다.
Ⓓ 그녀는 출판물을 대학원 입학 신청서에 사용할 수 있다.
Ⓔ 출판물은 학점으로 인정받을 수 있다.

5.

여학생이 다음에 할 가능성이 가장 높은 일은 무엇인가?

Ⓐ 데이비스 교수님과 협업에 대해 상담할 것이다.
Ⓑ 그녀가 등록한 커뮤니티 칼리지에 갈 것이다.
Ⓒ 그녀는 졸업 논문 준비를 할 것이다.
Ⓓ 그녀는 다른 대학교에서 수업을 들으라고 마이크를 설득할 것이다.

Lecture 3

 AT06_5

[1-6] Listen to part of a lecture in a social science class.

Man: Student | Woman: Professor

W After the invention of the movable-type printing press, books became cheaper and easier to produce, which led to a dramatic increase in literacy. It also led to the beginning of a new medium: the newspaper. As reading and education expanded people's minds, they became curious about what was happening in the world around them. To satisfy this thirst for knowledge about current events, the first newspaper was produced in 1605 in Strasbourg. They spread quickly throughout Europe, and the first successful English daily newspaper was printed in England from 1702 to 1735.

The first American newspaper was published by Benjamin Harris in Boston in 1690 titled *Publick Occurrences Both Foreign and Domestick*. However, only one edition was published before the government shut him down. The governor later had a change of heart, allowing *The Boston News*

사회과학 강의의 일부를 들으시오.

남자: 학생 | 여자: 교수

여 이동식 인쇄기의 발명 후, 책 생산이 더 저렴해지고 수월해졌고, 이는 읽고 쓰는 능력의 급격한 성장으로 이어졌습니다. 이것은 또한 새로운 매체, 즉 신문의 출발을 이끌었습니다. 독서와 교육이 사람들의 정신을 고양시킴에 따라 그들은 자신들을 둘러싼 세상에서 무슨 일이 일어나고 있는지에 관심을 가지게 되었습니다. 시사에 대한 지식의 갈망을 충족하기 위해 1605년 스트라스부르에서 최초의 신문이 제작되었습니다. 그것은 빠르게 유럽 전역으로 퍼졌으며, 최초의 성공적인 영국 일간 신문이 영국에서 1702년부터 1735년까지 간행되었습니다.

최초의 미국 신문은 벤자민 해리스에 의해 〈Publick Occurrences Both Foreign and Domestick〉라는 제목으로 보스턴에서 1690년에 발행되었습니다. 하지만 정부가 그를 중단시키기까지 1쇄만 발행되었죠. 후에 주지사는 마음을 바꾸어 1704년 〈보스턴 뉴스 레터〉의 발행을 허락하였으며, 그것이 식민지에서 성공적으

Letter to begin publication in 1704, and it went on to become the first successful continuously published newspaper in the colonies. It was a weekly newspaper, and others cropped up in New York and Philadelphia, the other two largest colonial cities.

The first American daily newspaper was *The Pennsylvania Evening Post* which started in 1775. At first it was a weekly paper, but it had to compete with five other Philadelphia papers, so Benjamin Towne, its creator, began to publish it three times a week. His newspaper was a vocal supporter of the rebellion until the British occupied Philadelphia. Towne then published pro-British articles until the Continental Army recaptured the city, at which point he printed a patriotic edition. His shrewd decisions allowed his paper to survive the war while the competition did not, leaving him the only printer left after the conflict ended. This also allowed him to secure very lucrative contracts with the state government as well as the Continental Congress. Over the course of the century, papers expanded their coverage, and editorial articles and opinion pieces became increasingly popular. The invention of the telegraph made it, so news stories about events in California could be printed in the morning edition in New York City the next day. Two new styles of journalism also developed: muck-raking and yellow journalism. Today, both terms have negative connotations, but muck-raking began as a public service. Corruption was rampant and took many forms, from city and state governments down to retail practices. Reporters would investigate these stories and reveal the truth to the people through newspaper articles. In one such case, reporter Winifred Black infiltrated a San Francisco hospital, where she observed the staff treating homeless women with what she called "gross cruelty." The morning the article was printed the entire staff was terminated.

The term yellow journalism developed out of the competition between Joseph Pulitzer's newspaper *New York World* and William Randolph Hearst's *New York Journal*. As these men vied for dominance, their papers became extremely sensational, with exaggerated headlines and articles, as well as a large amount of space devoted to reporting on crime. They were heavily criticized for these practices, but they still published detailed accounts of domestic and foreign issues.

M Wasn't Hearst partly responsible for the Spanish American War? I remember reading about that somewhere…

W Ah, that is debatable. Hearst was certainly a supporter of the cause, and his paper definitely agitated for military intervention in Cuba. He has been quoted as replying to a report of peaceful conditions in the country from artist Frederick Remington, "Please remain. You furnish the pictures and I'll furnish the war." Although, it is considered unlikely that the Journal's articles actually influenced the government to declare war. During the conflict, Hearst himself went to Cuba and reported on the fighting. His articles were sober and accurate, and gained him much praise.

In the twentieth century, newspapers faced increasingly stiff competition from other media. First, radio allowed journalists to broadcast stories directly to the public's ears. By the 1960s, American families were watching the Vietnam War unfold on their evening TV news. But, newspapers continued to publish their print editions. That is, until the 1990s, when Internet news rose up as a new threat. Today, many publications that failed to make the transition to the World Wide Web have disappeared. The survivors continue on Web sites bearing their print edition's names. While newspapers have not disappeared from the world yet, their eventual demise appears certain.

남 허스트는 미국-스페인 전쟁에 일부 책임이 있지 않나요? 어딘가에서 읽었던 기억이 나는데요…

여 아, 그건 논란의 여지가 있어요. 허스트는 확실히 대의명분을 지지했던 사람이었으며 그의 신문은 분명히 쿠바에 대한 군사적 개입을 선동했지요. 그는 예술가 프레데릭 레밍턴이 보낸 조국의 평화로운 상태에 대한 보고에 "가만히 계시오. 당신이 그림을 그리면, 나는 전쟁을 시작하겠소"라고 답신하였다고 인용된 바 있습니다. 하지만 〈저널〉의 기사가 실제로 정부가 전쟁을 선포하는 데 영향을 끼쳤을 리는 없을 거라 짐작됩니다. 분쟁 기간 동안 허스트는 직접 쿠바를 찾아가 교전 상황에 대해 보도했습니다. 그의 기사들은 냉철하고도 정확했으며, 그는 많은 칭송을 받았습니다.

20세기에는 신문이 다른 미디어와의 점점 더 치열한 경쟁에 부딪혔습니다. 우선, 라디오 덕분에 기자들은 대중들의 귀에 직접 뉴스거리를 방송할 수 있었습니다. 1960년대에는, 미국 가정이 저녁 TV 뉴스에서 방송되는 베트남 전쟁을 보게 되었습니다. 하지만 신문은 계속해서 인쇄판을 출간했습니다. 1990년대에 들어 인터넷 뉴스가 새로운 위협 요소로 등장하기 전까지 말이죠. 오늘날 인터넷으로 전환하는 데 실패한 많은 출판물들이 사라졌습니다. 살아남은 신문사들은 자신들의 인쇄판 이름을 그대로 유지하면서 웹사이트를 통해 계속해서 보도를 이어나갑니다. 신문이 전 세계에서 아직 사라진 것은 아니지만, 그들의 궁극적 종말은 확실해 보입니다.

어휘

movable adj 움직일 수 있는 | **printing press** 인쇄기 | **dramatic** adj 극적인 | **literacy** n 읽고 쓸 줄 아는 능력 | **medium** n 매체 | **expand** v 확장하다 | **publication** n 출판 | **continuously** adv 지속적으로 | **colony** n 식민지 | **crop up** 돌연히 나타나다 | **compete** v 경쟁하다 | **rebellion** n 반란, 모반 | **occupy** v 점령하다 | **recapture** v 탈환하다, 다시 붙잡다 | **patriotic** adj 애국적인 | **shrewd** adj 상황 판단이 빠른, 기민한 | **conflict** n 갈등 | **lucrative** adj 수익성이 좋은 | **contract** n 계약 | **editorial** adj 편집의 | **article** n 기사 | **telegraph** n 전신, 전보 | **muck-raking** n 추문하기 | **yellow journalism** 황색 저널리즘, 선정적 언론 | **connotation** n 함축, 암시 | **public service** 공공 서비스 | **corruption** n 부패 | **rampant** adj 만연한 | **retail** n 소매 | **investigate** v 수사하다 | **infiltrate** v 잠입하다, 침투하다 | **gross** adj 역겨운 | **cruelty** n 잔혹함 | **terminate** v 끝나다, 종료되다 | **vie** v 다투다, 경쟁하다 | **dominance** n 권세, 지배 | **sensational** adj 선정적인, 세상을 놀라게 하는 | **exaggerate** v 과장하다 | **devote** v 바치다 | **debatable** adj 논란의 여지가 있는 | **agitate** v 불안하게 하다 | **intervention** n 중재, 조정 | **declare** v 선포하다 | **sober** adj 술 취하지 않은, 냉철한 | **broadcast** v 방송하다 | **threat** n 위협 | **demise** n 종말

1. **Main Idea**
What is the main idea of the lecture?
- (A) **How newspapers in the U.S. developed over time**
- (B) Why U.S. newspapers were able to succeed overseas
- (C) How newspapers gained popularity in the 18th century
- (D) Why U.S. citizens started reading newspapers

2. **Connecting Contents**
Why does the professor mention *Publick Occurrences Both Foreign and Domestick*?
- (A) To compare the characteristics of it with the first daily newspaper
- (B) To distinguish it from the other daily newspapers at the time
- (C) To compare Benjamin Harris's experience with Benjamin Towne's
- (D) **To highlight the importance of the first American newspaper**

3. **Detail**
What is a key feature of *The Pennsylvania Evening Post* mentioned in the lecture?
- (A) It published editorial articles for the first time.
- (B) **It was the first American daily newspaper.**
- (C) It contained detailed stories about crimes.
- (D) It was unable to survive against harsh competition.

4. **Function & Attitude**
What does the professor mean when she says this:
> Today, both terms have negative connotations, but muck-raking began as a public service.

- (A) She believes that muck-raking is not different from public service.
- (B) She feels annoyed because muck-raking is so undervalued these days.
- (C) **She wants to explain that muck-raking had a positive impact at first.**
- (D) She knows that the students do not appreciate muck-raking at all.

5. **Detail**
According to the lecture, what is true about William Randolph Hearst?
- (A) He devoted most of his newspaper to opinion pieces.
- (B) He was heavily criticized for his reports on the fighting.
- (C) **He contributed to the development of yellow journalism.**
- (D) He was responsible for the Spanish American War.

1.
강의의 주제는 무엇인가?
- (A) 세월이 흐르면서 미국 신문이 어떻게 발전했는지
- (B) 미국 신문들이 왜 해외에서 성공을 거둘 수 있었는지
- (C) 18세기에 신문이 어떻게 인기를 얻을 수 있었는지
- (D) 미국 시민들이 왜 신문을 읽기 시작했는지

2.
교수가 〈Publick Occurrences Both Foreign and Domestick〉을 언급한 이유는 무엇인가?
- (A) 최초의 일간지와 특징을 비교하기 위해
- (B) 당대의 다른 일간 신문과 구분하기 위해
- (C) 벤자민 해리스의 경험을 벤자민 타운의 경험과 비교하기 위해
- (D) 미국 최초 신문의 중요성을 강조하기 위해

3.
강의에서 언급된 〈펜실베니아 이브닝 포스트〉의 핵심적인 특징은 무엇인가?
- (A) 최초로 사설을 실었다.
- (B) 최초의 미국 일간 신문이었다.
- (C) 범죄에 대해 상세한 보도 기사를 실었다.
- (D) 극심한 경쟁에서 살아남을 수 없었다.

4.
교수는 다음과 같이 말하며 무엇을 의미하는가:
> 오늘날 두 용어 모두 부정적인 의미를 담고 있지만, 폭로 저널리즘은 공공 서비스로 시작되었습니다.

- (A) 폭로 저널리즘이 공공 서비스와 다르지 않다고 생각한다.
- (B) 폭로 저널리즘이 요즘 매우 과소평가되고 있다는 사실이 못마땅하다.
- (C) 폭로 저널리즘이 처음에는 긍정적인 영향을 끼쳤다는 것을 설명하고 싶어한다.
- (D) 학생들이 폭로 저널리즘의 진가를 전혀 알아보지 못한다는 것을 알고 있다.

5.
강의에 의하면, 윌리엄 랜돌프 허스트에 대해 옳은 것은 무엇인가?
- (A) 신문의 대부분을 의견 기고란에 할애했다.
- (B) 전쟁에 관한 보도로 신랄한 비판을 받았다.
- (C) 황색 저널리즘의 발전에 기여했다.
- (D) 미국-스페인 전쟁에 책임이 있었다.

6. Inference

According to the professor, what can be inferred about the future of newspapers?

Ⓐ They will start competing with TV news.
Ⓑ They will focus more on foreign issues.
Ⓒ They will try to print more editions.
Ⓓ They will eventually cease publication.

6.
교수에 의하면, 신문의 미래에 대해 무엇을 추론할 수 있는가?

Ⓐ TV 뉴스와 경쟁하기 시작할 것이다.
Ⓑ 해외 이슈에 좀 더 집중하게 될 것이다.
Ⓒ 더 많은 쇄를 찍으려고 할 것이다.
Ⓓ 결국 출판을 중단할 것이다.

Actual Test 07

본서 | P. 124

Conversation 1	1. Ⓑ	2. Ⓑ	3. Ⓒ, Ⓔ	4. Ⓒ	5. Ⓐ	
Lecture 1	1. Ⓓ	2. Ⓒ	3. Ⓑ	4. Ⓒ	5. Ⓐ	6. Ⓐ, Ⓒ
Lecture 2	1. Ⓐ	2. Ⓑ, Ⓒ	3. Ⓓ	4. Ⓓ	5. Ⓐ	6. Ⓒ
Conversation 2	1. Ⓒ	2. Ⓑ	3. Ⓑ	4. Ⓐ	5. Ⓓ	
Lecture 3	1. Ⓐ	2. Ⓓ	3. Ⓑ	4. Ⓒ, Ⓓ	5. Ⓐ	6. Ⓒ

● 내가 맞은 문제 유형의 개수를 적어 보고 어느 유형에 취약한지 확인해 봅시다.

문제 유형	맞은 개수
Main Idea	5
Detail	12
Connecting Contents	3
Function & Attitude	4
Inference	4
Total	28

Conversation 1

[1-5] Listen to part of a conversation between a student and a library employee.

Man: Student | Woman: employee

W Hi! How can I help you?

M Hello! I'm trying to write a literature review for my psych class, and I'm not very familiar with the psychology section of the library. To be honest, I'm not very familiar with writing literature reviews either!

W I wish I could help you with the latter! But I can definitely help you with finding resources. Did you say psychology? What's your literature review on?

M Yes, it's for PSYCH 201. My topic is psychoanalysis.

W Ah! With Dr. Meyer! Yes. Well, for starters, you can visit the psychology section on the fourth floor.

M I've looked there. And I can see there's a huge range of resources, but I can't quite find much that will help me zero in on contemporary psychoanalysis.

W Okay. Can you tell me more about what you're interested in? Do you have any psychologists in particular that you want to research?

M I'm looking for stuff on relational psychotherapy. The subfield I'm interested in is self-psychology, which I understand is still a developing field. Heinz Kohut would be an author that I'm very interested in.

W Okay, I'm searching our database at the moment, and it seems like we only have journal articles written by this man. Have you had the chance to check our psychology journals section? Our library is subscribed to the Journal of Contemporary Psychoanalysis. Seems there are a few articles that cite this Kohut guy.

M Huh? I've looked everywhere for them but couldn't find any.

W It sounds like you were looking for physical copies! We don't have those anymore. Everything is electronic now. If you need immediate access to them, you can use the library computers. Since you're registered for a psychology course at the moment, you can use your student ID number and course code as your credentials.

M I had no idea. That's really good to know.

W: Sure! That's probably your best bet aside from the stuff that's on reserve.

M: On reserve?

W: Yes. Actually, that's how I knew who your professor was. Dr. Meyer has kept a huge stack of resources on reserve for your class to use on this assignment.

M: Oh! I thought I'd heard something along those lines, but I wasn't clear on the details. I'm so glad you said something about it!

W: Me too! That was a close one. Dr. Meyer has placed the sources on reserve on the same floor as the psychology section. It's right behind that section if you're facing it from the elevators.

M: Thank you. This is really a great help.

W: Good. Oh, I forgot to mention that we also have some psychology books in the rare books collection. I know literature reviews are usually on more contemporary sources, but you might want to compare them with some older stuff. Plus, some of these books are originals from Melanie Klein herself! I bet you'd enjoy seeing some of them firsthand.

M: How did I not know about this? Is this also all included in the books Dr. Meyer put on reserve?

W: No. The rare books collection is locked away in a completely separate location. It's located on the 5th floor, but in order to access it, we're going to need your student ID and driver's license.

M: Wow, I can't think of anything more inspiring than getting my hands on an original Klein publication!

W: Actually, we need to be a little careful about that. In fact, we have to get you fitted with a pair of special gloves. Can you show me your hands for a second?

어휘

literature review 문헌 검토 | **familiar** adj 익숙한 | **latter** n 후자 | **resource** n 자료 | **psychoanalysis** n 정신분석 | **contemporary** adj 현대의 | **relational psychotherapy** 관계 심리치료 | **subfield** n 하위 분야 | **developing** adj 발전 중인 | **database** n 데이터베이스 | **journal article** 학술 논문 | **physical copies** 실물 자료, 실물 사본 | **electronic** adj 전자적인 | **credentials** n 자격 | **on reserve** 예약 중인 | **assignment** n 과제 | **rare** adj 희귀한 | **original** adj 원본의 | **access** n 접근 | **driver's license** 운전면허증 | **inspiring** adj 영감을 주는 | **publication** n 출판물 | **pair** n 쌍 | **special gloves** 특수 장갑

1. **Main Idea**

Why does the student meet with the employee?

Ⓐ The student needs help finding resources for a final paper for a psychology class.
Ⓑ **The student needs help locating sources for a literature review.**
Ⓒ The student doesn't know where to find the rare books collection.
Ⓓ The student is unfamiliar with writing psychology reviews.

2. **Detail**

What is the topic that the student is trying to write on?

Ⓐ Contemporary psychoanalysis
Ⓑ **Self-psychology**
Ⓒ Relational psychotherapy
Ⓓ Melanie Klein

3. **Detail**

What errors has the student committed? Choose 2 answers.

Ⓐ He couldn't find the writing books in the reserved books section.
Ⓑ He tried to touch rare books without the required specialized gloves.
Ⓒ **He didn't understand what Dr. Meyer meant when he mentioned books on reserve.**
Ⓓ He thought the rare books collection was located within the reserved books area.
Ⓔ **He didn't realize that psychology journals now come in electronic form.**

4. **Function & Attitude**

Listen again to part of the conversation. Then answer the question.

> Ⓜ Oh! I thought I'd heard something along those lines, but I wasn't clear on the details. I'm so glad you said something about it!
> Ⓦ Me too! That was a close one.

Why does the employee say this:

> Ⓦ Me too! That was a close one.

Ⓐ The employee is also relieved that she got the chance to explain the location of the psychology section.
Ⓑ The employee is sympathizing with the student's panic regarding the project.

1.
학생은 왜 직원을 만나러 갔는가?

Ⓐ 학생은 심리학 수업의 기말 논문을 위한 자료를 찾는 데 도움이 필요하다.
Ⓑ 학생은 문헌 검토를 위한 자료를 찾는 데 도움이 필요하다.
Ⓒ 학생은 희귀 도서 컬렉션이 어디에 있는지 모른다.
Ⓓ 학생은 심리학 리뷰 작성에 익숙하지 않다.

2.
학생이 쓰려고 하는 주제는 무엇인가?

Ⓐ 현대 정신분석
Ⓑ 자기 심리학
Ⓒ 관계 심리치료
Ⓓ 멜라니 클라인

3.
학생이 어떤 오류를 저질렀나? 두 개를 고르시오.

Ⓐ 그는 예약 도서 코너에서 작문 교재를 찾을 수 없었다.
Ⓑ 그는 특수 장갑 없이 희귀 도서를 만지려고 했다.
Ⓒ 그는 마이어 교수님이 예약 도서에 대해 언급했을 때 무슨 뜻인지 이해하지 못했다.
Ⓓ 그는 희귀 도서 컬렉션이 예약 도서 구역 내에 있다고 생각했다.
Ⓔ 그는 심리학 저널이 이제 전자 형태로 제공된다는 사실을 몰랐다.

4.
강의의 일부를 다시 듣고 질문에 답하시오.

> 남 아! 그런 얘기를 들은 적이 있는 것 같긴 한데, 정확한 내용을 몰랐어요. 말씀해 주셔서 정말 다행이에요!
> 여 저도 마찬가지예요! 큰일 날 뻔했네요.

직원은 왜 이렇게 말하는가:

> 여 저도 마찬가지예요! 큰일 날 뻔했네요.

Ⓐ 직원은 심리학 코너의 위치를 설명할 기회를 얻게 되어 안도하고 있다.
Ⓑ 직원은 프로젝트에 대한 학생의 당혹감에 공감하고 있다.

- Ⓒ **The employee realizes how fortunate it is that the topic of reserved books came up.**
- Ⓓ The employee is pointing out the location of a psychology journal.

5. **Inference**
What will the student most likely do next?
- Ⓐ **Read an original edition of a book by Melanie Klein**
- Ⓑ Obtain a new ID card
- Ⓒ Search for articles by Heinz Kohut
- Ⓓ Search the psychology books on reserve

Lecture 1

[1-6] Listen to part of a lecture in a geology class.

Man: Student | Woman: Professor

W: Before we begin to discuss the possibility of intelligent life—well, any form of life, actually—existing outside of our solar system, we need to answer a basic question. In our solar system, why is Earth the only planet on which life exists?

M: Because of the size and brightness of the Sun relative to the size and distance of the Earth, I remember that from the reading.

W: Excellent, those are very important factors, but what do they determine? **You have outlined the boundaries of a zone wherein what can exist? What does life as we know it need to exist?**

M: Water!

W: Yes, water. Without water there is no life. But, there is actually a large amount of water throughout the universe. What makes that zone special, and the Earth special in our solar system, is that water can exist there in a liquid form. On most planets, water would either freeze or evaporate due to the extreme temperatures. As I'm sure you already know, around 71 percent of the Earth's surface is covered in water, and it accounts for 0.02 percent of the planet's mass. I know that doesn't sound like much, but it's actually spread pretty thinly over the surface. Now, the important question to answer is how it even got here. There are a few overlapping theories for this, the first of which is volcanic activity.

When the solar system formed, the inner planets were all balls of molten rock. As they began cooling, volcanic activity continued, spewing various gases into the Earth's atmosphere. Many of these gases, including carbon dioxide, are what we call greenhouse gases, and they trapped some of the Earth's heat, which allowed water to remain in a liquid state after most of the surface activity had ceased. But, some scientists have questioned whether this is the full story. They do not think that this could account for the volume of greenhouse gases or the total amount of water that exist. So, they looked for other large sources of water that could have reached the Earth, and they settled on comets.

Comets are balls of ice, rock and gases, and many of them orbit our sun, so a few could have easily impacted the Earth early in its history. However, recent probe surveys of comets have discovered a flaw in this concept. All of the water in the universe contains varying amounts of a hydrogen isotope called deuterium. Normal hydrogen has a single proton in its nucleus, while deuterium has one proton and one neutron. Deuterium is consumed inside of stars more rapidly than it is created, so scientists believe that all the deuterium in the universe came from the Big Bang. That means that objects that exist farther away from the Sun have more deuterium than those that are closer to it. The oceans on Earth contain 99.98 percent normal hydrogen and only a tiny fraction of deuterium. However, comets come from outside the solar system and appear to have a far higher concentration of deuterium, so they could not have been a significant source. So, what other objects have impacted the Earth in its history? Meteors. Millions upon millions of them...

Many of the meteorites that have been discovered on Earth date back to about 4 billion years ago, when the Earth, its moon, and Mars were all being battered with meteoroids. This celestial assault lasted for around 200 to 300 million years. Called the Late Heavy Bombardment, it created much of the Moon's surface as it exists today. Not long after the LHB ended, the first single-celled organisms began to emerge, and there may be a connection. When a meteor enters the Earth's atmosphere, its surface temperature suddenly and drastically increases due to friction. It begins to disintegrate, and usually loses much of its mass

속되었고, 다양한 가스를 지구의 대기에 뿜어냈죠. 이 가스들의 다수가 이산화탄소를 포함해 우리가 온실가스라 부르는 것들이고, 그것은 일부 지구 열을 가두었고 대부분의 지표면 활동이 멈춘 뒤에도 물이 액체 상태로 남아 있도록 만들었습니다. 그러나 어떤 과학자들은 이것이 전부가 아닐 거라고 생각했습니다. 그들은 이것이 온실가스의 부피, 혹은 존재하는 물의 총량을 설명하지 못한다고 생각합니다. 따라서 지구에 도달했을 만한 다른 큰 원천의 물을 찾았고, 혜성이라는 결론에 도달했습니다.

혜성은 얼음, 암석, 가스 덩어리이고 많은 수가 태양을 공전하기에 그 중 일부는 지구 역사 초기에 쉽게 영향을 미쳤을 수 있습니다. 그러나 최근의 혜성 탐색침 조사는 이러한 개념에 오류가 있다는 것을 밝혀냈습니다. 우주의 모든 물은 중수소라는 수소 동위 원소를 각기 다른 양으로 포함하고 있습니다. 일반 수소는 핵에 하나의 양성자를 갖고 있는 반면, 중수소는 하나의 양성자와 하나의 중성자를 가지고 있죠. 중수소는 생성되는 것보다 더 빠르게 별의 내부에서 소모되기 때문에 과학자들은 우주의 모든 중수소가 빅뱅에서 유래한 것이라고 믿습니다. 이는 태양으로부터 멀리 떨어진 물체일수록 태양과 가까운 물체보다 더 많은 중수소를 가지고 있다는 뜻입니다. 지구의 바다는 99.98%의 일반 수소로 이루어져 있으며, 오직 일부만 이 중수소입니다. 그러나 혜성은 태양계 바깥에서 오는데도 훨씬 많은 중수소를 가지고 있는 것으로 보이므로 그들은 중요한 원천이 될 수 없었습니다. 그러면 어떤 다른 물체들이 지구의 역사에서 지구에 영향을 주었을까요? 유성들입니다. 수십억 개의 유성들...

지구에서 발견된 많은 운석들은 지구와, 달, 그리고 화성이 모두 유성에 강타당한 약 40억 년 전으로 거슬러 올라갑니다. 이 천체 공격은 약 2백~3백만 년 동안 계속되었습니다. 후기 대폭격으로 불리는 이 시기는 오늘날 존재하는 달 표면의 대부분을 만들어냈습니다. 후기 대폭격이 끝나고 얼마 지나지 않아 최초의 단세포 생물체가 출현하기 시작했으므로 무언가 연관성이 있을 것입니다. 유성이 지구 대기에 들어오면 그것의 표면 온도는 마찰로 인해 갑작스럽고 급격하게 상승합니다. 그것은 분해되기 시작하고, 보통 착륙하기 전 대기에서 질량의 대부분을 잃게 됩니다. 그래서 과학자들은 운석 조각들을 섭씨 1000도까지 올리기 위해 전기를 사용했습니다. 그들은 많은 양의 이산화탄소와 산소를 방출하였고, 중수소의 양은 바닷물과 비

into the atmosphere before landing. So, scientists used electricity to raise meteorite pieces to 1,000 degrees Centigrade. They released large amounts of both CO_2 and H_2O, and their deuterium quantity was similar to ocean water. Therefore, it seems likely that a large percentage of Earth's water came from meteors.

M What about Mars? You said the LHB affected it, too. Why is there no liquid water there?

W An excellent question. There is evidence that liquid water did exist on Mars at one time. However, Mars has a very thin atmosphere compared to Earth due to its much weaker magnetic field. It could not hold on to its greenhouse gases, so much of its water was lost into space, and what little that remains is frozen at its poles.

숫했습니다. 따라서 지구에 있는 많은 양의 물이 운석으로부터 왔다는 것이 그럴듯해 보입니다.

학 화성은 어떻죠? 교수님께서 후기 대폭격이 화성에도 영향을 미쳤다고 말씀하셨잖아요. 그런데 화성에는 왜 액체 형태의 물이 없나요?

여 매우 좋은 질문입니다. 화성에 한때 액체 형태의 물이 존재했다는 증거가 있습니다. 하지만, 화성은 지구와 비교하면 자기장이 매우 약해서 매우 얇은 대기층을 가지고 있어요. 그것은 온실가스를 잡아둘 수 없었을 것이고, 따라서 대부분의 물이 우주로 방출되어 버렸고 남아있는 물의 일부는 극지방에 얼어 있습니다.

어휘

possibility n 가능성 | **solar system** 태양계 | **outline** v 윤곽을 잡다 | **boundary** n 범위 | **evaporate** v 증발하다 | **account for** ~를 설명하다, 처리하다 | **overlap** v 겹치다 | **inner planet** 지구형 행성 | **molten** adj 녹은 | **volcanic** adj 화산의 | **spew** v 뿜어져 나오다, 분출되다 | **carbon dioxide** 이산화탄소 | **greenhouse gas** 온실 가스 | **trap** v 가두다 | **cease** v 중단하다 | **comet** n 혜성 | **orbit** v 궤도를 돌다 | **impact** v 충돌하다, 영향을 주다 | **probe** n 탐색침 | **flaw** n 결함, 흠 | **isotope** n 동위 원소 | **deuterium** n 중수소 | **proton** n 양성자 | **nucleus** n 핵 | **consume** v 소모하다 | **fraction** n 일부, 부분 | **significant** adj 중요한 | **meteor** n 유성, 별똥별 | **batter** v 강타하다 | **celestial** adj 천체의, 하늘의 | **assault** v 폭행하다 | **emerge** v 나타나다 | **connection** n 관련성, 연관성 | **drastically** adv 철저하게 | **friction** n 마찰, 저항 | **disintegrate** v 해체되다, 분해되다 | **evidence** n 증거 | **magnetic field** 자기장

1. Main Idea

What is the lecture mainly about?

Ⓐ Volcanic activity contributing to the formation of water on Earth
Ⓑ The different atmospheric structures of Earth and Mars
Ⓒ The Late-Heavy Bombardment period on Earth, the Moon and Mars
Ⓓ **Theories regarding the process of water formation on Earth**

2. Function & Attitude

Why does the professor say this:

> W You have outlined the boundaries of a zone wherein what can exist? What does life as we know it need to exist?

Ⓐ To tell the students to focus on some other interesting points
Ⓑ To request different opinions from as many students as possible

1.
강의는 주로 무엇에 관한 것인가?

Ⓐ 지구 물의 형성에 대한 화산활동의 기여
Ⓑ 지구와 화성의 다른 대기 구조
Ⓒ 지구와 달, 화성의 후기 대폭격기
Ⓓ **지구 물의 형성 과정에 대한 이론들**

2.
교수는 왜 이렇게 말하는가:

> 여 어떤 것이 존재할 수 있는 구역의 범위를 규정한 건가요? 우리가 알기로 생명이 존재하기 위해 필요한 것은 무엇이죠?

Ⓐ 학생들에게 다른 흥미로운 점에 주목하라고 말하기 위해
Ⓑ 가능한 한 많은 학생들로부터 다양한 의견을 요청하기 위해

- Ⓒ **To prepare to introduce the topic of the lecture to students**
- Ⓓ To indicate that no one really knows the answers to her questions

3. **Inference**

What can be inferred about the volcanic theory?
- Ⓐ It is the main source for the formation of water on the Earth's surface after all.
- Ⓑ **It is questionable since volcanoes could not generate enough greenhouse gases.**
- Ⓒ It is flawed because the concentration of deuterium was higher after the volcanic activity.
- Ⓓ It is significant since it produced various gases for more than 200 million years.

4. **Connecting Contents**

Why does the professor mention deuterium?
- Ⓐ To provide evidence of how meteors burn up when they enter the Earth's atmosphere
- Ⓑ To show how volcanoes erupted and emitted various gases, including greenhouse gases
- Ⓒ **To explain that the comet theory cannot be the main reason for water formation**
- Ⓓ To point out that deuterium had a significant impact on the formation of the ocean

5. **Detail**

What connection does the professor make between comets and meteors?
- Ⓐ **Meteors contributed more to the formation of water on the planet than comets did.**
- Ⓑ The theory of meteors depositing water on Earth has been discredited by the comets theory.
- Ⓒ They both had significant influence on the formation of oceans and land masses.
- Ⓓ Meteorites and comets hitting the Earth's surface eventually led to volcanic eruptions.

6. **Detail**

According to the professor, what is true about the Late Heavy Bombardment? *Choose 2 answers.*
- Ⓐ **It set the stage for creating life on Earth.**
- Ⓑ It activated volcanoes all over the globe.
- Ⓒ **It produced greenhouse gases.**
- Ⓓ It lasted more than a billion years.

Lecture 2

[1-6] Listen to part of a lecture in a history class.

Man: Professor | Woman: Student

M Among the many cultures that lived in the Middle East between the Neolithic Period and the rise of Islam, one of the more obscure has been the Hurrians. They arrived in the northern part of the Fertile Crescent in the Middle Bronze Age and quickly spread to occupy an area that stretched from the Zagros Mountains in the east to the Khabur River Valley in the west. Although they adopted the cuneiform writing system of the Akkadians by around 2000 BCE, they actually spoke a language that was unrelated to the Indo-European and Semitic ones spoken by most of the other cultures in the area at that time.

Many historians believe that they originated in the Caucasus region, and some respected Russian linguists have drawn comparisons between Hurrian and Northeast Caucasus languages, but their true origins remain unknown. Despite their linguistic differences, they greatly influenced their neighbors, and the Hittites in particular, and they eventually came to dominate their region for a brief time as the kingdom of Mitanni.

One reason that researching their culture is difficult is that the Hurrians did not urbanize on the scale that their Assyrian and Egyptian neighbors did. The cities of Babylon and Thebes were huge urban centers, while the majority of Hurrrian city mounds in the Khabur Valley are rarely larger than one square kilometer. The notable exception to this rule is the city of Urkesh, which is their oldest city. The Hurrians appear to have been much more decentralized, with a more feudal organization that precluded large palace or temple complexes. However, they were still very influential.

The Hurrians are noted for their masterful pottery, exceptional metal work, and their pervasive religion. The ceramics that the Hurrians produced are referred to as Khabur ware and Nuzi ware. Both types of pottery are made on a wheel, and they were highly valued as far away as Egypt. Khabur ware predates Nuzi ware, and its construction tends to be somewhat heavier. It is decorated with red lines and geometric patterns, while Nuzi is more delicate and painted black or brown.

역사 강의의 일부를 들으시오.

남자: 교수 | 여자: 학생

신석기 시대와 이슬람의 출현 사이에 중동 지역에 생존했던 많은 문화권 가운데, 좀 더 베일에 싸여 있는 이들 중 하나는 후르리인들입니다. 이들은 청동기 시대 중기에 비옥한 초승달 지대의 북쪽에 도착했고 빠르게 수가 증가하여 동쪽의 자그로스산맥부터 서쪽의 하부르강 유역의 지역을 점령했어요. 기원전 약 2000년경에 아카드인들의 설형 문자 체계를 도입했지만, 그들은 그 시기 그 지역에 살던 다른 대다수 문화권에서 쓴 언어였던 인도유럽어나 셈어와는 관계가 없는 언어를 썼습니다.

많은 역사학자들은 이들이 코카서스 지방에서 왔다고 생각하며 몇몇 명성 있는 러시아 언어학자들은 후르리인과 동북 코카서스의 언어를 비교해보기도 했지만 이들이 어디에서 왔는지는 여전히 알려지지 않고 있습니다. 언어적인 차이에도 불구하고 이들은 이웃들, 특히 히타이트인들에게 매우 많은 영향을 주었고 이들은 결국 짧은 기간 동안 미탄니제국이라는 이름으로 그 지역을 지배하게 됩니다.

그들의 문화를 연구하기 어려운 이유들 중 하나는 후르리인들이 그들의 이웃인 아시리아나 이집트가 행했던 규모로 도시화하지 않았기 때문이에요. 바빌론과 테베의 도시들은 거대한 도심지였던 반면 하부르계곡의 대다수 후르리 도시 언덕들은 1평방 킬로미터보다 컸던 적이 거의 없었습니다. 이 법칙을 깬 주목할 만한 예외는 우르케쉬라는 도시인데, 후르리인들의 가장 오래된 도시이죠. 후르리인들은 큰 성이나 사원 건물들이 생기는 것을 막은 더 봉건화된 조직을 갖춘 훨씬 분산된 민족으로 보입니다. 그러나 여전히 영향력은 컸죠.

후르리인들은 원숙한 도예, 우수한 금속 가공, 그리고 보편화된 종교로 유명합니다. 후르리인들이 생산한 도자기들은 하부르 도자기와 누지 도자기라고 불리죠. 두 종류 모두 녹로에서 만들어졌고 멀리 이집트에까지 높이 평가받았습니다. 하부르 도자기는 누지 도자기보다 앞서며 구성이 어느 정도 육중한 경향이 있죠. 그것은 붉은 선과 기하학적 패턴으로 꾸며진 반면 누지 도자기는 더 섬세하며 검은색이나 갈색으로 칠해졌습니다.

W: The Khabur Valley was located in the center of the metal trade, and copper, silver, and tin were mined from Hurrian controlled areas and traded there. The Hurrians also had a reputation as skilled smiths, and their terminology for copper working was adopted by the Sumerians. This shows that they were superior artisans, and that they may have even introduced the technology to some local cultures. Unfortunately, few samples of their metal work have survived except from the latter part of their civilization, but a few small lion figurines found in Urkesh show fine craftsmanship. In a variety of ways and forms, the Hurrian religion affected nearly the entire ancient Near East, with the exceptions of Egypt which already had a well established pantheon of gods, and southern Mesopotamia. Perhaps its greatest impact was on the religion of the Hittites, but their gods and the legends about them pervaded the region. Some have even been said to have inspired some of the earliest legends of the Greeks, especially those regarding the creation of the Olympians.

W: Professor, you mentioned that the Hurrians also gained political influence; will you go into that more?

M: I was just getting to that. The Hurrian kingdom had been reduced to a vassal state by the early 20th century BCE. But, as the Babylonian civilization continued to fragment in the 18th century BCE before the conquest of the Hittites, the Hurrians steadily expanded their territory until they were able to form a distinct kingdom once again. They eventually possessed lands extending to the Mediterranean Sea, which brought them into conflict with Egypt. Under a king named Kirta, they established the kingdom of Mitanni around 1500 BCE, which developed into the most powerful kingdom in the region and lasted until about 1300 BCE. Afterward, they were absorbed by the Assyrians, and became a subservient state once again.

어휘

Neolithic Period 신석기 시대 | **obscure** adj 잘 알려지지 않은 | **Fertile Crescent** 비옥한 초승달 지역 | **Middle Bronze Age** 청동기 시대 중기 | **cuneiform** n 설형 문자 | **originate** v 비롯되다, 유래하다 | **respected** adj 훌륭한, 소문난 | **linguist** n 언어학자 | **urbanize** v 도시화하다 | **notable** adj 주목할 만한 | **decentralize** v 분산되다 | **feudal** adj 봉건의 | **preclude** v 못하게 하다 | **masterful** adj 능수능란한 | **pervasive** adj 만연하는, 스며드는 | **predate** v ~보다 앞서다 | **construction** n 구성 | **geometric** adj 기하학의 | **delicate** adj 섬세한 | **reputation** n 평판, 명성 | **terminology** n 용어 | **superior** adj 우월한

figurine n 작은 조각상 | **craftsmanship** n 손재주, 솜씨 | **pantheon** n 신들 | **pervade** v 만연하다, 배어들다 | **vassal state** 속국 | **fragment** v 부서지다, 해체되다 | **conquest** n 정복 | **steadily** adv 꾸준히, 서서히 | **expand** v 확장하다 | **absorb** v 흡수하다 | **subservient** adj 종속하는

1. Main Idea
What is the main topic of the lecture?
- Ⓐ **The influence of the Hurrians on their neighboring cultures**
- Ⓑ Hurrian religion and its influence on Greek religion
- Ⓒ Recent research and excavations regarding the Hurrians
- Ⓓ The discovery of the location of the Hurrians' central city

1.
강의의 주제는 무엇인가?
- Ⓐ 이웃 문명들에 후르리인들이 끼친 영향
- Ⓑ 후르리 종교와 이것이 그리스 종교에 끼친 영향
- Ⓒ 후르리인들에 관한 최근의 연구와 발굴
- Ⓓ 후르리인들의 중심 도시 위치의 발견

2. Detail
According to the lecture, what is true about the Hurrians?
Choose 2 answers.
- Ⓐ They dominated the Middle East by 2000 BCE.
- Ⓑ **They spoke a different language from their neighbors.**
- Ⓒ **They started using a cuneiform writing system around 2000 BCE.**
- Ⓓ They had a great influence on the Assyrians in particular.

2.
강의에 의하면, 후르리인들에 대해 옳은 것은 무엇인가?
두 개를 고르시오.
- Ⓐ 기원전 2000년경까지 중동을 지배했다.
- Ⓑ 이웃들과 다른 언어로 말했다.
- Ⓒ 기원전 2000년경에 설형 문자 체계를 쓰기 시작했다.
- Ⓓ 특히 아시리아인들에게 큰 영향을 끼쳤다.

3. Detail
What resulted from the Hurrians' small-scale urbanization?
- Ⓐ It helped with determining when they began settlements.
- Ⓑ It led to higher levels of migration to other countries.
- Ⓒ It increased the attacks from their enemies in general.
- Ⓓ **It made studying their culture and cities rather difficult.**

3.
후르리인들의 소규모 도시화로 어떤 결과가 발생했는가?
- Ⓐ 언제 정착을 시작했는지 알아내는 데 도움을 주었다.
- Ⓑ 다른 나라로의 이민이 더욱 증가하게 되었다.
- Ⓒ 일반적으로 적들의 침략을 증가시켰다.
- Ⓓ 이들의 문화와 도시를 연구하는 것을 다소 어렵게 만들었다.

4. Connecting Contents
Why does the professor mention Khabur ware and Nuzi ware?
- Ⓐ To support the opinion that they were widely used for decoration
- Ⓑ To describe their influence on their contemporaries
- Ⓒ To introduce another benefit of making pottery
- Ⓓ **To emphasize the skillful pottery making of the Hurrians**

4.
교수는 왜 하부르 도자기와 누지 도자기를 언급하는가?
- Ⓐ 장식에 널리 사용되었다는 의견을 뒷받침하려고
- Ⓑ 동시대 도자기들에 미친 영향을 설명하려고
- Ⓒ 도자기 제작의 또 다른 이점을 소개하려고
- Ⓓ 후르리인들의 뛰어난 도자기 제작 능력을 강조하려고

5. Inference

What can be inferred about the religion of the Hurrians?

Ⓐ **It was recognized throughout the region, affecting certain cultures.**
Ⓑ It spread very quickly to other countries, becoming their state religion.
Ⓒ It helped Egyptians shape the concept of their own gods and religion.
Ⓓ It ended up disappearing with the rise of the new religion of the Hittites.

6. Function & Attitude

Listen again to part of the lecture. Then answer the question.

> W: Professor, you mentioned that the Hurrians also gained political influence; will you go into that more?
> M: I was just getting to that.

Why does the professor say this:

> M: I was just getting to that.

Ⓐ To start a discussion regarding the Hurrians' political influence
Ⓑ To show the student that he is the one who is in charge
Ⓒ **To indicate that he was just about to discuss the Hurrian kingdom**
Ⓓ To tell the student not to rush to the next topic so fast

Conversation 2

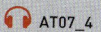

[1-5] Listen to part of a conversation between a student and a university staff.

Man: Student | **Woman:** University Staff

> M: Hello, who should I talk to about issues regarding tuition payment?
> W: Anyone who stands at this counter, which is just me at the moment. What is the issue you are trying to deal with?
> M: Well, it looks like I am not going to have enough money to pay for next semester. I am fully registered for next semester, but I discovered a problem when I went to the bookstore yesterday. Some of my courses require many large textbooks, and others have many copyrighted illustrations, so I won't have enough money to pay for my tuition when the bill comes if I purchase them all.

W: I see. Some textbooks can be unbelievably expensive. Have you tried looking for those expensive textbooks online? Since the bookstores rarely buy back books, and when they do it is for a mere fraction of the cost they sold them for, many students try to sell their old books online.

M: Yes, my roommate suggested that, too. I found one or two of them, but many of the books I need are new editions, so the older editions have some different contents. That makes them very difficult to use for class.

W: Yes, that does happen a lot. Have you thought of applying for a student grant?

M: Oh, no! I don't want to have that kind of debt hanging over my head. My sister got student loans, and she doesn't know if she will ever fully pay them back.

W: Student loans can be a burden, it's true. But I said a grant, not a loan. Students can often qualify for small one-time grants based upon their academic record. There are also some that are based upon your field of study. Those often involve essay contests or something similar. You never have to pay the money back. They are kind of like a reward.

M: That sounds like a great idea, and I will look into them. But, I need something quick.

W: Okay, have you thought about getting a part-time job? There are many businesses in the area looking for workers. Since the students have not moved into the dorms, many positions are still open.

M: I am already working full-time right now, and I will be working part-time during the semester.

W: Ok. That's good, but it might be worth your while to try to find a better paying position than the one you have. Where do you work and how long have you worked there?

M: At a restaurant, for one and a half years.

W: Then I would definitely take the time to look around. You started that position during the school year when very few jobs were available. I'm sure you could find something better now.

M: Hmm, I do have tomorrow off. I guess that would be worth my time.

W: Am I correct in assuming that you will be a junior next semester?

M: Yes. I will be.

W May I see your schedule?
M Yes, here it is.
W So, you're a biology major. You're taking seven courses next semester and working part time? That is going to be a major burden. Maybe we should see if we can trim down your schedule. For your required courses, some may be available later on while others may not. Plus, I can see that you have some elective courses here. If we can cut one of your courses from this semester, that could save you money on tuition and books.
M Okay, that sounds good. Thank you for being so helpful.
W No problem; that's why I'm here.

여 한 번 시간표를 봐도 될까요?
남 네, 여기 있습니다.
여 생물 전공이로군요. 다음 학기에 일곱 과목이나 들으면서 시간제 아르바이트를 한다고요? 정말로 힘들 거예요. 학생의 시간표를 좀 줄일 수 있을지 한 번 봅시다. 필수 과목들의 경우 몇몇은 다음에도 수강 가능하고, 다른 것들은 아닐 수 있으니까요. 그리고 여기 교양 과목들도 몇 개 있군요. 이번 학기에 과목들 중 하나를 줄일 수 있으면 등록금과 교과서에 들어갈 돈을 줄일 수 있겠어요.
남 아, 좋은 생각이에요. 도와주셔서 정말 감사합니다.
여 물론이죠. 그게 제가 여기 있는 이유니까요.

어휘

tuition n 등록금 | **counter** n 카운터, 계산대, 판매대 | **copyrighted** adj 저작권이 있는 | **illustration** n 삽화 | **purchase** v 구매하다 | **unbelievably** adv 믿을 수 없을 정도로 | **buy back** 되사다 | **fraction** n 일부, 부분 | **edition** n 판 | **content** n 내용 | **grant** n 보조금 | **hang over a person's head** ~의 머리에서 떠나지 않다 | **academic** adj 학업의, 학술적인 | **trim down** 줄이다 | **elective course** 교양 과목

---

1. Main Idea
Why did the man come to the woman's counter?
Ⓐ To change his major from biology to another subject
Ⓑ To complain about the university's tuition application system
Ⓒ **To see if he can find help to pay for his tuition and textbooks**
Ⓓ To get information about elective courses that he should take

2. Connecting Contents
Why does the man mention new editions and older editions?
Ⓐ To explain the process of buying books from an online store
Ⓑ **To point out that using older editions does not always work**
Ⓒ To tell the woman that they both cost almost the same
Ⓓ To show how both of them could be used in classes

1.
남자는 왜 여자가 있는 카운터로 왔는가?
Ⓐ 생물 전공에서 다른 분야로 전공을 바꾸기 위해
Ⓑ 학교의 등록금 지원 체계에 대해 불평하기 위해
Ⓒ 등록금과 교과서 비용을 내는 데 도움을 얻을 수 있는지 알아보기 위해
Ⓓ 들어야 하는 교양 과목에 대한 정보를 얻기 위해

2.
남자는 왜 새 개정판과 구판을 언급하는가?
Ⓐ 온라인 서점에서 책을 구매하는 과정에 대해 설명하기 위해
Ⓑ 구판 교과서를 사용하는 것이 늘 효과적이지 않다는 것을 지적하기 위해
Ⓒ 이 둘의 가격이 거의 비슷하다고 여자에게 말하기 위해
Ⓓ 두 가지 모두 수업에서 어떻게 사용될 수 있는지 보여주기 위해

3. Detail

Why does the man not want to apply for a student loan?

Ⓐ He has to take more elective courses to apply for it.
Ⓑ **It usually takes a very long time to pay back completely.**
Ⓒ The deadline for the application process has already passed.
Ⓓ Biology majors are rarely given student loans.

4. Detail

What does the woman recommend the man do?

Ⓐ **Get a job that would pay him more than his current one**
Ⓑ Ask his academic advisor for help with his schedule
Ⓒ Try to look for other locations to major in biology
Ⓓ Find another part-time job at the library

5. Function & Attitude

Why does the woman say this:

> W You're taking seven courses next semester and working part time? That is going to be a major burden. Maybe we should see if we can trim down your schedule.

Ⓐ To praise the man for trying to take so many classes
Ⓑ To see if the man can really handle this situation
Ⓒ To imply that the man doesn't know what he is doing
Ⓓ **To indicate that the current schedule would be too hard to manage**

3.
남자가 학자금 대출을 신청하고 싶어하지 않는 이유는 무엇인가?

Ⓐ 신청하려면 교양 과목을 더 들어야 한다.
Ⓑ 다 갚는 데 매우 오랜 시간이 걸린다.
Ⓒ 지원 과정을 위한 마감 기일이 이미 지났다.
Ⓓ 생물학 전공 학생들에게는 학자금 대출이 거의 주어지지 않는다.

4.
여자는 남자에게 무엇을 제안하는가?

Ⓐ 현재 일자리보다 더 돈을 많이 주는 일자리를 찾는다
Ⓑ 지도 교수에게 시간표에 대해 도움을 청한다
Ⓒ 생물 전공을 할 수 있는 다른 곳들을 알아본다
Ⓓ 도서관에서 다른 시간제 일자리를 알아본다

5.
여자는 왜 이렇게 말하는가:

> 여 다음 학기에 일곱 과목이나 들으면서 시간제 아르바이트를 한다고요? 정말로 힘들 거예요. 학생의 시간표를 좀 줄일 수 있을지 한 번 봅시다.

Ⓐ 이렇게 많은 수업을 들으려고 하는 것에 대해 남자를 칭찬하려고
Ⓑ 남자가 정말 이 상황을 잘 해결할 수 있을지 보려고
Ⓒ 남자가 자신이 무엇을 하는지 모르고 있다는 점을 암시하려고
Ⓓ 현재의 시간표를 감당하기 너무 어려울 것임을 알리려고

Lecture 3

 AT07_5

[1-6] Listen to part of a lecture in an art history class.

Man: professor | Woman: student

M Alright, class. Let's get straight into it. I want to continue our discussion on cave paintings. We've been talking about the Lascaux cave paintings. The use of color and pigments was of particular interest to us, how the variety in colors was achieved using natural pigments such as iron oxide for red, manganese dioxide for black, and charcoal for black as well. We also talked about how the preparation of these pigments involved grinding the minerals into fine powders and mixing

미술사 수업의 강의 일부를 들으시오.

남자: 교수 | 여자: 학생

교 좋습니다, 여러분. 바로 시작하겠습니다. 동굴 벽화에 대한 논의를 계속해 보겠습니다. 저희는 라스코 동굴 벽화에 대해 이야기했었죠. 특히 색상과 안료의 사용에 관심이 많았습니다. 붉은색을 위해 산화철을, 검은색을 위해 이산화망간과 숯을 사용하는 등 다양한 색상이 자연 안료를 사용하여 어떻게 만들어졌는지요. 또한, 이러한 안료를 만드는 과정에서 광물을 곱게 갈아 가루로 만든 후, 물, 동물성 지방, 또는 심지어 식물 수액 같은 결합제와 혼합해 반죽 같은 일관성을 만드는 것을 포함한 안료를 준비하는 과정에 대해서도 이야기했습니다. 네, 브렛?

them with binders like water or animal fat, or even plant sap to create a paste-like consistency. Yes, Brett?

W I just wanted to add that they worked well with the brushes the painters designed.

M Thank you for that. Yes, good point. We talked about how they used animal hair and plant fibers to make brushes, and this was well-suited for the pasty consistency of the paint. Of course, the painters also used their own fingers, a practice common in many cave paintings.

Today, I want to shift gears and discuss another famous site called the Chauvet cave paintings. I want to really zero in on the artistic aspects that scholars appreciate about this site.

Okay, so when we talk about the Chauvet cave paintings, we're talking about some serious artistic skill. These clearly weren't just quick sketches done in passing. The artists who created these masterpieces used a range of techniques to bring these animals to life on the cave walls. Working with natural pigments, they did an excellent job of capturing the movement, anatomy, and essence of animals like these horses, lions, and bison you see on the slide up here. Most remarkably, they didn't just paint flat images; they used shading and perspective to create a sense of depth and three-dimensionality. This artistic finesse is particularly evident in how they utilized the contours and shapes of the cave walls themselves. By incorporating these natural features, these artists made the animals seem almost like they were moving right there in front of you. See this slide here? There's a slight bulge on the rock on this part, which they used to add dimension to the bison they painted on top of the bulge. What's even more impressive is the attention to detail. The fur on a bison's back, the muscles of a running horse, the intense gaze of a predator—these elements show a connection with and observation of the natural world and a deep understanding of animal behavior. It's like they were not only capturing the physical appearance of these creatures but also their spirit and energy.

Now, alongside these lifelike animals, we find something more enigmatic: abstract symbols. Let me get to the next slide. There we go. These include geometric shapes, lines, and patterns that

여 화가들이 디자인한 브러시와 잘 어울린다는 점을 덧붙이고 싶었어요.

남 고마워요. 네, 좋은 지적입니다. 우리는 화가들이 동물의 털과 식물 섬유를 사용해 붓을 만든 방법에 대해 이야기했었고, 이 붓은 안료의 반죽 같은 질감과 잘 맞았어요. 물론, 화가들은 손가락을 사용하기도 했으며, 이는 많은 동굴 벽화에서 흔히 볼 수 있는 방식입니다.

오늘은 방향을 바꿔서 또 다른 유명한 장소인 쇼베 동굴 벽화에 대해 이야기해 보려고 합니다. 이곳에 대한 학자들이 높이 평가하는 예술적인 측면에 대해 집중적으로 다뤄보겠습니다.

자, 쇼베 동굴 벽화를 이야기할 때, 우리는 상당한 예술적 기술을 다루고 있습니다. 이는 단순히 지나가는 길에 그린 스케치 같은 것이 아닙니다. 이 작품을 만든 화가들은 동굴 벽에 동물의 생명력을 불어넣기 위해 다양한 기법을 사용했습니다. 천연 안료를 사용하여, 그들은 여기 슬라이드에 보이는 것처럼 말, 사자, 들소 같은 동물의 움직임과 해부학적 구조, 그리고 본질을 훌륭하게 표현해 냈습니다. 가장 놀라운 것은 단순히 평면적인 이미지를 그린 것이 아니라, 음영과 원근법을 사용해 깊이감과 입체감을 표현한 점입니다. 이 예술적 섬세함은 그들이 동굴 벽 자체의 윤곽과 형태를 어떻게 활용했는지에서 특히 두드러지게 나타납니다. 이러한 자연적 요소를 활용하여 이 예술가들은 동물들이 마치 눈앞에서 움직이는 것처럼 보이게 만들었습니다. 이 슬라이드를 보세요. 이 부분의 바위에는 약간의 돌출부가 있는데, 그들은 그것을 활용하여 그 위에 그린 들소에 입체감을 더했습니다. 더 인상적인 것은 디테일에 대한 섬세한 표현입니다. 들소의 등 위 털, 달리는 말의 근육, 포식자의 강렬한 눈빛—이러한 요소들은 자연계와의 연결 및 관찰과 동물 행동에 대한 깊은 이해를 보여줍니다. 이들은 단순히 이 생명체들의 외형만이 아니라, 그들의 정신과 에너지까지 포착한 것 같습니다.

자, 이러한 살아 있는 듯한 동물들과 함께 우리는 더 불가사의한 것을 발견합니다. 다음 슬라이드로 넘어가 볼까요. 여기 있습니다. 특정 동물이나 물체를 직접적으로 나타내지 않는 기하학적 모양, 선, 그리고 패턴들

don't directly represent specific animals or objects. These symbols are scattered throughout the cave. The interpretation of these abstract symbols is still a subject of debate among archaeologists and researchers. They could have held spiritual or ritualistic meanings, perhaps serving as markers of territory, signs of group identity, or even elements of a primitive language or communication system. Some might have been used in ceremonies or rituals, invoking the power of the animals depicted nearby. These abstract symbols add another layer of complexity to the Chauvet Cave paintings. They suggest that the artists were not only skilled in naturalistic representation but also engaged in abstract thought and symbolic expression. They were communicating ideas and concepts that went beyond the visible world of animals around them. You can even argue that they were among the first abstract paintings in history!

I want to look at another striking feature of the Chauvet Cave paintings, which is the dynamic nature of their compositions. These are not just static images of animals; they depict scenes of movement, interaction, and drama. You'll see predators in pursuit of prey, animals in combat, and groups of animals interacting with each other. These dynamic compositions suggest that the artists were not merely documenting the animals they encountered in their environment. They were storytellers, capturing moments of tension, action, and survival. Look at this slide. Notice how there is a subtle emotion expressed in the faces of these bison running away from the lion. I hope you can see that the subtlety conveys a distinct realism. Once again, this really shows a deep connection these painters had with nature. How about the movement of these horses here? What do you notice?

1. **Main Idea**

What is the lecture mainly about?

Ⓐ **The artistic value of the Chauvet cave paintings**
Ⓑ The techniques used by the Chauvet cave painters
Ⓒ An analysis of the Chauvet cave painting's subjects
Ⓓ The similarities between the Chauvet and Lascaux cave paintings

2. **Detail**

According to the lecture, which of the following is NOT something that painters of the Lascaux cave painting used to paint?

Ⓐ Paint brushes made of animal hair
Ⓑ Their own fingers
Ⓒ Plant material
Ⓓ **Bones of small animals**

3. **Detail**

According to the lecture, how did the painters of the Chauvet cave use the surfaces of the cave walls to their advantage?

Ⓐ They used the contours of the walls to make shapes of animals.
Ⓑ **They used the uneven surfaces to add dimensionality to the figures.**
Ⓒ They used shading and perspective to make the animal paintings realistic.
Ⓓ They incorporated the color of the cave itself into the depicted scenes.

4. **Detail**

According to the lecture, what might the abstract symbols on the Chauvet paintings indicate? Choose 2 answers.

Ⓐ Identities of animals
Ⓑ Indicators that aided in hunting
Ⓒ **Religious or spiritual symbols**
Ⓓ **A basic written language**
Ⓔ Sorcery practices

5. **Detail**

How does the professor organize the lecture?

Ⓐ **By different elements of the painting, in no meaningful order**
Ⓑ From an earlier cave painting to a slightly newer one
Ⓒ From concrete features of the cave painting to more abstract ones
Ⓓ From more-obvious to less-obvious components of the painting

1.
이 강의는 주로 무엇에 관한 것인가?

Ⓐ 쇼베 동굴 벽화의 예술적 가치
Ⓑ 쇼베 동굴 화가들이 사용한 기법
Ⓒ 쇼베 동굴 벽화의 주제에 대한 분석
Ⓓ 쇼베와 라스코 동굴 벽화의 유사성

2.
강의에 따르면, 라스코 동굴 화가들이 그림을 그릴 때 사용하지 않은 도구는 무엇인가?

Ⓐ 동물의 털로 만든 붓
Ⓑ 그들의 손가락
Ⓒ 식물 재료
Ⓓ 작은 동물의 뼈

3.
강의에 따르면, 쇼베 동굴 화가들은 동굴 벽 표면을 어떻게 그들의 장점으로 이용했는가?

Ⓐ 벽의 윤곽을 사용하여 동물의 형태를 만들었다.
Ⓑ 울퉁불퉁한 표면을 이용해 입체감을 더했다.
Ⓒ 음영과 원근법을 사용하여 동물 그림을 현실감 있게 표현했다.
Ⓓ 동굴 자체의 색상을 장면에 녹여냈다.

4.
강의에 따르면, 쇼베 동굴 벽화에 있는 추상적 기호들이 나타내는 것은 무엇일 수 있는가? 두 개를 고르시오.

Ⓐ 동물의 정체성
Ⓑ 사냥에 도움을 주는 표시
Ⓒ 종교적 또는 영적 상징
Ⓓ 기본적인 문자 언어
Ⓔ 주술적 실천

5.
교수는 강의를 어떻게 구성하는가?

Ⓐ 그림의 다양한 요소를 특별한 순서 없이
Ⓑ 더 오래된 동굴 벽화에서 조금 더 새로운 것으로
Ⓒ 동굴 벽화의 구체적인 특징에서 더 추상적인 요소로
Ⓓ 그림의 더 명확한 요소에서 덜 명확한 요소로

6. **Inference**

What will the class most likely do next?

Ⓐ They will move on to another important element of the paintings.
Ⓑ They will continue the discussion on emotional depictions.
Ⓒ They will discuss more examples of dynamism in the cave paintings.
Ⓓ They will study the role of animals in the cave paintings' depicted scenes.

6.
수업에서 다음으로 할 가능성이 가장 높은 것은 무엇인가?

Ⓐ 벽화의 또 다른 중요한 요소로 넘어갈 것이다.
Ⓑ 감정적 표현에 대한 논의를 계속할 것이다.
Ⓒ 동굴 벽화의 역동성에 대한 더 많은 예를 논의할 것이다.
Ⓓ 동굴 벽화에 묘사된 장면들에서 동물의 역할을 연구할 것이다.

PAGODA TOEFL Actual Test Listening | 해설서